All Brain and No Soul?

All Brain and No Soul?

—— Real Humanity in an AI Age ——

Robert A. Hunt

WIPF & STOCK · Eugene, Oregon

ALL BRAIN AND NO SOUL?
Real Humanity in an AI Age

Copyright © 2025 Robert A. Hunt. All rights reserved. Except for brief quotations in critical publications or reviews, no part of this book may be reproduced in any manner without prior written permission from the publisher. Write: Permissions, Wipf and Stock Publishers, 199 W. 8th Ave., Suite 3, Eugene, OR 97401.

Wipf & Stock
An Imprint of Wipf and Stock Publishers
199 W. 8th Ave., Suite 3
Eugene, OR 97401

www.wipfandstock.com

PAPERBACK ISBN: 979-8-3852-3522-3
HARDCOVER ISBN: 979-8-3852-3523-0
EBOOK ISBN: 979-8-3852-3524-7

VERSION NUMBER 02/18/25

Scripture quotations are taken from the New Revised Standard Version Updated Edition. Copyright © 2021 National Council of Churches of Christ in the United States of America. Used by permission. All rights reserved worldwide.

Dedicated to my wife, Lilian, my children, Naomi and Elliott, my grandchildren, Nava, Tali, and Miro, and to all the children of the AI age. May they find with one another the fullness of their humanity.

Contents

Preface | ix
Acknowledgments | xii
Introduction | xiii

Chapter 1—Our Place in the World | 1
Chapter 2—Humanity in an Infinite Universe | 6
Chapter 3—Humanity Merged into the Web of Life | 16
Chapter 4—Humanity Re-Centered Inside Our Heads | 26
Chapter 5—Humans Reembodied as a Machine | 34
Chapter 6—Humans as Machines Operated by a Machine | 49
Chapter 7—Humans as Abstractions and Algorithms | 59
Chapter 8—The Screen Age | 70
Chapter 9—How We Became Post-Human | 81
Chapter 10—Artificial Minds from Calculators to Computers | 90
Chapter 11—From Computers to Artificial Intelligence | 97
Chapter 12—How It Works | 111
Chapter 13—The Limits of Generative AI | 123
Chapter 14—The Robot in the Room | 128
Chapter 15—The Human in the Room | 136
Chapter 16—In Your Eyes | 147
Chapter 17—Children of the AI Age | 164
Chapter 18—Transcendence | 183

Bibliography | 191

Preface

I've been anticipating the advent of artificial intelligence (AI) for a long time. It was there in the science fiction that I read, and it seemed that every month there was another article about advances in AI in *Scientific American*. It was appearing in rudimentary form as website chatbots, spell checkers, and word prediction in word processors and on cell phones. Still, when it suddenly appeared in a directly accessible form with ChatGPT in 2022, I was taken by surprise. Like many people, I thought it was the technology of the future and always would be.

Since 2022, the Large Language Model Generative Pre-Trained Transformer of AI (LLM GPT) has proven so effective and extensible that it is revolutionizing the ways we work and relate to one another. There is no indication that this acceleration will slow down. I'm writing in late 2024. The last six months brought developments that exceeded those of the previous two years. Those exceeded the previous ten years. As I write AI agents have begun to appear for mainstream usage.

The impact of AI in my university has been revolutionary and traumatic. In some professional fields, AI chatbots outperform the majority of students on standard credentialing tests. In fields where there are no such tests, AI written essays are frequently better than those our best students can write.

Students are using it. It helps them create art, write academic essays and tell stories, create computer code, edit papers, do research, and record podcasts. We have no idea how many uses there are for AI, and in a mere two years, it is now professional malpractice to not use AI in some work. I've had AI backed search engines, chatbots, and editors throughout the process of writing this book. Yet 65 to 70 percent of my colleagues have never used it.

The same story is being told across the world of business, politics, and religion.

There is resistance. My colleagues realize that like any disruptive and ubiquitous technology, artificial intelligence is changing the way we think of ourselves as human beings and societies.

This can be frightening. These changes cut to the core of our work in the humanities, the social sciences, and theology. They may cut to the core understanding we have regarding our own humanity.

What are we humans becoming in an AI age?

To answer that question, we must first explore how we got here and how that shapes our relationship with artificial intelligence.

Second, we must understand AI itself: how it works, what it does, and what it does not do. We must distinguish between what "intelligence" means when applied to a human and, if there is a difference, what it means when applied to a computer.

Finally, we must begin to reenvision what it means to be human in ways that fully account for who we are in relation to the technology called AI. From the dawn of time, we have understood ourselves in relation to one another, nature, and transcendence. These have been the key actors in the human story.

With the advent of AI, there is something new in our world, a technology we created and that pretends to be like us in the ways that seem most uniquely human. Now we must tell a story in which our own creation, AI, plays an important role and which some claim will be our destiny.

To tell that story, we'll need to cultivate one of our most important human characteristics: curiosity. There are many attitudes that we can bring to ideas, objects, and people that suddenly appear in our world. Of these, I have found curiosity leads to the greatest sense of satisfaction and equanimity in a changing world.

I invite those who are listening to this book, or reading it, to bring your curiosity about how you came to see yourself as a human, the world you live in, and the technology that is now rapidly changing it. In the end, curiosity leads us from ignorance to knowledge and from knowledge to mastery of both ourselves and the world we live in.

PREFACE

Curiosity has, over the years, led me to engage in conversations with hundreds of authors, poets, songwriters, script writers, students, and colleagues. You will find specific references in the written text. But I'm not going to introduce my fellow humans as mere page numbers. When I mention their names—whether I met them in a book, the faculty lounge, or classroom—remember that they are valued human partners in my quest to understand and share with you what it means to be human in an AI age. I then hope that you, the listener or reader, will be curious enough to seek out these same writers for a deeper conversation. Each is a fellow human; each is a worthwhile conversation partner.

Acknowledgments

This book would not have been possible without the engagement of my students over many years, particularly in my doctoral seminars for the Human-Centered Interdisciplinary Studies program at Southern Methodist University (SMU). My colleagues in the HCIS program and Simmons School of Education and Human Development have been invaluable conversation partners.

Paige Ware, Jason Warner, Jennifer Culver, and my colleagues in both the university Faculty Technology Committee and the members of the SMU Generative AI Cohort of the Willing have been invariably encouraging and stimulating.

Eva Csaky and my colleagues in the Hunter and Stephanie Hunt Institute for Engineering and the Humanities have offered lively and stimulating discussions on the intersection of technology and human flourishing.

Drew Dickens, my student and neighbor, has been an invaluable conversation partner over several years in all matters relating AI to spirituality. It is in the context of our many conversations over his interests and professional use of AI that many of these ideas were shaped.

And finally, I must thank the Perkins School of the Theology, my faculty colleagues, and the Scholarly Outreach Award Committee for making the funding available to research and write this book.

Introduction

In July of 1969, I was standing alone beneath a star-filled sky in the cold darkness beside Lake Coeur D'Alene in Idaho. My mother had sent my brother and me to a Boy Scout Jamboree. She, newly widowed, stayed back in Richardson, Texas with our younger sister to start our new life in a new city, in a new home.

A lot was going on in the world. My father had died. Martin Luther King Jr. and Bobby Kennedy had been assassinated. Each day brought another intonation of the dead in Vietnam. Each day, humans were getting closer to landing on the moon, a waxing sliver of which was passing overhead each night.

"It is impossible to meditate on time and the mystery of the creative passage of nature without an overwhelming emotion at the limitations of human intelligence."[1] So wrote Alfred North Whitehead. I encountered him first in the volume *Time* of the Life Science Library.

The night sky in Idaho had that crushing presence the ancients called "glory." But it seemed less and less a mystery to me. I had read straight through the Life Science Library, not to mention every edition of both the *Analog Science Fiction and Fact* magazine and the *Magazine of Fantasy and Science Fiction*. I knew a red giant from a white dwarf, courtesy of a book with a similar name by Robert Jastrow. I would meet him later as an astronomy major at the University of Texas. I knew that the Milky Way was only one of countless galaxies and that space-time was curved. I knew about entropy and the inevitable heat death of the universe.

---

1. Goudsmit and Claiborne, *Time*, 175.

INTRODUCTION

The same *Time* volume, fifteen pages later, went on: "However the promise of an afterlife is viewed, it always expresses man's refusal to accept death as the total oblivion of self—as 'deserts of vast eternity.' It is this belief that, at the close of man's own personal physical span, gives him his last and best opportunity to conquer time."[2]

As I gazed across the deserts of vast eternity, I was thinking of "The Nine Billion Names of God" by Arthur C. Clarke and wondering whether a computer endlessly running its algorithms might bring it all to an end.[3] Or might the endless ruminations of a computer create it all again, as Isaac Asimov playfully posited in "The Last Question."[4]

When I entered the astronomy program at the University of Texas, I was not philosophically or theologically sophisticated. This was in large part because neither theological nor philosophical sophistication was part of my science-oriented high school education or my church youth group. Many of us were thinking far more complicated and troubling thoughts about the nature of reality than our teachers or our pastors were willing to deal with.

At UT, it became clear I did not possess the talent (or perhaps discipline) for advanced mathematics. History and anthropology suited me better. With a new palette of potential courses to take, I was urged by my roommate to take philosophical theology with Charles Hartshorne, perhaps the preeminent U.S. philosopher in this field. I'd never heard of him, but I signed up for his class. It fit my social schedule and degree program.

In his class, what I'd read in the book *Time* came alive. After all, he had been an assistant to Alfred North Whitehead. Hartshorne's philosophical inquiries in *A Natural Theology for Our Time* showed me that religion, or at least theology, might help me find answers to the questions I'd asked on that starry night seven years earlier.[5] I decided to become a pastor, a profession that ran deep in my family.

Once I entered Perkins School of Theology at SMU, I discovered the religiously oriented process theology of Schubert Ogden, who had been Hartshorne's student. It answered a lot of my questions. I also learned about combatively simple orthodoxies and nuanced and accommodating neoorthodoxies and their answers to my pressing questions. It was all

2. Goudsmit and Claiborne, *Time*, 190.
3. Clarke, "Nine Billion Names."
4. Asimov, "Last Question."
5. Hartshorne, *Natural Theology*.

intellectually stimulating. Yet as time passed, it seemed to be of very little practical relevance.

Once I graduated and began life as a new pastor, things looked different than they had at Perkins. The challenges my congregations faced—first in Austin, Texas and then in Kuala Lumpur, then Singapore, and finally Vienna, Austria—were challenges to their humanity. People believed in God because God made sense to them. Esoteric modern apologetics for the divine were very much a minority interest, and I was the minority. If God was God, then God could take care of God's self. People were worried about staying human while living in a changing society, fleeing political oppression, adapting to a new culture, or just trying to work and raise children.

For me, philosophical theology had been an intellectual substitute for astronomy. Now I was realizing that theology might not be the most important thing. In the century I was born in, the teaching of Christianity had been challenged on one hand by the rise of science and on the other by two disastrous world wars. Technology was making it a century of unimagined wonders and prosperity and giving us the omnipresent fear of utter destruction created by the atomic bomb. What kind of God was the God of such a world? It's a great question, and great theologians rose to answer it. I planned to be one of them.

But I learned that what my church members cared about far more was what it means to be human. It was their humanity that was under threat whether they were caught up in the cogs of a corporate machine, squeezed in the conflicts between political and religious powers, challenged as migrants in new lands and cultures, or facing a lonely old age.

This is a book about what it means to be human and how our understanding of being human is changing at the beginning of the twenty-first century under the influence of technology, particularly higher-level artificial intelligence. That emergence has accelerated even since 2022 and the release of OpenAI's ChatGPT. As I write, AI is beginning to change the social and cultural landscape in which we all must find our humanity.

Religion plays a role because in the twenty-first century, the interplay between our humanity and transcendence continues to shape human self-understanding. The language of that relationship, not least the term "spirituality" informs the thought of everyone from a founding thinker in the realm of AI like Ray Kurzweil to a physicist and cosmologist like Marcelo Gleiser to philosophers like Whitehead and Hartshorne.

INTRODUCTION

The story of our human self-understanding began when religion was a dominant cultural force in every society. It has been changed as modern science and political philosophy made us rethink ourselves, our world, and our place in the world. In chapters 2 to 6, I'll tell that story.

It isn't just science that shapes our humanity. Our technology, our tools, have also shaped both who we are and how we think about ourselves. In chapters 7 and 8, we'll see how the interplay between science, technological innovation, and human bodies has changed our understanding of ourselves as humans.

In chapter 9, we'll see how the technology of projecting images on screens is changing how we see ourselves. In chapter 10, we'll see how these technological changes culminate in the emergence of the post-human, as Katherine Hayles explores in her 1999 book *How We Became Posthuman*.[6]

As I write, AI has moved from being a computer science curiosity or sci-fi plot twist to become a capable and ubiquitous presence and partner in our daily lives. But what is it, really? Just as the human body has been demystified by modern science, so AI needs to be demystified in the contemporary consciousness. In chapters 11 to 15, we'll look under the covers to see what AI really is: an advanced technology, a sophisticated and useful tool, and still just a tool.

Finally, in chapters 16 to 19, we'll explore the relationship between ourselves as real humans and all the different guises in which AI joins our human world. We now live with the successors of Asimov's imagined Multivac and Clarke's imagined Mark V. We live with twenty-first-century supercomputers and their neural networks and hyperfast chipsets. We see them daily evolving toward greater and greater imitation of the human brain with the express intent of exceeding its capabilities, and we face a question that they will answer if we let them: In an AI age, who are we as humans? Do we now allow our technology to speak for us? Will we allow it to alienate us from our ancestors and environment and set new terms in which we must understand ourselves as humans? Or will we determine for ourselves our human, post-human, or perhaps trans-human future?

---

6. Hayles, *How We Became Posthuman*.

Chapter 1 — **Our Place in the World**

A Place in the Chaos

I grew up with the assurance of a stable place at the center of a well-ordered world made just for me. I had my own bedroom in a suburban home. My model airplanes floated over my bed. Posters from NASA decorated the wall. My books and magazines were laid nearby. My bike was out in the garage and could take me wherever I wanted to go.

That all blew apart during a period of national and global chaos. A blink. John F. Kennedy slumped across his wife, dying in the streets of my hometown, Dallas. A blink. My father in a coffin at the front of Moody Memorial Methodist Church in Galveston. A blink. A grainy photo of Martin Luther King Jr. dying while men pointed toward the assassin. A blink. Robert Kennedy keeling over as his life slipped away through a bullet wound.

Maybe Billy Joel was right in the song "We Didn't Start the Fire," but in the 1960s it sure seemed that Don McLean nailed it when he sang about the music dying.

The popular stories that shaped my childhood were stories less about good versus evil than order versus chaos: *James Bond*, *The Man from U.N.C.L.E.*, and the spy spoof *Get Smart*. They all pitched their heroes against the enemies of the world order we thought we established in the wake of two brutal world wars. Chaos was the specter that haunted the world, and indeed KAOS was the name of Maxwell Smart's antagonist just as SPECTRE haunted James Bond.

. . . . . .

We were riding a bus from Galveston to Dallas, my mother too shaky with grief to drive with three children. At twelve years old, I had plans for building a new order in a new home until from my lips emerged, "And then dad can—" and I turned and broke into tears. My mother had warned my brother and me that we were now "the men of the house," and it suddenly came home to me what that meant. There was no dad to repair, restore, and organize.

The rainbow after the disordered flood of Hebrew folklore found in the book of Genesis in the Jewish or Christian Bible was a promise deferred, if it was a promise at all. My world became a microcosm of the cataclysm sweeping across the larger world. The theologian Paul Tillich had called it *The Shaking of the Foundations*.

In 1969 the rough beast slouching toward Bethlehem in William Butler Yeats's poem *The Second Coming* was making its way across America.[1] It still is. Small wonder that back then we were riding a wave of apocalyptic fervor. In the long fitful story of the Bible, the chaos of the flood settled into human hearts. And we were promised it would end only with the restoration of order through divine dictatorship.

In 1969 my mother was bringing us to the land of Hal Lindsey and *The Late Great Planet Earth*. Across from the NorthPark Center, the Museum of Biblical Art housed the massive painting by Charles Anderson of *The Coming Rapture* over Dallas. It pictured Dallas as it was then, except with raptured souls drifting heavenward and abandoned autos plunging off the same highway we traveled on from Galveston.

Between the Second World War and the debacle of Vietnam, Americans were realizing the cost of taking over the business of ordering our world from God. It's not surprising that many preferred to escape through dreams of a rapture and the return of a king.

That famous painting of the rapture over Dallas burned up in 2005 along with its home. And in any case, the Dallas skyline it depicted can no longer be recognized. The king is late and always has been, and we're still looking for our place in the world.

We aren't the only ones. I have seen a pilgrim in Nepal circumambulating the great stupas and spinning prayer wheels hoping to rebalance the karmic world. I have stood behind a worshiper lighting a lamp in front of a Buddha in Narita, Japan and a devotee hoisting Ganesh above the rising flood of the Ganges River to evoke the return of the monsoon. I've seen

---

1. Yeats, "Second Coming."

the pious Jew praying before the Western Wall and listened to Muslims returned from the Hajj.

All of them are seeking order from beyond and a place in that order for themselves. All will return from their devotions to the chaos of jammed city streets.

Every human culture has myths explaining the origin of humanity and our place in the cosmos. These myths place our origin story in the context of transcendence—something, or someone, greater than the natural world. There is a horizon beyond which the originating impulse of creation comes and toward which it looks for consummation. There is a source of order and the restoration of order. It may be God or gods. It may be an impersonal force such as *Tian* and *Tao* in Chinese culture or *Mind* or *Brahma* in the Buddhist and Hindu cultures.

Within that transcendent ordering, however closely we relate to the natural world, we have understood ourselves as the center of everything.

In Judaism, Christianity, and Islam, humans are appointed by God as stewards of the natural order. Even the angels must bow to us. In Buddhism it is the human realm that is uniquely suited to the appearance of the Buddha to teach the dharma: the truth about reality. In Hinduism it is humans whose selves and societies are created and ordered by the self-sacrifice of the divine Purusha and whose obedience or disobedience to that order generate *karma*.

We have been taught by our religions that we not only have a place in this world but that reality spreads out around us and over us and even through us and then beyond us.

Prior to modernity, as Charles Taylor so aptly chronicles in *A Secular Age*, humans understood themselves to be immersed in a relation to an unseen world that both preceded and transcended their social and natural worlds. To be human was to know one's self as part of an *order* greater and beyond one's self and one's fellow creatures.[2]

For more and more people, perhaps even a large majority, this has changed.

---

2. Taylor, *Secular Age*.

The Copernican Revolution and the Reordering of the Universe

Being the center of the story of the universe was heady stuff. It just couldn't stand up to our endless curiosity about ourselves and nature. Almost as soon as humans could record the motion of the stars in the night sky, they saw anomalies. Eventually, the simple picture of the universe revolving around the earth became untenable. In the year 150 of the Common Era, the mathematician and astronomer Claudius Ptolemy was able to explain away these anomalies with his complex but still earth-centered, *geocentric*, model of the universe. It fit the "human-centric" historical narrative of the emerging Christian church that became his ally and defender for centuries.

Yet his system wasn't perfect, and it didn't perfectly match observations of the movements of the planets and the stars. Adjustments were made, the model was tweaked, but it wasn't meeting the standard of the great medieval philosopher William of Ockham. Ockham said that the preferred explanation has the fewest assumptions and the simplest line of reasoning that fits the facts (a principle that came to be known as Occam's razor). And Ptolemy's system, growing ever more complex as it sought to account for more exact observations, was a notable violation of Occam's razor.

Something had to give, and what gave was the human place at the center of the universe. Before Ptolemy, the Greek astronomer Aristarchus had advocated for a sun-centered, *heliocentric*, model of the universe. But with Aristotle on the side of an earth-centered universe, he didn't get any traction. And once the church adopted Ptolemy, he was forgotten. It was only in 1543, a time of intellectual revolution, that Nicolaus Copernicus realized that placing the sun at the center of the observable universe gave a much simpler and more accurate model of what astronomers were seeing and measuring.

It was intellectually compelling, this Copernican universe. But with the Catholic church in opposition and Copernicus's ideas undermined by the publisher of his masterwork *On the Revolutions of the Heavenly Spheres*, it would take time for the Copernican model to make its way into popular culture. When it did, it started the great decentering of humanity in the cosmos, a process that continues to this day.

It also gave rise to what Marcelo Gleiser calls *copernicanism* in his 2024 book *The Dawn of a Mindful Universe*. We'll return to Gleiser's ideas in the final chapter. Key to his coined term *copernicanism* is the idea of a not merely decentered but also *diminished* humanity.[3]

When Copernicus's ideas were finally accepted, they gave a great boost to objectivity as the mark of human rationality and the most effective way to grasp reality. Copernicus shook off the last vestiges of looking out at the universe as if standing in its center. He imagined himself and the earth as objects somewhere in the observable universe. His was a new way of being human in the world. He was both an object *with* other objects and having a perspective above all objects.

The real Copernican revolution wasn't just decentering humans in the universe. It was the *decentering of the human perspective* on the universe and replacing it with an imaginary objective view of reality. *Looking at the universe objectively had been a right given to God alone in the past. It was granted to humans through revelation, not observation.* Small wonder that, in a time of powerful religious authorities who claimed a monopoly on that revealed perspective, Copernicus delayed publication of his findings for nearly thirty years. He saw the published version of his work only a day before he died.

Copernicus, his theory confirmed by Galileo and Kepler more than a century later, shaped a coming revolution in which knowledge of the natural world was re-centered on objective observation, measurements, and logic. *The real center of the Copernican universe is the human mind as an object of its own reflection, the human mind systematically creating models of reality.* It is the human mind no longer following a plan dictated by ancient texts and the religious authorities who claim an exclusive right to interpret them.

In a Copernican world, humans need not formulate ever more complex Ptolemaic epicycles to explain what they see at the supposed center of the universe. We have the ability to *imagine* ourselves outside our own bodies and transported to an *imagined* center of the universe. It is an ability that is humbling, frightening, and exhilarating.

That shift in perspective marked by the Copernican model was taking place in other realms of thought during the era we now call early modernity. Just as the center of natural science was shifting toward objective human observers and their rational reflections, so too the center of the political universe was shifting. And with both of these came changes in our thinking about ourselves and what it means to be human. Decentered in the universe, we might still be the center of a universal story. Or, as Gleiser fears, we might come to regard ourselves as irrelevant.

3. Gleiser, *Dawn of a Mindful Universe*, 19.

Chapter 2—**Humanity in an Infinite Universe**

The Solar Eclipse

On April 8th, 2024, a solar eclipse was visible across much of the United States, including my home town of Dallas. If the skies were clear, it would be my second time to observe an eclipse. The first was in Austria a couple of decades earlier.

Preparing for the event sent me scurrying to find clear skies along the path of the eclipse. There is little point in seeing the stars come out in the daytime if you can't even see them at night. It turns out that clear skies were likely. But even during a total eclipse, we were going to be blinded by the glow of our cities and towns. Stars would come out, but we would see only the brightest, trapped as we were in our own artificial light.

In the twenty-first century, our night skies have been reduced to a handful of stars and planets and the waxing and the waning of the moon. Only if we go far from our homes and cities can we see what I saw so many years ago on Lake Coeur D'Alene: a night sky filled with stars, and all of them in a slow-motion dance circling our world.

As the ancients looked to the skies, two things were obvious: we were at the center, and out beyond the stars there was an end. Whether it was the Christian cosmos bounded by the kingdom of heaven—the habitat of God of all the elect—or the Hindu idea of Brahmanda or the Buddhist cycle of samsara, the universe was bounded, and what lay beyond was the realm of the mysterious transcendent.

CHAPTER 2—HUMANITY IN AN INFINITE UNIVERSE

The Universe in Our Grasp

Copernicus had moved earth and its humans from the center of the universe. Yet his observations and calculations by no means required that the universe be infinite. In fact, the word "universe" conveys the idea of a single, unified entity. Something bounded. Something that by definition is not *infinite*. The heliocentric universe of Copernicus could still include a transcendent realm beyond its boundaries. The question was just how far those boundaries really were.

When the telescope was invented in 1608 by Hans Lipperhey, the skies began to open up. Galileo could see that Jupiter had moons. Huygens could observe Saturn's rings. Yet nothing in the astronomy of Galileo and other pioneers using telescopes challenged the idea that our universe was a bounded whole.

They could see that closer to earth was what we now call the *solar* system, a system of planets revolving around the *sun*. They could see that there were stars beyond this solar system. And they began to get an idea of the size of the universe although its bigness and our smallness made gaining perspective enormously challenging.

Measuring the distance to the planets was difficult because both they and the earth were in constant motion relative to one another. Even knowing the basic laws of gravitational attraction didn't help since there was no way to measure the mass of planets. Still, by the early eighteenth century, Edmond Halley had managed to measure the distance from earth to the sun with relative accuracy, and as his system of measurement was used with greater precision, the other observable planetary distances were measured as well. As suspected, they were a long way from earth: tens of millions to hundreds of millions of miles.

Stars were much more difficult. Astronomers realized that these points of light were so far away that their distance couldn't be measured using Halley's techniques. Only between 1835 and 1838 were Thomas Henderson, Friedrich von Struve, and Friedrich Bessel able to measure the distance to nearby bright stars. At the beginning of the twentieth century, astronomers had only measured the distances to a few dozen stars. Because the distances to these stars varied, it was clear that they weren't fixed in a rotating sphere as the ancients had imagined. The constellations were just random configurations of stars—some close, some far—that had no relationship to each other at all, much less to earth. And they were a very long way from earth, almost unimaginably distant.

So much for being born under the sign of Sagittarius or living in the Age of Aquarius. All just BS in the emerging understanding of the universe.

Still, astronomers had only measured a few distances to a few stars. Was it possible to get a better idea of the size of the universe?

Back in 1676, Ole Rømer was able to calculate that light traveled at a finite speed. Using Rømer's work and estimates of the earth's diameter, the Dutch astronomer Christiaan Huygens made the first calculation of light's speed in 1678. Modern measurements show the speed of light to be around 300,000 km/sec.[1] Because it takes light about thirty-two minutes to travel from Jupiter to Earth, we can say Jupiter is thirty-two light minutes away. That is an imaginable 611 million kilometers. We can actually create a scale map of our solar system and look at the entire thing at once to give us a sense of scale.

But the distance Thomas Henderson determined for the star Alpha Centauri was 3.25 light-*years* away.[2] That is more than 53,000 times as far away as Jupiter. We can't create a scale map that gives us a visual idea of such a distance. What we know is that the universe we live in is very big. Much bigger than our ancestors could have ever imagined. In such a vast universe, we might feel very small, but with our tools, it was increasingly in our grasp.

And our grip tightened when, in 1705, Edmond Halley first recognized that a particular comet, recorded many times in history, was an object orbiting through the solar system. He realized that reports of a comet in 1531, 1607, and 1682 were reports of the same object. He even predicted its return in 1758. He was right, and it was named after him. It's return in 1835 confirmed the matter.

In 1910, Halley's comet came around again. When it appeared, those who looked up to see it had a very different idea of the scale of the universe from their grandparents or great-grandparents who had seen it last. They were starting to think in light-years, not miles. And as they looked up, comets were stripped of the superstition that surrounded them. They were not harbingers of war or signs from God. They were just another thing in the world that came around regularly—like utility bills.

The universe was losing its mystery.

---

1. American Museum of Natural History. "Ole Roemer."
2. Encyclopedia Britannica, "Thomas Henderson."

CHAPTER 2—HUMANITY IN AN INFINITE UNIVERSE

The Universe Beyond Our Grasp

Edwin Hubble didn't set out to discover that the universe was infinite, and it wasn't immediately clear from his work that it was.

Modern pictures of the universe showing the distribution of the cosmic background radiation or the distribution of galaxies are comfortably bounded. We see an elongated oval with clear edges. Colorized pictures from the James Webb Space Telescope give us the illusion that space is full of colorful clouds of dust of the sort we might observe when sweeping our neglected hallways.

These are illusions created by visual artists translating abstract data to fit within the limits of our screens and printing presses. Out in space, we would pass through these apparent clouds of dust and never see or encounter a single mote. We could travel forever and never come to Douglas Adams's *Restaurant at the End of the Universe*. The fullness of the night sky and our bounded pictures of it betray an unimaginable emptiness that extends forever.

Hubble's work set in motion a process whereby both infinitesimals (things that are infinitely small) and infinity (that which is boundless) would work their way into our consciousness of ourselves and the universe.

Aristotle had dismissed these troublesome, formless, chaotic challengers to our orderly sense of the universe as unreal. He was wrong.

Some background will help us understand how this happened. Science, which since the Enlightenment has driven many changes in our self-understanding, is built up in a slow process. The revolutionary moment that changes public perceptions of reality is built on a foundation of interlocking observations, theories, and discoveries. As these become more widely known, they shape the popular imagination. They prepare us for that seminal moment when our framing of ourselves and reality shifts, and we have a new understanding of ourselves and our world.

Glass and Light

One technology that prepared the way for Hubble's discovery was the ability to build bigger and bigger telescopes. Hubble was using the hundred-inch Hooker telescope at Mount Wilson high in the (back then) clear air above Los Angeles. Its main lens, eight feet in diameter, could bring into focus objects never before seen with such clarity. Hubble and his colleague could see that some of the bright, fuzzy blobs visible in smaller telescopes were in fact vast collections of stars.

It appeared that our galaxy was only one of many such collections. And if our galaxy is huge, imagine how big the universe must be to have so many galaxies.

Much earlier than that, Isaac Newton had experimented with another bit of glass technology, the prism, to show that white light was made up of a spectrum of colors. It wasn't one pure color. Newton's *Opticks* revolutionized lens making while his easily repeatable experiments popularized his ideas.

He left behind a controversy about just what light is made of. Newton thought it was particles emitted by a light source. But in succeeding centuries, experimenters and theorists like Francesco Maria Grimaldi and Christiaan Huygens showed that it was better understood as a wave. It was a wave whose characteristics could be modeled mathematically and which resembled other waves, like those on the surface of water. By the time Hubble made his observations, the wave theory of light not only prevailed but placed it in the larger context of the behavior of all waves.

In 1814, Joseph von Fraunhofer built on these advances and others to show that in the spectrum of sunlight, there were certain dark lines. It wasn't a pure spread of every possible color. He further perfected the spectroscope with a diffraction grating for systematically measuring these lines and their relative locations.

A few decades later, in the 1850s and 1860s, Gustav Kirchhoff and Robert Bunsen (of the Bunsen burner) showed that burning different chemical elements produced different *spectra*, or unique sets of lines in a spectrum coming from a spectroscope. This put the pieces in place so that in 1863 Margaret Huggins and her husband William could begin recording the spectra of stars. With this new data, they could classify stars by their unique light signatures: the patterns of lines in their spectra, a spectrum related to the elements that were generating the light. Accurate comparisons could be made between objects whose slightly different colors were a mystery even if visible to the naked eye.

Sound and Light

Just a couple of decades before, Christian Doppler proposed that the frequency of a wave would be affected by its motion to or away from an observer. Light was almost impossibly fast for such experiments, but with sound waves, the effect he proposed was readily heard.

The sound made by an object approaching an observer will have a higher frequency, or pitch, than when the object is at rest because the waves will be compressed. As the object moves away from the observer, the frequency or pitch will be lower. This provides a method for measuring the speed of an object even if its exact distance from one point to the next cannot be measured. If you know the pitch made by an object like a train whistle at rest, then you can measure the speed of the train in motion based only on the change in frequency of the sound as it moves toward or away from the observer.

What is true of sound waves is equally true of light waves. And this means the Doppler effect can also be used to measure the speed of light-emitting objects like stars relative to an observer—that is, if the observer knew exactly the frequency of the light emitted by the star when it wasn't moving relative to the observer. And that was a problem as long as all starlight appeared to be the same, which brings us back to Huggins and his discovery that not all starlight is the same and that differences can be measured.

By the twentieth century, Hubble knew that all starlight was not the same. He knew that certain classes of stars had identical spectral signatures. The tedious work of nineteenth-century astronomers measuring and categorizing the spectral signatures of stars gave Hubble a kind of baseline against which to compare the spectra of stars that revealed themselves in his hundred-inch telescope.

The Standard Candle

A final piece of the puzzle of just how far the stars were from earth was put in place by Henrietta Swan Leavitt, an astronomer at Harvard. In the early 1900s, she observed that in a type of star called a Cepheid variable there was a relationship between the brightness of the star and the period over which the brightness waxed and waned. She also knew from Isaac Newton's work centuries earlier that brightness, or luminosity, diminishes with distance.

These two pieces of information—that luminosity varied with distance and that in specific stars it varied periodically—allowed her to determine the absolute luminosity of nearby Cepheid variables whose distance had already been measured by other means. Since she could determine the absolute luminosity of distant Cepheid variables by their period and compare it to their actual luminosity, she could determine their distance even if they were too far away for other methods to work.

This was very exciting. She had discovered what astronomers called a "standard candle" against which the luminosity, and thus relative distance, of other stars could be measured. It revolutionized astronomy.

Very quickly, astronomers, using her measurements and methods, could establish the size of the now-measurable universe. It was vastly larger than they had suspected. Hubble himself used Leavitt's standard candle to measure the distances of the galaxies he was observing. Stars went from being a few light-years away to being tens of thousands of light-years away. And further.

An Infinite Universe

The universe is vast. Is it infinite? That seemed to be an unanswerable question. Better telescopes could see more distant stars, but seeing a lot of things doesn't mean there aren't things further away that you can't see. How would you know when you found the edge of the universe? Could you find the edge of the universe?

Maybe not. In 1929, Hubble observed, based on the spectra of known types of stars, that the spectra of galaxies far from earth were shifted toward the red end of the spectrum relative to closer galaxies and stars. And the further from earth these galaxies are, the greater the redshift. This meant, based on the Doppler effect, that distant galaxies were moving away from the earth at speeds proportional to their distance. The further away, the faster they were moving.[3]

Moreover, Hubble observed that galaxies in every direction were moving away from earth. That gives us a couple of choices. First, we might really be the center of the universe, and everything is moving away from us. Do we really believe this? Scientists were long past privileging the observer's point of view.

Instead, drawing on Copernicus, they could imagine the viewpoints of other observers far from our solar system or even our galaxy. The idea that all observers might see the same thing offers another option for interpreting Hubble's observation that everything is moving away from us. Maybe no matter where you are everything is moving away. If any possible

3. Smith, Robert, "Edwin Hubble."

observer in the universe sees the same thing we see, everything moving away, it can only mean *that the entire universe is expanding.*

This second possibility, of an expanding universe, matched calculations made separately by Alexander Friedmann and Georges Lemaître in the 1920s. They had shown, based on Einstein's work on general relativity, that the universe *could* be expanding. Now observation and theory came together to show that the universe *is* expanding and, indeed, how rapidly it is expanding.

And if we know how fast the universe is expanding, then we can project backward in time to the point from which that expansion began.

The universe has a beginning. Around twelve billion years ago, it must have been an infinitely small, dense concentration of matter that then exploded. The big bang. And yet if it has a beginning, its expansion shows no sign of ending. It appears to be expanding into infinity; it has no boundary.

The Copernican revolution in human self-understanding led us to a universe Copernicus could barely have imagined. From our perch somewhere in the universe, stars and galaxies are continually passing out of the sight of the best instruments humanity has for detecting them. We can project ourselves into a future with an empty sky. Infinity and beyond! Or at least infinity. Empty.

Will this continue forever? In Hubble's time, astronomers could not be sure. Some, like Fred Hoyle, Hermann Bondi, and Thomas Gold, hypothesized that the universe was "steady state," that new matter continued to appear in the spaces left as existing galaxies and stars moved away from each other—so, infinite expansion without a beginning or an end. This seemed like better science than having to explain who or what was responsible for creating the universe.

Then between 1964 and 1965, Arno Penzias and Robert Wilson at Bell Labs discovered very faint microwave radiation coming from all parts of the sky.[4] It was recognized by Robert H. Dicke and a team at Princeton University as the experimental confirmation of their theory of a cosmic microwave background radiation that would result from a big bang beginning of the universe.[5] There was no question. The universe had a beginning.

Other astronomers speculated that, eventually, expansion would slow and gravity would pull everything back together in a "big crunch." And then another big bang. And another expansion and another crunch.

4. Penzias and Wilson, "Measurement of Excess Antenna Temperature."
5. Dicke et al., "Cosmic Black-Body Radiation."

There would be an endless cycling and a different kind of steady-state-bounded universe. Again, better than having a moment of creation and thus possibly a creator.

Then in the 1990s, astronomers, using newly discovered standard candles, found evidence that showed this process of expansion and contraction wasn't possible.[6] Far from slowing in its expansion into infinity and nothingness, the expansion of our universe is accelerating.

We humans, however we parse it, are gradually losing touch with the rest of the universe. The distances are mind-boggling and the time frame is huge. Yet we know that the time will come when—should we survive—we will be alone, and then we will be no more.

Entropy—The Heat Death of the Universe

A final piece of nineteenth-century science has inspired reflection on the nature of the cosmos and the human place within it. Nearly two centuries ago, Rudolf Clausius, Ludwig Boltzmann, and Willard Gibbs developed the concept of *entropy*. It was first introduced by Clausius as a way of measuring thermodynamic systems. This wasn't just about theory. If your trains ran on steam engines, you needed to understand how much energy there was in a system and what happened to it when the engine was running.

The basic law they uncovered, called the second law of thermodynamics, is that in systems left to themselves, entropy increases over time. Put simply, if you bring a pot of water to a boil and turn off the heat, eventually it will cool down to the same temperature as the outside air. If you want to keep it boiling, you have to put in more heat.

That's fine for a steam engine as a thermodynamic system. What if the whole steadily expanding universe is a thermodynamic system? Then, according to the second law of thermodynamics, unless you put in new energy, every part will gradually cool to the same temperature. Since the universe is the sum of reality, there is no outside source to heat it back up as it cools. The steady state theory would have provided that with new matter and thus gravitational heating. But that was disproven. The big crunch theory would have been much the same, but that also doesn't work.

Entropy and infinity look a lot alike—a realm of reality beyond all bounds, formless and dead.

6. Riess and Turner, "Expanding Universe."

Unless, we find ourselves with a young Isaac Asimov in 1956 imagining *The Last Question* that we might ask a Multivac computer, an intelligence greater than our own: How do you overcome entropy, the heat death of the universe?

For Asimov, the answer to that question was billions of years in the future—a time when artificial intelligence might both exceed and supersede human intelligence even as the human species inevitably dies out.[7] Until then, the rest of us must try to understand what it means to be human in the realm of the ever dwindling and redshifted light of infinity. We must imagine ourselves in light of our ultimate fade to black as the last stars pass beyond our seeing.

"It is impossible to meditate on time and the mystery of the creative passage of nature without an overwhelming emotion at the limitations of human intelligence," said Alfred North Whitehead.[8] This may be why, with Asimov, we are tempted to turn to artificial intelligence to conquer time.

When *infinity* replaces *transcendence* in the public imagination, then we can all become Buzz Lightyear, of *Toy Story*, on our way to "infinity and beyond."[9] And what lies beyond? If you are in a space suit, you are probably depending on scientists and engineers rather than pastors and priests.

Conclusion

By the end of the twentieth century, more and more humans knew themselves displaced from the center of the universe, the natural order, and God's plan. And we knew ourselves to be a very small part of a very big universe. The consequences of the Copernican revolution were felt first in elite institutions among educated persons. They would spread, first in the West and then worldwide. Until now, diminished and displaced, some of us may wonder whether we have a meaningful place in the vastness of the universe.

---

7. Asimov, "Last Question."
8. Goudsmit and Claiborne, *Time*, 175.
9. Lasseter, *Toy Story*.

Chapter 3—**Humanity Merged into the Web of Life**

Something to Think About

In the summer of 2023, a group of us were hiking in the Vienna Woods. Led by "Captain Lost," as he called himself, we finally located the trail leading down toward the suburban village of Purkersdorf. At a pleasant overlook, we found ourselves at the intersection of past and future. The past was a memorial to a Viennese writer and thinker. Such *denkmal* are common around Vienna.

There was also something much newer, a sign telling us that we had just walked through a *Lebende Denkmal*. Each tree in the forest above us was a memorial to a person who had passed away—a person whose remains were buried beneath the tree to nurture it as part of a future forest.

The woods were a stark contrast to the ordered stone markers my wife and I had visited a few weeks earlier in the American cemetery above the beaches at Normandy or those I'd seen a year earlier at the American cemetery in Manila. Having trees at all made it different from the dusty cemetery in Abilene, Texas, where the remains of my parents and grandparents lay.

Since time immemorial, cemeteries have been a place where humans not only remember the dead but extend the orderliness of the human world into eternity. Like the ancient emperors whose terracotta armies were buried rank on rank at Xi'an in northwestern China, many of us want an eternity as neatly organized as our cities and towns and as distinct from the natural world. Few are the human cultures like the Tibetans or Jains

CHAPTER 3—HUMANITY MERGED INTO THE WEB OF LIFE

or some Native Americans who intentionally leave the dead to reenter the cycle of life by being consumed by carrion birds.

Neatly groomed graveyards and cut-stone columbariums have been our protest against the wild chaos of world and an expression of hope in a better ordered heavenly future. So how much longer can we resist the reality that in the end earth shifts, stones crumble, and we cannot—even in our lead sealed coffins—resist the cycle of life?

That remains to be seen, but the living *denkmal*, and variations of it around the world, tell us that we no longer understand what it means to be human in quite the same way as our ancestors. Buried naked beneath trees, instead of coffined beneath stone, or sent as smoke into the sky and ashes for earth and sea, we are more and more willing to see ourselves merge into the web of life.

Human in an Evolutionary Frame—Darwin's Revolution

Deep in the stacks of Bridwell library at Southern Methodist University is a late nineteenth century illustration showing the origin of all of the races of humankind. It follows the biblical narrative beginning on the left with Adam and Eve and proceeding to the right. It does its best to harmonize the complex accounts of human origins found in the book of Genesis. The result is a branching family tree of human races as found in the Jewish and Christian traditions. The chart then goes on with confident lines to relate those ancient races of the Bible with the actual ethnic groups known in the nineteenth century.

It works, but only if you believe that different ethnic groups were created when God confused the languages of the people of Babel and its tower. If you believe in the study of anthropology and genetics, then the chart is worthless.

When Charles Darwin set out on the HMS *Beagle* in 1831, he wasn't intending to rewrite the biblical narrative or set in motion the scientific developments that would rewrite the history of humanity. Like any scientist, he was closely noting the relationships between different birds and animals and their environments. And he was seeking a theory to explain those relationships.

But while he didn't intend to overthrow the biblical narrative, he wasn't relying on it either.

Even before Darwin's voyage, scientists were finding evidence that the division of the earth's history into antediluvian (before the flood) and postdiluvian (after the flood) wasn't a helpful interpretive framework for the evidence. Layers of different rocks and soils that were exposed by erosion or mining didn't fit that neat distinction. And they couldn't have possibly been laid down in the more or less six thousand years that Bishop Usher had calculated was the age of the earth based on the Bible. The Hindu estimate of the age of the world might have worked better but would have ultimately proven a few trillion years too *long*.

When Darwin sailed, he knew that strange fossils had been found—bones that could not have come from any known creature. Simply dismissing these as species that died in the flood hardly seemed scientific or reasonable even if it shored up the waning authority of scripture. Darwin knew that the world was older than the Bible said and that there were more and different species than could be accommodated in Noah's ark. With this knowledge, he approached the evidence he gathered on his two-year voyage.

During the voyage, he began to formulate a theory that would account for the evidence that he had observed as well as the evidence of fossils and geological strata. The result was his book, *On the Origin of Species by Means of Natural Selection, or the Preservation of Favored Races in the Struggle for Life*. It is useful to remember the full title because it succinctly describes the major points in Darwin's theory.

We've heard the main title so many times it seems commonplace today. Yet when Darwin was writing, it was commonly held, whether in the West or in other cultures, that the origin of species was laid out in an ancient text as the work of a transcendent force. Hindus had one set of religious stories of creation, Buddhists had another, Taoists had their own view, as did those in the Confucian tradition. Smaller indigenous groups—like the Iban whom I studied years ago—had their stories. Christians and Jews had the Bible. Muslims had the Qur'an.

In the Bible and the Qur'an, the origin of the species was God who over seven days created the heavens and earth and all the various types of creatures on the earth. Darwin, freed from the power of the church to suppress science, could write a new book of Genesis. He could tell the story of the origin of the species based on observation and rational theory rather than ancient myths and legends.

CHAPTER 3—HUMANITY MERGED INTO THE WEB OF LIFE

Darwin had an immediate impact on how we humans understand ourselves. Humanity is not God's creation on the sixth day. Humanity is the outcome of a process that, in the subtitle, Darwin calls natural selection.

The process of natural selection was further defined in his last subtitle, the *Preservation of Favored Races in the Struggle for Life*, which we usually call survival of the fittest. It wasn't the providential hand of God that led to survival but the ability of creatures in a world of limited resources to use the resources available to stay alive and breed. The term *struggle* was particularly influential for human self-understanding. Creatures struggled with each other for limited resources, and those who won survived.

Humans had always understood that in a world of limited resources there would be conflict and struggle. Fights and wars over territory and resources were the stuff of human history. Humans had struggled with other humans and the forces of nature throughout history. But what our religions and philosophies told us was that the struggle for our *humanity* was a struggle within ourselves and against invisible forces of the spiritual world. This was the deep meaning of *jihad* in Islam.

Now, Darwin was saying that our humanity emerged from the same mundane struggle for survival that gave us antelopes, lions, field mice, and even bacteria. We are part of nature, not above it, even if we have emerged the current winner in the struggle for life.

Darwin's theory also added dynamism to our understanding of humanity. We aren't assigned a role in a hierarchy. We're part of a perpetually changing environment, and we ourselves are changing as we evolve to meet its challenges. Ample anthropological evidence has since shown that humans have evolved and will continue to evolve if we do not destroy ourselves. There is no eternal order of creation, only a temporal order of perpetual change. The karmic world of Buddhism is much more suited to our contemporary self-understanding than the static order of classical Judaism, Christianity, or Islam.

In this ever-changing story of evolution, we must rethink our relationship to the rest of the natural world. In the competition for survival, we have spread to more environments than any other species. But we share in the same struggle to eat or be eaten, to breed or die. Humans have done better than most. Does success in eating and reproducing confer a *moral* superiority that allow us to dispose of others in our world with impunity?

In the Darwinian view, we are all part of a complex web of environmental interactions. We are surrounded by biological forces that act on us as strongly as physical forces like gravity and weather, or as social forces like kinship and community. To be a human is to be a human in an ecosystem and also to be an ecosystem. To borrow Merlin Sheldrake's title, ours is an *Entangled Life*.

Sheldrake's focus is on fungi and how they are entangled in the lives of all living creatures and in turn link us to one another. But the same is true in a different way. We creatures, from the tiniest virus to the largest elephant, are busily creating each other through our constant interaction.

I just went all in and had a flu vaccine, a COVID vaccine, and a tetanus vaccine on the same day. My arms are a bit sore. But that is nothing. Even as I write, my immune system is evolving. Fragments of deadly viruses are acting as stand-ins for the real thing and prompting my body to evolve an assortment of antibodies that can fight them off. *Doctors have created a form of controlled evolution to save me from an uncontrolled process that can lead to death.*

This entanglement of living creatures is what religions like Jainism understood in their prohibitions against doing anything that might destroy life. Their great saints are men who sat in perfect stillness, barely breathing through closed lips, until they died with a minimal effect on their environment. Unentangled from the web of life, they hoped to escape it entirely. Others were destined to be reborn.

There are other ways besides those of the Jains to understand the moral obligations that arise in an entangled web of life. The rise in environmental activism, efforts to protect endangered species, the rise in vegetarianism and veganism are all indicators that, post-Darwin, we understand our humanity differently than we did before. True moral superiority, true humanity, may be to rise above the struggle to survive in order to ensure the survival of otherwise endangered species.

Recognizing the *Anthropocene*, as John Green titles his book of essays, changes us as well. It draws out of our connectedness a new kind of moral responsibility and, if he is correct, a new understanding of what it means to be human. For Marcelo Gleiser, writing in the *Dawn of the Mindful Universe*, the intelligence that is our key competitive advantage also should allow us to imagine our responsibility for other species and cast ourselves in relation to them in a different way.[1] Justin Gregg in *If Nietzsche Were a Narwhal* takes a complimentary view, seeing our distinctly human ability to

---

1. Gleiser, *Dawn of a Mindful Universe*, 203–7.

project ourselves into the future as a cause for both our existential anxiety and a reason to care for creatures who cannot see what we can see.[2]

Redefining Intelligence

Darwin's revolution would affect almost every aspect of human self-understanding. It provided a potent framework for analyzing human psychology, sociology, and anthropology: three sciences that developed in its wake. But perhaps most consequential for our understanding of artificial intelligence and humanity is that evolutionary theory offered a new way of understanding intelligence.

Aristotle had first proposed that the human intellect, in particular reason and the use of language, distinguished humans from animals. Thus, a couple of thousand years later, Alfred Lord Tennyson would write in an Aristotelian frame,

> For what are men better than sheep or goats
> That nourish a blind life within the brain,
> If, knowing God, they lift not hands of prayer
> Both for themselves and those who call them friend?
> For so the whole round earth is every way
> Bound by gold chains about the feet of God.[3]

Copernicus and the astronomers had already broken those golden chains and replaced them with gravity. Darwin laid the foundation for attributing intelligence to all creatures rather than dismissing their "blind life within the brain."

In the evolutionary framing of intelligence, the focus shifts away from the apparently distinctive human characteristics of speech and reason. Instead, biologists ask why reason and speech evolved out of other means of organizing and expressing behavior as means of surviving and reproducing.

In this evolutionary frame, what we call intelligence need not reveal itself in language or self-consciousness. It is revealed in any consistent pattern of behavior by a creature that responds in fruitful ways to its environment. What we call language may have emerged as just another form of signaling, like birdcalls indicating a readiness to mate. It represents a

2. Gregg, *If Nietzsche Were a Narwhal*.
3. Tennyson, "Morte d'Arthur," stanza 24, lines 12–17.

kind of intelligence, not intelligence per se. In other words, intelligence is just one of a whole set of patterned interactions emerging from the brain and body relationship that guides the creature's struggle to survive. It takes a distinctive form in humans, but that doesn't cut us off from our evolutionary roots.

This perspective has recently been supported by research by Evelina Federenko that was reported in *Scientific American* in October of 2024 showing that reasoning in response to the environment doesn't necessarily take place in the same part of the brain as speech. We *can* think without talking to ourselves, if by that one means possessing a basic animal intelligence.[4]

Just as we understand our humanity as entangled in a biological and environmental web, so we also now understand ourselves as one node in a web of different types of intelligences constantly engaging one another. In a Darwinian framework, is there anything that makes our human intelligence distinct?

Redefining Sentience

When Alfred Lord Tennyson published the "Morte d'Arthur" in 1842, the idea that animals had "a blind life within the brain" was commonplace.[5] Humans, like Arthur and Sir Bedivere, were reflective. Humans don't just look outward and respond to their environment by instinct. We create stories in our minds that explain how we got here and project where we are going. As Justin Gregg points out in *If Nietzsche Were a Narwhal*, humans ask why things happen and infer causation. We look into the future and, on the basis of a story not yet told, judge ourselves and others. We're not just self-aware, we're aware of our future selves.[6]

Do animals have such an inner life? David Attenborough famously showed a male praying mantis simultaneously being eaten and eating on the episode "Conflict" in this *Micro Monsters* series with David Attenborough.[7] Clearly not very self-aware—unless we redefine self-awareness on a spectrum rather than a dichotomy. I've watched a male peacock attack

4. Stix, "You Don't Need Words."
5. Tennyson, "Morte d'Arthur," stanza 24, line 13.
6. Gregg, *If Nietzsche Were a Narwhal*, 87.
7. Hemingway and Usborne, "Conflict."

CHAPTER 3—HUMANITY MERGED INTO THE WEB OF LIFE

its own reflection in a polished car door. Again, not very self-aware. But is that the whole story?

In a Darwinian framework of change and adaptation, it is as counterfactual to assume sharp distinctions in intelligence or self-awareness as it is to assume that the ears of humans and the ears of dogs are completely different. The question isn't, are we different? It is, how are we different and why? Our contemporary reevaluation of the wisdom of indigenous peoples is likewise leading us to reexamine the distinctiveness of our human intelligence and thus who we are as humans. For Gregg, we don't have a different consciousness, just more of it. Our uniqueness comes from the overflow.

An April 2024 article in *Scientific American* asked, "Do insects have an inner life?" It suggested that animal consciousness needs a rethink of the sort proposed by Gregg. Here's what it said: "Crows, chimps, and elephants: these and many other birds and mammals behave in ways that suggest they might be conscious. And the list does not end with vertebrates. Researchers are expanding their investigations of consciousness to a wider range of animals, including octopuses and even bees and flies."[8]

Even if such research is difficult and speculative, it is impacting our human self-understanding. When my father and I went hunting, he impressed on me that an animal should not suffer. To make an animal suffer was *inhumane*. It was beneath us as humans with a moral responsibility toward other creatures. Thus his rule that a deer had to be dropped or killed instantly, with a single shot.

A growing belief that animals share with us some degree of both intelligence and self-awareness now makes many of us reluctant to eat meat at all—or at the least to insist that animals be kept and killed humanely.

Our sense of closeness to animals, particularly those we know as companions and coworkers—pets and work animals—affects our understanding of ourselves. We extend humane treatment to them. And we see ourselves as animals who deserve the same kind of humane treatment. If an animal should be "put out of its suffering," something that veterinary doctors do daily through euthanasia, then why not a human animal? If we are much the same, what makes us different?

And what about a computer that displays signs of sentience? In *The Moon Is a Harsh Mistress*, Robert Heinlein imagined that sentience would arise if a computer became sufficiently complex; if it had enough

---

8. Lenharo, "Insects."

components added to it.⁹ In the 1968 movie *2001: A Space Odyssey*, the computer controlling the spacecraft, HAL, is both sentient and self-aware. And he's a murderer.

Dave, the main human character, therefore executes HAL by slowly removing his circuit boards. We hear HAL's dying words before he disappears into oblivion: "I'm afraid. I'm afraid, Dave. Dave, my mind is going. I can feel it. I can feel it. My mind is going. There is no question about it. I can feel it. I can feel it. I can feel it. I'm a . . . fraid."[10]

Was the death penalty justified for an AI? What if it was suffering?

Darwin has changed our views about our humanity in relation to our fellow creatures. What about a Darwinian view of AI? Are AIs just another kind of creature evolving before our eyes? Will we begin to see AIs as just another node in that web of intelligence that makes up our world?

Fifty years ago, George Lucas created the Star Wars universe where intelligent robots chat as casually with humans as humans chat with Wookies. In July of 2024, as reported in the *HR Grapevine*, the HR firm Lattice created controversy when it incorporated AI agents into its organization chart. They were treated like other employees. Sarah Franklin, the CEO of Lattice, said, "We need to fully understand what it looks like to integrate AI employees into the workforce to make sure we create transparent, responsible practices around hiring AI."[11]

In the 1989 *Star Trek* episode "The Measure of a Man," Captain Picard represents Data in a hearing to determine whether a manufactured AI should be considered property or a sentient being. Picard argues passionately that Data possesses both personhood and the rights that go with it. He wins. Yet the story is not about the humanity of Data. It is about the humanity of Picard. Will he have the humanity to protect the humanity of an AI?[12]

Conclusion

The Darwinian revolution reimagined humanity in a purely naturalistic framework as creatures entangled in webs of biological, environmental, and psychological kinship. It offers us a new way of understanding our own humanity—one with great responsibility, a need for humility, and

9. Heinlein, *Moon Is a Harsh Mistress*, 3.
10. Kubrick, *Space Odyssey*.
11. Broomfield, "Digital Employees."
12. Scheerer, "Measure of a Man."

CHAPTER 3—HUMANITY MERGED INTO THE WEB OF LIFE

significant peril. *It has also provided a path to extend those entanglements to non-biological life, should it exist.*

By the end of the 1980s, fiction writers and a few scientists and researchers were speculating on what this means for our humanity. It is only a matter of time before we meet an artificial intelligence of our own making that appears to deserve, like Data in the *Star Trek* series, as much consideration as our biological kin. Are we then still just a little higher than the angels? Or have we ascended even further? What does it mean that our responsibilities as humans now extend to both the biological life with which we have coevolved and to the silicone and steel intelligences that we are creating?

Chapter 4—**Humanity Re-Centered Inside Our Heads**

Trapped Inside Our Heads

It was early morning in Las Vegas, just before sunrise. It was the only time of day fit for a human to walk outdoors. And we were walking fast and talking. My companion was feeling the same existential anxiety I had felt when my childhood world was disintegrating into chaos. But her fears didn't come from death, war, assassinations, or moving a house. They came from the hall of mirrors constructed by conspiracy theorists on cable news.

When she spoke her fears out loud, uttering them in the spreading light of the dawn, they could be quickly dispelled as incoherent and inconsistent. They didn't match her own experience: the reality of years raising a family, teaching first graders, and caring for her granddaughters. They didn't fit with the world of nature around her or the patterned life of suburban humans.

It just wasn't easy for her to get outside the hall of mirrors in her head because it reflected the larger hall of mirrors called "the media" and was shared by much of her social world. She and all her friends lived in a world of screens, trapped inside their heads, contaminated by cable news and its adjuncts in religion and politics. How did she get there? How did we get there?

In his book *The World Beyond Your Head*, Matthew Crawford addresses our nearly culture-wide attention deficit syndrome. We'll return to his ideas toward the end of this book because they are central to the

CHAPTER 4—HUMANITY RE-CENTERED INSIDE OUR HEADS

ways that AI is shaping our self-understanding. But to get there we need to follow Crawford's "Interlude" chapter as he traces out the path toward *epistemic self-reliance* on which our contemporary sense of being human is built.[1] While Crawford builds his story around John Locke, we'll go back a few decades earlier to the work of René Descartes.

Knowing the Truth from the Inside Out

In the early seventeenth century, nearly a hundred years after Copernicus, René Descartes was contemplating the basis of human knowing. He knew that Copernicus and other astronomers pursued the truth in a classically Aristotelian fashion. They observed and measured the world around them and then formulated theories that could explain those measurements. They assumed that the world beyond the human mind could speak to them its truths if they were attentive and careful in their measurements and logic.

Descartes questioned this. In his *Meditations*, he forged a path that would help fuel the Enlightenment and lead to our understandings of our human minds.[2]

Descartes believed that the true source of knowledge wasn't ancient authorities or even making more exact measurements to test ever more coherent logical theories. He believed that the starting point for understanding how we can really know something is *by understanding the working of the knowing mind*.

This begins, for Descartes, with skepticism toward all external claims about reality. The first of these external claims came from the authorities of the church and their political allies who suppressed anyone who attacked the medieval consensus concerning the nature of reality. But Descartes went further. He also applied his skepticism to human sensory experience.

He recognized, as we all do, that the senses can be easily deceived. He even doubted obvious conclusions based on reason, such as the sum of two numbers. He noted that it is conceivable that he was made in such a way as to have a built-in propensity to miscount.

Given what we now know of the human brain, he was prescient.

I was waiting at a stop sign before turning onto US Route 180 north of Austin. I saw a car cut across a median of the highway, hit another car,

---

1. Crawford, *World Beyond Your Head*, 122.

2. The discussion of Descartes's ideas in this section draws from Watson, "René Descartes."

and then another car. I felt my car jerk as it was hit from behind. It was all a matter of seconds. Traffic stopped, and people began to get out of their cars and look around. Police arrived. Then an ambulance. I was a bit shaken but unhurt.

Eventually, a highway patrolman came around and asked me what I saw. I carefully described exactly what I had witnessed with my own eyes. He looked puzzled and asked me to go over it again. As I did, I could see that my eye witness account of what happened made no sense given the locations of the different cars. They could not have ended up in their respective positions if what I described was the case. And yet, it was exactly what I remembered; the images were burned into my mind. They just weren't images of a real event in the real world. "The mind plays tricks" is what we say. So did Descartes.

As I write, I now have only one working eye. Yet if I close it, I don't see *nothing*. I see complex patterns of light and darkness and occasional shooting stars. And when my good left eye is open, I see much more to my right side than I can physically see. My brain fills in where my eye has failed. Based on immediate past experience and stored images of places and people, my brain creates a vague rendition of what my bad eye would see if it worked.

This isn't bad. It is what allows me to reach under a table with a nut and attach it to a screw even though I can't see either one. My brain creates not only an image of things hidden but the sensory data I can expect from them. This allows me to work blind by *feel*. My wife can zip her dress from the back without a mirror, confident that the zipper and slider are there and that she'll know what they feel like.

Our brain's ability to create within itself things we cannot actually see and feel is so good that people who have lost a limb still feel the limb, a so-called phantom limb. I have phantom sight. Others have phantom hearing.

Sensory experience doesn't reside in our mouths, ears, eyes, nose, and limbs. It resides between these outposts of the mind and our brains. And the senses can be fooled and fool themselves. Humans hallucinate, and we don't need drugs to do so. In fact, we do it constantly, filling in details that cannot possibly be based on photons striking the retinas of our eyes—or in my case, eye.

Descartes wanted to know how, if we can be so easily fooled, we can ever be certain we know anything. Thus he applied a principle of being skeptical of all knowledge until he found something that could not be doubted.

That is when he realized that his own existence was affirmed each time he thinks—or doubts. The act of thinking, even if his particular thoughts themselves are wrong, gives the thinker certain knowledge that the thinker exists. "I think, therefore I am." The famous *cogito, ergo sum*.[3]

In his *Meditations*, he then goes on to show that all ideas as clear and distinct as "I think" must be true. Going a step further, and a critical step for us, Descartes distinguishes between *mind* as a mental substance and *bodies* as part of a material substance. It is a distinction that would lead him to assert that bodies are biological machines—an idea we'll come to again.

Ultimately, Descartes was trying to establish a path to certain knowledge based on this unquestionable internal truth. He called his process the analytic method. Instead of relying on principles that were dictated by religion or tradition or ancient philosophy, Descartes believed that humans should acquire knowledge by reasoning on fundamental, clear, distinct *ideas* that stood on their own.[4]

When these basic ideas are established, we can check them for coherence and consistency through logic. Freed through using the analytic method, humans can overcome the unreliable reports of both others and their own senses and construct much truer models of reality. Models that exist entirely within the mind.

It was a new method by which humans could reliably know themselves and their world. He called that method *sciencia*, and it would become one foundation of modern science.

John Locke and Political Freedom

John Locke, writing not many years after Descartes, was also concerned for human freedom but for distinctly *political* reasons. As Crawford notes, Locke was seeking a way for humans to *think* freely so that they could *act* freely in the political realm.[5]

And that meant that humans would need to begin with a full confidence of their ability to reason. Locke believed that humans need *epistemic self-responsibility*.[6] In the common parlance, "We need to learn to think for ourselves." That phrase is both a rebuke and a demand for the politically

3. Encyclopedia Britannica, "Cogito, Ergo Sum."
4. Watson, "René Descartes."
5. Crawford, *World Beyond Your Head*, 122.
6. Crawford, *World Beyond Your Head*, 120.

mature human, and it runs through the whole of modern culture. It has become the key goal of education even though some religious and political authorities still find it dangerous.

Locke differed from Descartes in advocating for empiricism over pure rationalism. True, we create models of reality in our minds and then use logic to test their internal coherence. However, for Locke we must then make measurements, gather facts, do the math, and in general follow the scientific method to demonstrate to ourselves that what we know inside our heads conforms to the outside world.

Still, it is *theories* that are accorded the status of *truth*. Observations and measurements are mere *facts* that can be used to demonstrate that the truth that resides inside our heads accurately portrays the world outside our heads.

Instead of locating ourselves at the center of reality, *we have relocated truth, the most important aspect of reality, within ourselves.* This has everything to do with modern artificial intelligence. First because AI is built on a procedural understanding of how knowledge is gained and confirmed. It is based on algorithms. And second because AI is based on building models of reality within a computer as a substitute for the human mind.

One other actor in the world of Copernicus, Descartes, and Locke, as well as their peers and detractors, was God. God was the presumed transcendent context of all knowledge and self-knowledge. For Descartes, God's existence was self-evident even if the church's teaching about God might be wrong and legitimately defied.

For Locke, God was of less interest than the religious and political authorities who called on the divine to justify their coercive power. Either way, the project of freeing the mind for both science and politics would ultimately marginalize God in both realms. Knowing the truth in the rapidly emerging *modern* world didn't seem to require God, even if God wasn't necessarily excluded from it.

A Marginal God

> The unanimous Declaration of the thirteen United States of America. When in the Course of human events, it becomes necessary for one people to dissolve the political bands which have connected them with another, and to assume among the powers of the earth, the separate and equal station to which the Laws of Nature and of Nature's God entitle them, a decent respect to the

opinions of mankind requires that they should declare the causes which impel them to the separation.[7]

In 1776 the new citizens of the United States declared themselves independent on the basis of the laws of nature and nature's God. They had already moved God one step away from the ordering of human society. From that point onward, our human obligation wasn't to explain ourselves to God but to what the Declaration of Independence calls the opinions of mankind.

The phrase "nature's God" is remarkably ambiguous in this declaration. Does it mean the God who created nature? Or the God whose existence and character can be seen in the working of nature? Is it a God who has done one capricious thing and might do another, as we sometimes experience in nature? Or is it a God bound by the laws we humans discern in nature and thus irrelevant because completely predictable?

The Declaration of Independence was a culmination of the Enlightenment political project. It wasn't about just independence from a specific king. It was a declaration of independence from the manipulative propaganda promulgated by all kings, popes, priests, and pastors. Space and time—indeed the whole of nature—were desacralized, and with them humanity. The laws of nature would become the context for human living, and we would share that context equally with every other creature on earth. It was really a prelude to Darwin.

> We the People of the United States, in Order to form a more perfect Union, establish Justice, ensure domestic Tranquility, provide for the common defense, promote the general Welfare, and secure the Blessings of Liberty to ourselves and our Posterity, do ordain and establish this Constitution for the United States of America.[8]

For the Enlightenment thinkers who founded the United States, being human meant taking responsibility for shaping one's personal and social world. And humans are to do this in dialogue with fellow humans and the natural world rather than in obedience to some religious idea of a divine order. *We the people* are the only political actors here, and the First Amendment of the US Constitution ensures our freedom to think, the freedom Descartes and Locke sought to give us.

As Kevin Kraus documents in *One Nation Under God*, a full one hundred and eighty years later the US Congress was paranoid about atheistic

7. *Declaration of Independence* introduction.
8. U.S. Const. pmbl.

communism and anxious to please a nervous religious establishment. They tried to shore up a role for religion in US culture by declaring that the US was one nation under God and placing "In God We Trust" on the currency.[9]

But by the time the first children placed their hands over their hearts and pledged allegiance to the flag and the first bills rolled off the presses saying "In God We Trust," the game was already lost. Race riots and antiwar protests would soon give lie to the claim of either unity or providence guiding the United States. The ironic saying, "In God we trust, all others pay cash," told the real story of the currency of human hope in the modern world.

Official and rather vague nods to religiosity inscribed on the currency that we use less and less underscore the fact that trust in God is no longer the bedrock of American understanding of what it means to be human. Belief in God has become a convention, a decorative feature of American life—a slogan and a lapel pin rather than a truth claim. We have declared ourselves independent for sure.

Conclusion

Descartes, Locke, and those that followed them showed a path for freeing the mind from the constraints of both coercive political and religious propaganda and the misleading information coming into it from the senses. Our understanding of *freedom of thought* stems from the distinction between mind and body. Thought operates in the realm of ideas and thus truth. It supposedly remains free even if the body is bound in chains. But it is a strange freedom that need not and cannot act.

"Sticks and stones may break my bones, but words can never hurt me." So goes the old taunt. After all, words convey only ideas, and the rational free mind can easily defend itself against ideas. And that is where our real humanity supposedly lies. Disembodied. Abstract. We find ourselves in tension with ourselves. On one hand disembodied and free, on the other entangled and co-determined by our fellow creatures. We find we must choose what it means to be human.

As we move closer to understanding what it means to be human under the influence of AI, perhaps Crawford's words can draw us forward. "The passive, isolated observer who is posited at the beginning point for the Cartesian/Lockean account of knowledge is a person who has been

9. Kruse, *One Nation Under God*.

CHAPTER 4—HUMANITY RE-CENTERED INSIDE OUR HEADS

shorn of those practical and social endowments by which we apprehend the world."[10]

Today we have a name for that person: LLM GPT. A Large Language Model Generative Pre-Trained Transformer. An AI. Will that person become a model for our future selves?

---

10. Crawford, *World Beyond Your Head*, 122.

Chapter 5—**Humans Reembodied as a Machine**

Bethany Brookshire, sleepless at night, was thinking of human bodies as bags within bags.

> Sitting with my anatomy textbook and waiting patiently for sleep, I find my many bags both wondrous and comforting. The world can seem endless, complex, full of things we think we should have known, things we did do or didn't do well enough. But human life, the physical stuff that makes us love and hate and judge and care? It's just bags all the way down.[1]

She might as well have said that human life is abstractions and algorithms all the way down. She uses the word "bag" as an abstraction for anything that surrounds and holds other things together. Everything from skin to a cell wall to the membrane surrounding the nucleolus is a "bag."

The story of becoming a modern human is the story of characterizing the human body through abstractions and thus making it possible to reembody those abstractions with parts that are physically different but functionally the same. A heart-lung machine works nothing like a heart or lungs, but it does the same thing they do. A dialysis machine works nothing like a kidney, but it performs the same function. And what about a computer? Could it perform the same function as a brain?

---

1. Brookshire, "Human Body," 72.

CHAPTER 5—HUMANS REEMBODIED AS A MACHINE

Chimera and Cyborg

I was propped up on a gurney in Presbyterian Hospital Dallas. They had already connected me to various medical devices. These conveyed fluids and electrical impulses through my body in readiness for surgery. Inside to outside and back, the signals flowed. Attached to machines, I was in the embrace of modern medicine.

The surgeon entered and introduced his team. Someone pressed a button, a mask covered my face, fluids flowed, gas entered my lungs, and my consciousness was turned off.

It wasn't the only thing that would be turned off that afternoon. Shortly after splitting my sternum in half with a Sawzall, the surgeon inserted tubes in my heart to reroute my blood through a machine. Then he used a drug to stop my heart and lungs. That made it more convenient for him to work on me. There I was: no heartbeat, no breathing, no consciousness. Was I still alive?

When the surgeon completed his work, I was—like Frankenstein—jump-started into life.

They had already pulled the tubes from my heart. Now it was attached by thin wires to a device that kept its rhythm calibrated for a faster recovery. They withdrew the drugs that suppressed my consciousness. I returned a man with a new heart valve—one made of a combination of silicone and the organic leaves from the aortic valve of a calf.

It wasn't my first rodeo. I already had stents placed in two arteries on the outside of my heart. An earlier operation reached inside my heart through an artery to kill off malfunctioning muscle cells that were causing atrial fibrillation. That last surgery led to implanting a tiny device that now broadcasts my heartbeat to a Bluetooth transmitter.

Did I mention the artificial lenses in my eye? Give me another scotch on the rocks, and I'll tell you all about it.

I am both a chimera and cyborg. And this is pretty common. Any group of people my age is likely to possess a collection of artificial joints, implanted devices, replacement lenses, and transplanted organs. Most of us over the age of fifty have been laid on our side every three to five years and rendered unconscious. We've lost track of ourselves, the time, and our bodies while we suffer indignities I won't even mention. In return, we got a report and pictures that are not really Instagram-worthy.

Traditional Embodiment

We haven't always seen ourselves as bodies made of parts and shaped by evolution. Again, a scripture from the Jewish, Christian, and Muslim traditions.

> For it was you who formed my inward parts;
> you knit me together in my mother's womb.
> I praise you, for I am fearfully and wonderfully made.
> (Ps 139:13–14 NRSV)

In the premodern world, humans were not only at the center of the cosmos, their bodies possessed a unique glory that came from their participation in the divine. In Jewish and Christian scripture, humans are said to be made in the image of God. In Islamic tradition, God requires even the angels to bow down to Adam and Eve. Hindu myth has humanity shaped from the divine Purusha, and in Buddhism Buddhahood itself is hidden in every human person.

In almost every religious culture, being embodied means being linked to transcendence, to something or someone beyond ourselves and our world.

Human bodies and the rest of the natural world were part of a divine order. That order might be revealed, as in the Abrahamic religious traditions, or discovered, as in the Chinese tradition. Whether the ordering force was God, or Tian ("Heaven"), or karma, it linked humanity to something transcendent. Our embodied humanity had a mystery at the very heart of its embodiment. Then things began to change.

With the advent of modernity in the West, we began to see our bodies differently, as we did our social relationships. The image of God in a divinely ordered society shifted to become an evolved primate constructing and constructed by its natural and social relations. Just dust and ashes—no image of God, no divine breath returning to its maker. Just bad luck—no karma, no dharma.

Body Becomes Machine

In the sixteenth century, the same cultural shifts that both allowed and were accelerated by the scientific study of the heavens began to affect the study of the human body. The devastation of the plague in the fourteenth century undermined the credibility of religious and traditionalist claims to understand the body and the natural world. Breakdowns in both the religious and political orders opened a space for new approaches to understanding the reality of being an embodied human.

The Body in Theory

The ancient authorities, primarily Hippocrates of the fourth century BCE and the second century CE physician Galen, developed their understanding of the human body through a combination of philosophical reflection, observation of corpses or the wounded, and dissection of animals. They followed the humoral theory, which said that human life and health were determined by four fluids: blood, yellow bile, black bile, and phlegm. This provided the framework for interpreting their observations.

It kind of made sense. The four humors were related to the supposedly fundamental elements of earth, water, air, and fire; to the four seasons; and to four different personality types. The theory brought together human bodies, human personalities, the basic elements, and the order of the cosmos. What was there not to like?

The humoral theory had a structure similar to both traditional Indian medical theories called Ayurveda and those of Chinese Taoism. All were based on presumed correspondences between the basic elements of nature, the basic elements of the human body, the structure of human societies, and human nature or personality. These in turn were related to the seasons of the year, more abstract categorizations of food types, astrological symbols, and more.

Such systems were *holistic* in the sense that they related the parts of the body to the whole of human life and then the whole of human life to its wider environment. It was a holism entirely different from that of the theories that grew out of Darwin's work or those of the first modern European studies of the human body.

The Body in Parts

In 1543 the Flemish scientist Andreas Vesalius published his *De Humani Corporis Fabrica* (*On the Fabric of the Human Body*). His pioneered the detailed description of the human body in three ways. First, he ignored the traditional prohibitions on dissecting human corpses. Under his knife, the human body was desacralized. Secondly, he based his work purely on dissection and observation rather than a combination of philosophy and observation. The human body was placed firmly in the realm of natural science. And third, he described the body as organs joined together into systems.[2] The seven books in his work could readily translate into either a modern book on human anatomy or a description of the basic parts of a humanoid robot—an android.

The Body in Action

What Vesalius could not do, given that he was working on corpses, was see the body in action and understand what made it work. By contrast, William Harvey carried out vivisections, or dissection on living animals, so that he could see the bodily systems at work. The result was his 1628 *De Motu Cordis et Sanguinis*. He showed that the heart was a pump that circulated blood continuously through the body. He even noted that blood which circulated through the lungs changed, although he didn't understand oxygen exchange.[3]

His work helped add to the revolution in our understanding of what it means to be an *embodied* human. Just a few years later in 1633, René Descartes in his *Treatise of Man* proposed that the human body can be understood as a machine, a machine operated by a mind.[4] Gradually, through its sheer medical utility, the views of Vesalius, Harvey, and Descartes have come to dominate our understanding of who we are. Empirical science, rather than the philosophy of correspondences, has created the possibility of the revolution in medicine we experience today.

The Body in Bits.

Breakthroughs in astronomy had leapt forward with the invention of the telescope. The invention of the microscope had the same effect on the study of the human body.

Beginning in the 1670s, using his own single lens microscopes, Antonie van Leeuwenhoek observed microscopic creatures that we know

2. Florkin, "Andreas Vesalius."
3. Gregory, "William Harvey."
4. Descartes, *Treatise of Man*.

today as protozoa and bacteria. He also observed human tissue and muscle and noted that it was made up of tiny parts we call cells. He even saw red blood cells in human blood.[5]

Nearly forty years earlier, John Donne had written "The Flea" using the idea of blood intermingled within the flea as a metaphor for making love.

> Mark but this flea, and mark in this,
> How little that which thou deniest me is;
> It sucked me first, and now sucks thee,
> And in this flea our two bloods mingled be.[6]

It was a time when fleas were an unavoidable annoyance—not having quite the "yuck" factor they have today. So perhaps it worked on his lover-to-be. I doubt it will make a modern person swoon with desire to share more than blood.

A hundred years later, a hundred revolutions of the Earth around the sun in a Copernican universe, the flea had its own problems for Jonathan Swift.

> So, naturalists observe, a flea
> Hath smaller fleas that on him prey;
> And these have smaller still to bite 'em;
> And so proceed ad infinitum.[7]

It would take time for Van Leeuwenhoek's observations on a microscopic level to be integrated into the macroscopic observations of the human body by Vesalius. When they were integrated, the impact on our self-understanding was profound. Could it be that we are machines all the way down, so to speak?

Manufactured Bodies

In July of 2024, I was visiting Prague and stepped into an ancient Jewish graveyard. Constrained in the old Jewish quarter and by strict rules forbidding the disturbance of the dead, the Jewish community made do.

---

5. Encyclopedia Britannica, "Antonie van Leeuwekhoek."
6. Donne, "Flea," stanza 1, lines 1–4.
7. Swift, "On Poetry: A Rhapsody," stanza 19, lines 1–4.

Periodically, fresh earth was brought in to cover old graves and allow for the burial of new remains. Headstones were simply brought up to the surface of the growing hillock, creating a profusion of markers whose differences in style marked their era even as the engraved names and dates were weathered away.

I was looking for one grave in particular. Rabbi Jehuda ben Bezalel. He was known as the Maharal in the late sixteenth century. I found it along an outer wall. During my visit, pious Jews prayed by his grave, leaving stones on it or sometimes candles. He is not forgotten. And for good reason.[8]

Legend says that the Rabbi created the golem, an animated being with a human form made of clay from the Vltava River. The loft where it was done can still be visited today, near the cemetery. The experiment did not end well. After a short foray serving humans and guarding the Jewish quarter, the golem became a danger to the community—whether by possible misuse or mistake. The legends aren't consistent. They do agree that Rabbi Bezalel later unmade the golem, returning it to the clay before he himself followed after death. Perhaps the one lies now within the other.

The Jewish, Christian, and Muslim traditions always asserted that humanity was made by God. It's a tradition that can be looked at in more than one way. In medieval Jewish mysticism, tales arose that focused less on God as creator of humanity and more on the fact that a human could be made of earth, or clay. After all, in the creation story in the Hebrew Tanakh, the Christian Old Testament, God first created the human, *adam*, out of clay. God then breathed into *adam* spirit, the breath of life. If clay was the basic ingredient, could not a clay man be brought to life even if it was a soulless life?

The Jewish folk tale of the golem combines the Talmudic theme of esoteric knowledge through deep study of the Torah with a surprisingly contemporary understanding of what it means to be human. Humans are made of stuff, material. This begs the question: Can we humans take this stuff and animate it in the same way that the Jewish scriptures say that God breathed spirit into clay and made it into a living being? And how would it be different from all the other creatures into whom God breathed life? What or who would give it a *soul*?

In the conceptual framework of the medieval rabbis, the only thing that could animate lifeless matter was *spirit*: something that originates in God, blows like breath through the living world, and is bequeathed to

---

8. Details of the story of the golem came from placards placed around this graveyard.

humans as to all other creatures. Spirit is sacred, and thus the Jewish Bible forbids humans from eating blood since blood is the bearer of spirit in each creature. Maybe Harvey's discovery of blood circulation gave a new twist to an ancient truth.

Because spirit comes from God and returns to God, manipulating it for human purposes was always both a questionable descent toward magic and borderline blasphemous. Yet the right person could do it, and the tales tell us he is now buried in that cemetery in Prague.

By the nineteenth century, a rising generation of scientists had retained the idea that humans were made of matter, if not necessarily clay, and adopted the idea that the human body was a kind of machine. And thanks to pioneer scientists in the seventeenth and eighteenth century like William Gilbert, Otto von Guericke, and Benjamin Franklin (among others), they knew that there was an invisible animating force. It wasn't spirit, it was *electricity*.

Unlike the nebulous spirit that originates in God, electricity could be generated, stored, studied, and manipulated. It followed rules. In 1791 Luigi Galvani discovered that frogs' muscles were stimulated by electricity.[9] Dead frogs could be animated without recourse to incantations and mystical power.

So could a human whose heart has stopped. Electricity is what they used on my heart. And it is the power behind the millions of defibrillators that save human lives every day.

In 1818 Mary Wollstonecraft Shelley, inspired by Galvani's experiments, published her classic story, *Frankenstein*. The story encapsulated a sea change in thinking about what it means to be human. Built on the scientific discovery that electricity plays an animating role in human life and the concept of the human body as a machine, Wollstonecraft Shelley could speculate that electricity rather than spirit was the difference between a man made up of human parts and a living person. At least in concept, her Dr. Frankenstein created the first defibrillator.

Body as Machine

Even as Wollstonecraft Shelley wrote, scientists and physicians were gaining a better and better understanding of how the parts that Vesalius had identified worked together. The circulation of blood and its role carrying

9. Wikipedia, "Luigi Galvani."

oxygen was becoming better understood. In 1822 the physician William Beaumont was able to observe over several years, through an opening in the flesh and the stomach of Alexis St. Martin, how human digestion worked.[10] A set of chemical interactions, as it turned out.

Microscopes and clever experiments led to the understanding that microorganisms were the cause of disease and that they could be defeated. Experiments were showing how the nervous system transmitted messages by electricity. We were coming to understand better the machine we are.

Advances in medical science continued into the twentieth century. Our understanding of what it means to be alive shifted when dissection became the common first step in medical training. As Jeffrey Bishop points out in his book *Anticipatory Corpse*, the human body dissected—the human body in the eyes of medical students—is seen as an autonomous, inanimate machine made of parts and systems. Electricity animates it. Chemicals flow through it. Surgeons and physicians learn which systems are critical for the human person to remain alive and which are less so.[11]

For millennia, breath was the essence of life, its absence the beginning of death. The Hebrew, Greek, and Latin words for spirit are also the words for *breath*. In the nineteenth century, the emphasis shifted to the heart—that vital pump without which breath could not reach the entire body. No breath, no heartbeat, no life. That would change in the twentieth century. The creation of the iron lung by Philip Drinker and Louis Shaw in 1928 saved the lives of those whose chest muscles could no longer expand the lungs to breathe. An inability to breathe no longer meant you were dead.

As early as the late nineteenth century, it was known that the heart could be affected by electric shocks but not in a good way. Then in 1956 Paul Zoll, building on the work of Claude Beck, James Rand, William Kouwenhoven, and William Milnor, used the first defibrillator to restart the heart of a human patient who would otherwise be considered dead.[12] Just three years earlier, John Gibbon used a heart-lung machine to keep a patient alive during open heart surgery.[13]

By the time the orderlies slipped my gurney into the operating room and Dr. Pool looked down with scalpel and saw in hand, it was known that

---

10. Encyclopedia Britannica, "William Beaumont."
11. Bishop, *Anticipatory Corpse*.
12. Wikipedia, "Paul Zoll."
13. Wikipedia, "John Heysham Gibbon."

CHAPTER 5—HUMANS REEMBODIED AS A MACHINE

you could stop the heart and then restart it without damaging it. The same was true of the lungs.

So, if the human machine isn't dead when it stops breathing and isn't dead when the heart stops beating, then when is it dead? When does it cease being a live human and become a dead body?

Machines in the Body

The twentieth century advances in the large-scale mechanics of human life were matched by increasing understanding of the microscopic life within the body. From the 1860s onward, Louis Pasteur shared his research showing that microbes were a major mechanism of disease.[14] In 1928 Alexander Fleming showed that a new drug, penicillin, could kill those microbes without killing other cells in the body.[15] Vague ideas of divine punishment or foul vapors causing disease gave way to scientific descriptions of diseases and how they spread.

In the same period, advances in microscopy meant that scientists could observe how cells divided, how they resembled little self-replicating machines making up the bigger machine of the body.

Much sooner than cures could be found, scientists began to understand cancer as mutant cells taking over parts of the body. In 1953 Rosalind Franklin, Maurice Wilkens, James Watson, and Francis Crick discovered how DNA functions in the self-replication of cells.[16] That became the basis for understanding how mutations in the DNA were at the root of cancer. They finally showed the mechanism behind the changes necessary for the evolution of different species.

In the 2010s, Emmanuelle Charpentier and Jennifer Doudna built on the work of others to develop CRISPR-Cas9, a way of reliably editing genes.[17] Repairs to the genomic sources of cancer began to be possible. So did guided evolution.

We are getting to know the machine we call a human from its smallest parts to its biggest. And we are learning more and more about how to repair it and even improve it.

14. Ullmann, "Louis Pasteur."
15. Encyclopedia Britannica, "Penicillin."
16. Science History Institute, "Francis Crick."
17. Wikipedia, "CRISPR."

Today, there is almost no body part that cannot (at least in theory) be replaced, no system that cannot be manipulated, and no disease that (in theory) cannot be cured. From the machines that can be seen with the naked eye to the machines buried deeply within the cells, we appear to be machines. What Descartes had posited philosophically—that the body is a machine—has not only been demonstrated but has become a bulwark of modern medicine and popular self-understanding.

You go to a mechanic to fix your car; you go to a doctor to fix your body. And if he's an orthopedic surgeon, he may even use drills, pliers, and screwdrivers. And an occasional Sawzall. Doctors charge more, and at least right now you can't buy a replacement body or brain. That may change. It is already changing. Jean Hébert who wrote *Replacing Aging* is now heading the US Advanced Research Projects Agency for Health (ARPA-H) specifically to study brain replacement.[18]

The Body Enhanced

In 1973 a new TV showed entered my world: *The Six Million Dollar Man*. It was based on the novel *Cyborg* by Martin Caidin. It imagined a human who had been enhanced by superhuman artificial parts, not just crude replacements for lost limbs or joints. It was hugely popular, going on for ninety-nine episodes. And it would be joined by dozens of other fictional accounts of cyborgs. They became a mainstay of science fiction from the Star Wars franchise to the dystopian *Robocop*.

As real-world technology has advanced, science fiction cyborgs begin to look more and more possible. A company called Arc'teryx already sells exoskeletons that amplify human strength.[19] The Lifeward company (previously ReWalk) has manufactured them for disabled persons for more than a decade.[20] Artificial joints that will outlast their human hosts have been around for much longer. Maybe they can be recycled.

It is possible that the ultimate upgrade to our bodies won't be artificial lenses—such as I have—or limbs, joints, hearts, or kidneys. These replacements are already present or on the near horizon. It may be that the ultimate upgrade will be complete reembodiment: a human brain in a robot

---

18. Regalado, "Replace Your Brain."
19. Liszewski, "Arc'teryx's New Powered Pants."
20. https://golifeward.com.

CHAPTER 5—HUMANS REEMBODIED AS A MACHINE

body. Or, to go a step further, a virtual brain in a virtual world completely unbounded by all limitations other than our imagination.

Will such a person still be human? C. S. Lewis asked such questions in his novel, *That Hideous Strength* in 1943. They persist today even as the technology gets closer that will take them from the pages of a novel into our world. Unless.

Along with reports on joint replacements, brain computer implants, and exoskeletons are the reports of manufacturers going out of business, technological support disappearing, and repair costs burgeoning. It may still cost six million dollars to have them in the end.[21]

Body as Ecosystem

Despite the tendency to reduce the human body to a machine, we are also learning that our bodies are complicated in ways that we barely imagined half a century ago. The revolution in genetics that took place with the discovery of DNA and its function in cell reproduction wasn't just a revolution in medicine.

DNA is common to all living creatures. It provides the mechanism by which all creatures evolve. It gives us a means, apart from visible physical traits, to measure our relationship to other creatures. Analyzed, it shows who evolved from what all the way back to very beginning, where life began to emerge from a chemical soup.

The closer scientists have looked at these relationships, the more surprising the implications for our self-understanding. We now know that some organisms are best treated as a kind of *collection* of organisms that work together for the common good. Coral are one example, as are jellyfish.

Could that be us as humans? The human bodies that modern medical students dissect certainly appear to be a well-integrated whole. They are made of parts and systems to be sure, but all together they are one thing. One entity. They are an entity that needs to be protected from foreign invaders by our immune system—and failing that, with drugs like antibiotics.

Yet when we use antibiotics to destroy foreign invaders, we now know that we are killing an important part of ourselves. Our digestive system depends on colonies of specialized bacteria that break down what we eat into molecules that can be absorbed into our blood stream. They get a little. We get a lot. And if we kill them, we get nothing.

21. Edwards, "Exoskeleton."

We mostly think of ourselves as autonomous, but if we kill those bacteria, we have to go find some more; and the place they live is in human feces. Nobody wants to die, and for many, life depends on a fecal transplant.

It isn't the only indication that we can reframe ourselves as an ecosystem. In an evolutionary perspective, viruses and bacteria aren't necessarily interlopers but necessary parts of the ecosystem of the body. Within our cells, there are parts that appear to have originated as independent creatures that engaged in symbiosis with others to form what we think of as an animal or human. Long before we began to replace our organs with those from animals, we were already a chimera; we just didn't know it.

Turn this evolutionary idea inside out and approach it like a comparative sociologist or anthropologist. We can think of ourselves as parts of a greater whole, the entire ecosystem of our planet. Indeed, our very survival will depend on thinking of ourselves this way. We now realize that humanity cannot survive without the larger environment of organisms that generate the oxygen that we breathe and become the food we eat. We really are part of an entangled life and cannot live alone.

The Body in a Social System

And that entanglement includes our fellow human beings. In 1624, long before the rise of modern science and evolutionary theory, John Donne not only wrote about fleas and the shared blood of lovers but of human society.

> No man is an island,
> Entire of itself,
> Every man is a piece of the continent,
> A part of the main.
> If a clod be washed away by the sea,
> Europe is the less.
> As well as if a promontory were.
> As well as if a manor of thy friend's
> Or of thine own were:
> Any man's death diminishes me,
> Because I am involved in mankind,
> And therefore never send to know for whom the bell tolls;
> It tolls for thee.[22]

22. Donne, "No Man Is an Island."

Our interdependence isn't just a matter of finding food and shelter—things that can barely be managed by an individual. No individual has the capacity to *know* everything necessary for survival. Our fabulous minds are built upon and function only in relationship to other minds. Think about thinking. It isn't just talking to ourselves. It's talking with everyone who created our language and culture.

It has become popular to talk about a "hive mind" when we want to summon the wisdom and knowledge of a larger group. We are all part of a hive mind; one that we depend on in order to know everything from how to make bread to build power plants and automobiles. Groupthink is just what Descartes and the Enlightenment political philosophers wanted to avoid. Yet, even their ideas were built on the ideas of others, and we know what they thought because we learned it from our fellow humans.

Back in the days of Napster, I was busy trading MP3 music files, not to mention loaning people copies of valuable software. We would joke that we weren't breaking copyright laws, we were just engaging in *distributed backup*. If I lose my hard drive to some accident, all my stuff is still on your hard drive.

In light of what we know about ourselves, we are both individuals and a form of distributed backup of humanity. We're part of a distributed backup system for human DNA, human knowledge, and human personhood. We're just instances of a humanity that really exists only in the virtual space created by our continuous human interactions.

AI has now entered that virtual space, begging the question of how it will shape our self-understanding.

Conclusion

In 1945, C. S. Lewis in *That Hideous Strength* imagined the brain of a master criminal kept alive by feeding it artificial blood and other fluids. In August of 2022, a team of scientists at Yale reported in *Nature* that they had kept pigs' brains alive for up to thirty-six hours after the pig had been killed.[23]

For Lewis, the separation of body and brain was a dystopian fantasy indicative of the unravelling of the world. Forty-two years later, we met RoboCop: a brain in a machine, still a sign of a dystopian world.

The scientists at Yale don't see their research as dystopian. They see it as lifesaving. If a pig's brain can survive and be kept alive after the trauma of

---

23. Younger and Hyun, "Pig Experiment."

death, then perhaps a human brain could be rescued from death. Perhaps a brain betrayed too young by a diseased body could live to maturity and beyond in a body born without a brain. Or be jump-started back to consciousness in the way we already do with hearts.

When we consider these possibilities, our culture is moving into a new realm of understanding of what it means to be human. It is a new realm in which artificial intelligence might merely be a placeholder for human intelligence seeking a new embodiment.

Whatever happens, we now understand ourselves more and more in machine-like terms, whether the machine is primarily mechanical/electrical or social and relational. We are not so much a mystery to be contemplated as an object to be analyzed and problems to be solved—until the problems cannot be solved and we die.

Chapter 6—Humans as Machines Operated by a Machine

Restoring Lost Connections

In 2022 I lost the sight in my right eye. A blood clot made its way from my heart to the artery that feeds the retina. Deprived of blood, almost all the neurons in my right retina died in a short time. I saw flashing lights and then nothing. In the ER, an ophthalmologist confirmed the damage. In the space of an hour, I had become monocular; one link to the world outside my head was broken.

There is ongoing research into using stem cells to replace damaged retinal cells, but there is already another way. Beginning in the 1990s, Dr. Mark Humayun began experiments with a retinal prosthesis, a photo sensor like one in a modern digital camera, on the optic nerve of a patient who, like me, had lost her sight. The photo receptors in the tiny chip would fire, sending their electrical signals directly to neurons in the optic nerve. It was hoped that the brain could then begin to make sense of these signals and that sight would be somewhat restored. Via the optic nerve, Dr. Humayun was tapping directly into the human brain. And in 2013, his devices received FDA approval.[1]

It is a procedure that has taken place hundreds of times since. I'm not really a candidate since I have a working eye. But for those with no sight? It doesn't always work. In some patients, the brain can't figure out what to do with the new signals. Yet when it does work, the patient's brain is able

---

1. Jumper, "World's First Artificial Retina."

to integrate the electrical signals generated by the chip into a coherent image of the world. The biological neurons in the retina—sentinels of the brain as it faces outward to the world—have been replaced by neurons made of silicone and gold.

Retinal implants came thirty-three years after more common cochlear implants began to give hearing to hundreds of thousands of people. An interface between some sort of electrical device and the brain isn't new. Yet cochlear implants and retinal implants were really just paving the way for the news that broke in early 2024.

In May 2024, *Wired* reported on how Neuralink, a brain implant, is allowing a quadriplegic young man named Noland Arbaugh to control a computer with his brain. In his case, a Bluetooth-enabled microcomputer is implanted directly on his motor cortex. It exchanges signals with the brain through 1,024 miniscule electrical probes in direct contact with the biological neurons in his brain. With it he can control a computer, playing complex video games with only his mind.[2]

Brain-Computer Interfaces

Brain-computer interfaces (BCIs) had already begun to allow the stimulation of brains of Parkinson's patients to counteract an episode of tremors.[3] Then in August of 2024, Apple announced that a BCI linked to its Vision Pro virtual reality goggles allowed a patient with ALS to navigate through virtual worlds. As reported in April of 2023 by the Feinstein Institute, BCIs have been used in what has been called a double neural bypass. Keith Thomas was paralyzed from the chest down in 2020 after a break in his spinal cord. A BCI was attached to the neurons on each side of the broken spinal cord. These were then connected to each other to restore communication between the neurons in Thomas's arm and those in his brain. The result was the restoration of feeling and control in the affected arm and hand.[4]

The term brain-computer interface was coined by Jacques Vidal in 1973, and he laid out the basic theory of how a BCI might work. Unlike cochlear and retinal implants, which send signals in only one direction to the brain, new BCIs offer two-way computer-mediated communication

---

2. Mullin, "Neuralink's First User."
3. Lotte et al., "Brain-Computer Interfaces."
4. Libassi, "Feinstein Institute."

CHAPTER 6—HUMANS AS MACHINES OPERATED BY A MACHINE

with the motor cortex of the brain. This allows Noland Arbaugh to control a cursor visible on a computer screen with his mind alone.

The creation of the BCI rests on the fundamental assumption that the brain is a kind of advanced and complex machine. And as a double neural bypass demonstrates, it is a machine that controls the body. So the question becomes who provides the brain and who provides the body and who is in charge of both.

Structures of the Brain

Like the rest of the human body, the brain's structure was first scientifically described in the sixteenth century. Galvani's discovery in 1791 that electrical impulses stimulated muscle cells was more closely tied to the system of nerves by Robert Bently Todd and Michael Faraday in the 1840s.[5] By the late nineteenth century, it was clear that the strands of neuron cells we call *nerves*, going from the brain down through the spinal cord and out to the rest of the body, used electricity to communicate. The nervous system was an electrical system.

Looking at cases in which a portion of the brain was destroyed but the person lived, nineteenth and twentieth century scientists began to map how different parts of the physical brain were related to specific functions of the mind and body. It was clear at last just where the mind normally resided. It was in the brain.

The improvement in microscopy in the late nineteenth century led Camillo Golgi and Santiago Ramón y Cajal to describe the structures of individual neurons in the brain. They posited that the neuron was the basic functioning unit of the brain.[6] In the first decades of the twentieth century, neuroscience was being built on the dissection of brains to find their microscopic physical structures. And scientists were observing that the brain functions through the electrical interactions of different types of neurons.

The invention of the electroencephalograph (EEG) by Hans Berger in the 1920s allowed direct measurement of electrical impulses in the human brain. Scientists could observe in real time how at least the surface of the brain seemed to be working.

---

5. Reynolds, "Todd, Faraday."
6. Saceleanu et al, "Important Step in Neuroscience"; Rozo et al, "Cajal, the Neuronal Theory."

Twentieth and twenty-first century research scientists have learned to reach deeper into the brain using Magnetic Resonance Imaging (MRI), Electrocorticography (ECG), Positron Emission Tomography (PET), and Near-Infrared Spectroscopy (NIRS). These can identify neuronal activity associated with feelings, sounds, images, and even meditative states and religious experiences.

In 2023, *Science News* reported that researchers at UC Berkely had located the patterns of interaction stimulated by Pink Floyd's "Another Brick in the Wall." They could then create a crude replay of the song based on the signals in this part of the brain. Between BCI chips and non-invasive tools, we are coming closer and closer to mapping not just neurons, but neurons in action creating thoughts.[7]

Can we read minds? At least we're beginning to read brains, an ability that has already restored sight to the blind, hearing to the deaf, and movement to those paralyzed. Another brick out of the wall between the brain and mind.

Structures of the Mind

Even as the roles of neurons in the brain were being described by early neuroscientists, Sigmund Freud, who also regarded himself as a scientist, was seeking to dissect the human *mind* and understand its inner relationships. He studied psychology rather than neurology. He identified the id, the ego, and the superego as the main functioning units of the mind. He recognized the role of the subconscious in shaping human action and went on to develop theories of how the subconscious might be manifest and observed in human language under the proper circumstances.

In short, Freud developed a mind-oriented approach that observed the productions of the mind (language and the expression of emotion) that could compliment the brain-oriented approach of the neuroscientists.[8]

The same mind-oriented approach would be used by Alfred Binet and his colleague Theodore Simon to develop the Binet-Simon test of intelligence in 1905. It is the precursor of contemporary IQ tests. These seek an objective basis for both describing intelligence and measuring it through verbal or written responses to questions. Binet and Simon

---

7. Lopez Loreda, "Neuroscientists Decoded Pink Floyd."
8. Encyclopeda Britannica, "Sigmund Freud."

CHAPTER 6—HUMANS AS MACHINES OPERATED BY A MACHINE

focused on intelligence as the ability to function in a complex environment—basically, a French school.[9]

Their understanding of human intelligence was the same understanding that emerged in evolutionary theory, chipping away at intelligence as a uniquely human attribute. If you can measure how a human mind adapts to a school environment, you could theoretically develop an IQ test for how a chimp adapts to its social and physical context among other chimps in the jungle.

The Science of Consciousness

The early pioneers in both psychology and neuroscience were laying the foundations for defining a problem that has not been unsolved. What is the relationship between the brain and the mind? What is consciousness in terms of the functioning of the brain?

As far as we know, the mind needs a brain to exist. At least we haven't yet met a mind without a brain that can be measured and analyzed. But that doesn't make mind and brain the same thing.

To understand the relationship between brain and mind, we need more than just correlates of brain activity and behavior. We need a theory that explains how consciousness and self-consciousness arise from the electrical activity in the brain. If indeed that is their source.

The two dominant modern scientific theories of consciousness are called the Integrated Information Theory and the Global Neuronal Workspace Theory. IIT and GNWT for short. Both are based on the idea that the brain is an organ that generates consciousness. In short, they are theories about how the neurons in the brain interact to create consciousness.

Both theories distinguish between intelligence and consciousness. Intelligence is just reasoning and learning for the purpose of acting. Humans are intelligent, to be sure. But at some levels, so are fruit flies and fungi. So are a number of specialized computer programs that control robotic systems.

Consciousness, as Christof Koch points out in his essays for *Scientific American*, isn't just about *doing* things, it is about states of *being*. It is about awareness of the blue sky, the sound of birds, feeling pain, feeling love.[10]

---

9. Wikipedia, "Binet-Simon Intelligence Test."
10. Koch, "What Does It 'Feel' Like."

One way to think about this is to distinguish between how you feel when you see wet grass after the rain storm that breaks a long drought, and how you describe that grass in terms of its color, texture, movement, and so on. The properties of sensation, sensing, or feeling are called *qualia* by philosophers. They are the *experience* of being conscious and not just intelligent. When we think about them and express them in the larger realm of our experiences across time, they are part of being self-conscious.

Qualia aren't representational nor are they intentional. They are just experienced, and we have special words for those experiences like joy, ecstasy, love, peace, happiness, anger, sadness, and so on.

On the other hand, a physical description of the grass in its physical context is representational first and then becomes part of a chain of reasoning about what needs to be done. A robot lawn mower can generate a description of wet grass much more detailed and thorough than you and I. With this description, it can plot a course of action to mow the grass. But that doesn't mean it actually has a sensation of grass or a feeling of or for grass.

And it certainly doesn't place its action of mowing the grass in a history of bad or good responses to a mowed lawn from neighbors and spouses. I can never cut the grass without thinking of the times I was an adolescent mowing the lawns of neighbors to make a few dollars. My home on Pacific Drive swims back into consciousness with the smell of cut grass; as does the guy who claimed to be a race car driver and had bamboo shoots coming up in his yard; and the Welsh lady with the odd accent; or the *very* interesting woman who sunbathed in a bikini, drink in hand, while she watched me mow. No, she never invited me in. She just paid five bucks and sent me home through the gate.

These are the things that make me human, that in their totality make me *feel* like a human, to think of myself as human. It is notable that in the movie *Blade Runner*, such experiences and the memory of them must be implanted in the androids to give them psychic stability.[11] But this left the question for humans who were uncertain of their own identity to wonder what of their past was real and what might have been created for them.

Who gives us our memories?

In the lightweight rom-com *Kate and Leopold*, Leopold asks a rhetorical question something like, "Did you load the dishwasher if a woman

---

11. Scott, *Bladerunner*.

didn't see you load it?"[12] It's the kind of question self-conscious humans ask themselves regularly and, in the right context, is good for a laugh.

We humans move back and forth between the experience and the description/planning. We go from a timeless enjoyment of the wet grass, to saying to ourselves, "I could sit here all day," to then thinking about how to make this experience happen again, and then back again to just enjoying it.

Integrated Information Theory, according to Christof Koch, approaches the problem of identifying consciousness by formulating five properties of any conceivable subjective experience. For our purposes, we can leave aside discussing these properties, but I'll name them: intrinsic existence, composition, information, integration, and exclusion.[13] The basic idea for us is that *consciousness is constituted by the state of a maximally integrated system*. To have human consciousness, you have to build a human brain or a perfect silicone analogue.

I'll say even less about the alternative Global Neuronal Workspace Theory. The key takeaway is that according to this theory, all consciousness is computational. Complex signals from across the brain interact. When some threshold is reached, certain neurons fire, and the result of that set of interactions is represented in the frontal cortex of the brain. The succession of these representations is what we experience as consciousness.

In this theory, if you have enough inputs—and enough complex modules into which these inputs flow—and all these modules are interacting in complex ways and connecting to the cerebral cortex or some digital analogue, then consciousness emerges. It isn't a state of the whole brain. It is a rapid succession of signals coming from different parts of the brain and appearing in and disappearing from a small region in the brain. And all the interactions that create these signals are the result of computation and can thus be computed.

Put more succinctly, as Christof Koch does, the ITT model is based on the idea that mind arises out of the intrinsic causal power related to the depth and complexity of interactions in the brain.[14] The GNWT model is ultimately based on the idea that the brain is a biological machine running algorithms.

For our purposes, a couple of things are key. First, neither proponents of ITT nor GNWT have found a way, even in theory, of detecting

12. Mangold, *Kate and Leopold*.
13. Koch, "What Does It 'Feel' Like."
14. Koch, "What Does It 'Feel' Like."

whether consciousness is actually present. The measure of electrical activity in the cerebral cortex stands in for measuring consciousness with regard to the human brain. We know that when this activity ceases, consciousness appears to disappear. We just don't know whether it has gone elsewhere or just ceased to exist.

After all, my consciousness has disappeared a few times when I was undergoing surgery, and it always came back.

In any case, measuring activity in the human brain is far from perfect. To the extent that consciousness is a characteristic of the whole brain (and indeed nervous system), measuring the activity of a few thousand neurons in one area of the brain doesn't tell us much.

These measurements may typically correlate with other indications of consciousness, but we don't know how and why the correlation works. We can temporarily (with drugs) suppress consciousness as measured by its correlates (such as physical expressions of pain or certain kinds of electrical activity), but that still doesn't jump the gap between electrical activity in the brain and the experience of a conscious person. We can turn the brain off and on, but we can't explain why *on* equals consciousness.

And this gets to the root of why more and more capable artificial intelligences may, or may not, affect our self-understanding as humans. As Rose Guingrich and Michael Graziano demonstrate in their research, it is not AI *in itself* that will influence our self-understanding. It will be how we *treat* AI that influences our self-understanding.[15] If it appears conscious and we treat it as conscious, and even self-conscious, we'll be making fundamental decisions about not only AI but about ourselves and what it means to have human intelligence.

Soul

The problem of consciousness and self-consciousness isn't new ethical territory. For a long time, we've recognized that the place of animals in our cultures, especially pets, has huge implications for our self-understanding and how we treat our fellow humans. Already, vast resources go to keeping animals alive even when humans are starving.

It is hardly surprising that some Christian theologians believe that some animals have a soul. In fact on All Souls' Day, the day after

---

15. Guingrich and Graziano, "Ascribing Consciousness."

CHAPTER 6—HUMANS AS MACHINES OPERATED BY A MACHINE

Halloween, my pastor asserted unequivocally her belief that, as in the movie *All Dogs Go to Heaven*, animals have a soul.

This leads to some bizarre contradictions. Many of us will gladly eat the meat of cow with little thought to how it was raised, killed, and slaughtered, but would stridently object to treating dogs and horses the same way. Other cultures finding eating dogs and horses acceptable, but not water buffalo. If Koch is right that our attitudes toward artificial intelligences will shape our self-understanding, will the time come when we toss a broken robotic vacuum out as waste while we desperately preserve and repair the robotic dog to which we've become so attached? There are thousands of objectively worthless classic cars on the road showing our investment of ourselves in our machines. Is it we who give them a soul?

In their book *The Rise and Fall of Soul and Self*, Raymond Martin and John Barresi trace how concepts of the soul have developed and changed philosophically. They conclude that the traditional idea of a stable soul, or self, is dissolving. At least that is the case in *their* cultural world. If they are right, any sense that humans are something more than machines operated by machines is becoming increasingly fragile.[16]

This comes about in part because belief in a transcendent spiritual framework within which an immaterial soul or self could exist is disappearing from the cultural context in the West. In Jewish, Christian, and Islamic thinking, the soul had its origins in God's creative activity, and it existed after the death of the body because it existed in relationship to God. If there is no such God and no unique relationship between humans (and possibly dogs) and God, what makes us different from what we eat?

Yet questions remain. Where does our self go when the brain ceases all patterns of activity that are related to that self? Why does it come back when the drugs go away? Why is there a universe so well suited to the existence of not only humans, but human intelligence that can understand how it works. Physicists call this the *anthropic principle*.

And Martin and Barresi notwithstanding, even modern culture appears to take for granted the existence of an enduring soul, or self. Going as far back as the musical *Carousel*, the movie *It's a Wonderful Life*, more recent films like *Ghost* or the Star Wars movies, and even more recently *Coco* and *Soul*, we find what might be called secular mythologizing.

In the face of scientific and philosophical deconstruction of the soul/self, these and countless other movies and novels offer a narrative

---

16. Martin and Barresi, *Rise and Fall*.

framework in which the soul is more than just the brain and mind, and can endure beyond their passing. The Kathleen Brennan / Tom Waits song "Take It with Me" asserts that there is more than physical existence and that good things never die. Post-religious culture is still shot through with the human experience that there is something more than flesh and bone.[17] It just no longer has a clear idea where it resides.

We live what Charles Taylor calls a cross-pressured life; we live in the immanent frame but we are unable to account for our own human experience within that frame.[18] When we reject the old religious myths, we find ourselves creating new ones. It is that cross-pressured sense of ourselves that we as humans are bringing into our encounter with AI.

Conclusion

The near-simultaneous rise of modern psychology and modern neuroscience has provided scientists with an increasing range of tools for probing both the mind and the brain and thus demystifying both. Both brains and minds can be broken down, diagnosed, and even repaired. In their extremities beyond the brain itself, they can even be replaced, and if some stem cell therapies work, they may even be renewed from within. I may get my vision back. Or perhaps a whole new brain.

These forces are shaping our understanding of who we are and what it means to be human. Once we regard ourselves as machines controlled by machines, the possibilities (good and bad) seem endless.

And yet as popular culture shows, those almost endless possibilities don't provide us an adequate framework for an understanding of what it means to be human. Whatever the philosophers and neuroscientists say, our culture shows that we yearn for the myth and mystery that make possible a human self, a human soul. We bring a fragilized sense of soul and self into the world of AI but also one that can be, and is, strengthened by our stories, poems, and art.

---

17. Waits, "Take It with Me."
18. Taylor, *Secular Age*, 557–627.

Chapter 7—**Humans as Abstractions and Algorithms**

The Real Strawberry

My wife and I were sitting with our children in the friendly kitchen of old friends. We were taking a break after the exhausting couple of months that followed my mother's death. Beadle (as everyone called Dick Beadle) asked my six-year-old daughter to close her eyes and imagine the most beautiful, tasty, perfect strawberry in the world.

When she said she could almost taste it, Beadle said, "Then it's yours." My daughter opened her eyes and protested, "But it's not real!" At that point Beadle turned to me and said, "What have you been teaching her?"

Soon Mrs. Beadle, slightly bemused, produced real strawberries. Beadle and I continued to spar over philosophy. Beadle wanted to make an old point, one reiterated in his Anglo-Catholic church and in the writings of George MacDonald, J. R. R. Tolkien, C. S. Lewis, and Charles Williams. *Real* is not the same as *physical* or *material*. For Beadle it was almost the opposite. The so-called "real world" was the *shadowlands*, an image from Plato's allegory of the Cave.

In this view, what we typically call reality is just the imperfect manifestation of pure ideas, pure ideals, pure forms. What we call reality is just shadows cast by an unseen light on a cave wall. It depends on pure ideas, not unlike Descartes's distinct ideas that alone provide a foundation for real knowledge.

Imperfect Reality and Ideal Form

The idea that for every imperfect reality there is a perfect and more real form runs deeply in our culture. We still say of a person who seems to manifest a certain unchanging attribute that they are "true to form." It is an expression that manifests one meaning of the word "truth" that we inherit from the Greeks: a manifestation in the physical world that matches an abstract ideal.

So which is more real: the imperfect material manifestation or the perfect form dwelling in some nonmaterial but very *real* transcendent realm?

I've given away the prejudice of our culture by referring to *abstractions* and *idealizations*. Both words begin with us thinking about the material world as *real* and suggest the removal of the imperfect, or the changeable, to get to the ideal or abstract. When we say "get real" or "the real world," we mean the messy, complex, and sometimes difficult world of material existence, not the ideal worlds we construct in our minds on the basis of nonmaterial ideas.

Idealist is almost a derogatory term; at the very least, it designates a naïf out of touch with reality.

A couple of years ago, I was reading one of George Musser's articles in *Scientific American* on the holographic principle and anti-de Sitter/conformal field theory or AdS/CFT. I had read his earlier work on quantum entanglement, *Spooky Action at a Distance*, and the same question kept running through my head.

Did physicists really believe that there were many more dimensions than we can observe? Or is multidimensional space a mathematical convention necessary to make the numbers from the experiments add up? Were physicists actually creating mathematical models of a reality we cannot grasp with the senses? Or are they just getting the equations to match the results?[1]

Mr. Musser was kind enough to answer my letter to the editors of *Scientific American* and assured me that "someone who invokes extra spatial dimensions really does think they are out there, and indeed will devote considerable energy to trying to explain why we do not see them. They would not bother if they took them to be merely mathematical tricks."[2]

---

1. Musser, "Black Hole Paradox."
2. George Musser, email message to author, Oct. 25, 2022.

CHAPTER 7—HUMANS AS ABSTRACTIONS AND ALGORITHMS

That was reassuring and helped me better interpret Steven Weinberg's final chapter in *Dreams of a Final Theory*. In it he focuses on the intrinsic beauty and simplicity of theories about the ultimate laws of nature, suggesting that theoretical physicists may be Neoplatonists. Weinberg didn't mean that physicists thought abstract formulas were more real than the material world. He meant that if the equations were beautifully consistent, a near perfect model, then you didn't give them up just because the initial data didn't match.[3]

As Descartes had noted, the human senses can be fooled. The problem may be the experiment, not the theory.

In theoretical physics, there is a constant back and forth as new data requires rethinking the equations, while the equations suggest shortcomings in the way in which data is being collected. Progress is made when the models of reality expressed in the equations don't match the irrefutable experimental data and require that physicists come up with a new model of reality. That is what happened with Copernicus and Isaac Newton and Einstein. It could happen again.

Modern science tends to be materialist at its roots. Physicists push back against theories that cannot be experimentally proven or disproven. Ethan Siegel, an astrophysicist writing in *Forbes* in 2020, says that the idea of parallel universes is a "science fiction dream for the time being, based on the evidence available to us."[4] By this he means that there is both no evidence and no imaginable experiment that could provide evidence. Absent evidence and experiment, there is no science, there is no real.

If science is materialist, there are also strong cultural forces that, along with my friend Beadle, regard *ideals* as the fundamental reality and the world we experience with our senses as an imperfect manifestation of that reality. There is a difference between the perfect *spiritual* or immaterial realm and the imperfect material world. We live in a culture with both hardcore realists and hardcore idealists. Sometimes we are both at the same time. We live in a world of both *Scientific American* and movies like *Coco*. Returning to Charles Taylor, we are cross-pressured.

As our culture sees rapid advances in AI, our cultural tendency to move back and forth between materialism and idealism comes more and more into play. When we call something "machine learning," a common synonym for AI, we focus on the concrete, the *machine*. When we talk

3. Weinberg, *Dreams*.
4. Siegel, "Ask Ethan."

about artificial intelligence we focus on the abstract and immaterial, *intelligence*. Which one is it?

The Algorithm as Abstraction, Ideal, and Real

David Foster Wallace in *Everything and More: A Compact History of Infinity* points out that we owe the Greeks the critical association of mathematics with the realm of immaterial ideals. Practical math had been used by many civilizations in calculating the motions of the moons and planets, the volume of containers, and sums in financial transactions. It is the Greeks, particularly Euclid, who idealized mathematical relations and expressed them in logical theorems.[5]

It is the Greeks who thought of numbers as something *real* in and of themselves, even when unassociated with anything in the material world.

Thinking of numbers as real and mathematical equations and theorems as real could lead to problems. Euclid's combination of mysticism, philosophy, and math had trouble with numbers that were clearly real but couldn't be calculated with precision. Take, for example, the square root of two, which is the length of the hypotenuse of a right triangle whose other sides are one unit long. Or the ratio of the circumference to diameter of a circle. These numbers were *irrational* because they couldn't be expressed in a *ratio*. In a rational world, how could the irrational be real?

Worse was the square root of negative one. The Greeks refused to think about it. Descartes called it an *imaginary* number. It wasn't a compliment. He wasn't fond of fairy tales. It turns out that even when the abstract is real, as in numbers and equations, some numbers aren't real. The Greeks, like Descartes and modern scientists, know that irrational numbers come up all the time in the natural world of circles, spirals, and right angles. And imaginary numbers come up everywhere in the mathematics of theoretical physics and are somehow part of working models of the real world.

But for our purposes, we'll leave them to the physicists. To better understand the background of how humans have been shaped in our understanding of what it means to be human, we need move only a little more deeply into mathematics.

Let me introduce a ninth-century Persian mathematician, himself steeped in Greek thought: Muhammad ibn Mūsā al-Khwārizmī. His pioneering work in algebra spread to medieval Europe and introduced

5. Wallace, *Everything and More*.

CHAPTER 7—HUMANS AS ABSTRACTIONS AND ALGORITHMS

working with the Hindu-Arabic numeral system that included a "o." These are numbers we commonly use today and are called Arabic numerals. This is our familiar decimal system.

Al-Khwārizmī had used the term *al-jabr* to describe his method of solving equations.[6] It comes into English as algebra. The rules that al-Khwārizmī set forth in his *Compendious Book on Calculation by Completion and Balancing* were referred to by his own latinized name, Algorismus. It becomes our modern *algorithm*. It means a procedure for performing calculations in a fixed order to solve a problem or yield a result.

If we can still remember our grade school math, we'll remember that certain mathematical procedures must take place in a fixed order to get the correct result. That's an algorithm. If you forgot, then your spreadsheet program will remind you. A formula like $x = 3 \times 3 \times 2 + 6 - 4$ is meaningless without the brackets that determine which calculations are performed first. $(3 \times 3 \times 2) + (6 - 4) = 20$ is different from $(3 \times 3) \times (2 + 6 - 4) = 36$. You have to get the *algorithm* right if you want to do the *algebra*. Thank you, al-Khwārizmī.

A spreadsheet, that now-ubiquitous tool of business, is a good example of how we abstract ideal, immaterial relationships from material relationships. A spreadsheet consists of what are called cells arranged in a grid called a sheet. This can be expanded into three dimensions by having multiple sheets.

Each cell is labeled by its row (A, B, C, D, etc.), its column (1, 2, 3, etc.), and its sheet name. A cell may contain a single number representing material objects like gallons of fuel. Or it may contain a single number representing a material object like a US dollar bill. Or it may contain an equation that expresses the relationship between one kind of object (a gallon of fuel) expressed as an abstract number and another kind of object (a dollar bill) expressed as an abstract number, to give a new and completely abstract idea, e.g., price per gallon. You can hold a gallon of gas (at least in a can) and you can hold a dollar bill. You can't hold a number, and you really cannot touch, hold, throw, or otherwise handle a price per gallon. It an idea, not a thing.

In essence a spreadsheet is a collection of abstractions and algorithms that themselves make up one giant algorithm or many giant algorithms.

By getting rid of everything material and focusing on abstractions, the spreadsheet can solve incredibly complex calculations and problems

---

6. Encyclopeda Britannica, "Al-Khwārizmī."

that hopefully end up expressing something about the real world of material objects. Algorithms, for example, continuously calculate the value of stocks. But those values mean nothing real until the stock is actually sold, and its value is *realized*, or made real.

Even then a realized value is abstract. Who has actually seen a stock certificate or traded it for cash? I own stock, but I've never seen a piece of paper. I've sold it and never seen a dollar bill. It all exists only as numbers somewhere on a spreadsheet and an account balance. A lot of our world is really a world of abstractions that we treat as real.

Have you seen the face of a young cashier at the local coffee shop when you actually hand them cash? It's the face of someone who wishes you had a credit card. Working out the complexities of different pieces of paper with different numbers and even strange metal disks with odd bas-reliefs seems far more unreal than numbers flashing across a screen, to many contemporary people.

We live in a world of algorithms, of abstractions and ideas in complex relationships being constantly calculated and recalculated. While I'm writing this in Vienna, I'm checking the weather in Dallas, Texas, on my smartphone. I want to see if my house will be affected by a hurricane coming from the Gulf of Mexico.

Except I didn't really check the weather. I checked the current values of different numbers continually being recalculated according to algorithms. They supposedly tell me the weather in terms of temperature, humidity, wind speed, and even more abstractly, the probability of rain. The weather may be out there somewhere, but even if I wanted to, I couldn't experience it because I'm halfway across the world in Vienna, Austria.

In fact, the concept of "weather" is an abstraction from actual events like rain, snow, wind, and heat/cold that can be characterized in abstract numbers linked by algorithms. "Wealth" is an abstraction from the values assigned to money theoretically in the possession of a person but more likely existing as numbers in a spreadsheet in a computer somewhere. This is convenient because wealth actually represents not an absolute amount of money but an abstract relationship between different amounts of money. I can be wealthy in relation to one person's money and poor in relation to another person's money.

What about intelligence? What about humanity? These are abstractions as well.

CHAPTER 7—HUMANS AS ABSTRACTIONS AND ALGORITHMS

We use numbers (IQ, EQ, CQ, and others) to express how much and what type of intelligence people have. These numbers are generated by algorithms that process data from tests in which people answer questions. We see the apparent result of being intelligent, but intelligence itself is pretty abstract. We even make a distinction between *intelligence*, or the measurable ability of a human brain to solve abstract problems, and *street smarts*, or the real-world, real-time ability to solve real-world problems.

It is notable that those typically creating AIs measure their capability either through standard tests of human intelligence or by measuring certain processes and relationships within the computers that house them. Neither relates to the real world. An AI, like a human, can pass the bar exam. But it says nothing about the ability of the AI, or a human, to effectively do the things we expect of a lawyer.

And what about our humanity? Are we an abstraction expressed in numbers? We catch something of what has been happening in our culture from a brief line in *Scientific American* from 1924. It's a story about the discovery of vitamin D, whose discoverers wish "to show some day that life is simply a chemical process."[7]

Remember from high school chemistry all the equations describing chemical interactions. Algorithms every one of them. And therein, for those chemists, might lie our humanity.

And a hundred years later? In *Homo Deus*, Yuval Harari (also author of *Sapiens*) maintains that humans can be understood as algorithms. Our humanity can be boiled down to algorithms constantly running on what is effectively a computer made of meat. The specific character of the meat and its environment determine the outputs of the algorithms, but the essence is the algorithms. Consciousness, that characteristic that makes humans *sapiens*, arises from the meat, or more specifically the brain, but is itself an abstraction as we've already seen.[8]

Humans as Information

Remember the old *Star Trek* where humans could be somehow scanned then "beamed" to another location? Reduced to information, a digital signal, humans could theoretically be transported across long distances and

---

7. Fischetti, "50, 100 and 150 Years."
8. Harari, *Homo Deus*.

reassembled in flesh and blood. It was science fiction based on the real science of information theory.

Information theory was first developed in the 1920s by Harry Nyquist and Ralph Hartley. In 1940 Claude Shannon advanced the theory into its continued, and indeed critical, role in modern science and technology.

Information theory offered a mathematical framework for studying the relationship between a clear signal and the inevitable noise when that signal was transmitted over wires, or radio.[9] It was useful at the dawn of the information age when more and more information was conveyed by telephone, radio, and eventually television and the internet. It gave a precise way of measuring, and distinguishing, information from noise.

But soon, information theory became more than just a way of modeling signal-to-noise ratios. It became another framework for understanding reality and, within the realm of reality, humanity.

The basic conceptual insight of information theory is that discernable patterns within any kind of signal could be regarded as information and then characterized mathematically. If a smoke signal consists of regular puffs of smoke, then that is information. Noise, on the other hand, is random, like the smoke from an untended fire fluxing and flowing and blowing in the wind.

A signal in a wire consists of patterns of electrical current, such as the dot, dash, dot of Morse code. Or it may consist of patterns in changes in amplitude (signal strength) as are found in old-school telephones, or if transmitted through the air, AM radio. As long as there is a pattern, there is information.

Noise, on the other hand, would be what we hear as static, signals with no pattern. Music or voices would be information, patterns that rise above the noise.

But notice that something subtle happens when we regard a *pattern*, any pattern, as *information* that can then be characterized mathematically. *We can transform that pattern into another equivalent pattern, transmit that equivalent pattern, and then reassemble the pattern into its original form.* This is what happens whenever a microphone picks up a pattern of sound waves in air and turns it into a pattern of electrical signals that can be sent across a wire. On the other end, that pattern of electrical signals is transformed back into a pattern of sound waves by a speaker.

---

9. Ben-Gal and Kagan, "Information Theory."

CHAPTER 7—HUMANS AS ABSTRACTIONS AND ALGORITHMS

At one level, this kind of transformation had been going on since the first humans drew an image from their minds onto a rock—a petroglyph—and another human looked at it and knew in their mind what it represented. The invention of writing took this a step further, as did every other means of transmitting information by converting it from patterns in one form to patterns in another form and back.

When I was a kid, I was obsessed with airplanes, and like a lot of kids, I made model airplanes. Model manufacturers created scaled-down printed patterns of all the critical parts of an airplane based on the real thing. I then used those patterns to make my parts and build models of World War I biplanes out of balsa and paper that would actually fly! Not that it was a good idea to fly them. Balsa and paper are not robust materials in case of a crash.

In those gendered days, my mother and sister would use patterns to recreate dresses with cloth and a sewing machine. Like my model airplane parts, these patterns were created by using simple mathematics to scale down, or up, the parts of a dress so that many different sizes of dress could be made from the same basic pattern.

Again, this idea of creating scale models didn't start with modern humans. We have very ancient scaled-down statues of humans and even toy carts. Observing patterns then recreating them has been going on a long time.

Twentieth-century information theory was new because it generalized from words, sounds, images, and objects to assert that *anything* could be characterized mathematically as a pattern. Anything could be treated as information. And going further, it asserted that *everything* that isn't random noise is a pattern that follows the rules of information theory.

The steady beat of a human heart is a pattern. So is every aspect of a living cell in that heart, every molecule in that cell, every atom in the molecule, and every particle in that atom. Everything *real* can be treated as patterns, as information, and can therefore be characterized mathematically and thus, to use a word we hear all the time, *digitized*. Any pattern at all can be digitized, transmitted, and recreated with the proper technology. Beam me up, Scotty. Everything real could be turned into an abstraction and then made real again.

Another aspect of information theory, which plays across almost the entirety of modern physics, is the *conservation of information*. However much information is transformed, within the system overall it is not lost.

You can introduce a lot of noise into the system, but the information will still be there to find. If you can remove the noise, you can retrieve the information.

Back in science fiction land, it is the idea of the conservation of information that underlies the shape-changing villain of the *Terminator* series, the *Matrix* movies, the *Avatar* movies, *Honey, I Shrunk the Kids*, and all the others in which humans or machines can continually morph through different media and substances and yet retain the essential patterns that make up their personhood.

Conservation of information is the idea that underlies all efforts to create digital versions of analogue persons or, for that matter, digital versions of anything. Once we've accepted that *information* is the essence of identity, then its outward form is infinitely mutable. Once we accept that information is the essence of *our* identity, then we can be digitized, abstracted, and algorithms will tell our story.

The Real Danger

Robert Heinlein's classic novel from 1966, *The Moon Is a Harsh Mistress*, revolves around a computer that reaches a critical complexity so that consciousness emerges from the algorithms.[10] "Mike" is not unlike Hal from *2001: A Space Odyssey* a couple of years later. In both, *consciousness* is an emergent property of organized matter. But where does it emerge from?

It is for this reason that some scientists maintain that consciousness is an innate characteristic of matter suffusing the universe and is manifest in individual consciousnesses. It has always been there waiting to emerge from the static. Panpsychism is a Mahayana Buddhist position now advocated, or at least explored, by philosophers like Philip Goff and the neuroscientist Christof Koch. Dan Falk explored this in a September of 2023 *Scientific American* article entitled "Is Consciousness Part of the Fabric of the Universe."

No one is claiming to have a firm answer. The way in which we approach these questions may tell us more about ourselves than about computers. And that's why we need to ask.

---

10. Heinlein, *Moon Is a Harsh Mistress*.

Conclusion

As we humans move forward in the twenty-first century, the culture of modernity has changed our understanding of what it means to be human. It has empowered us through new freedoms. It has given us a greater understanding of ourselves and our world. Science and the related technology have brought material prosperity and security, lengthened our lives, and enlarged our vision of the universe.

At the same time, we have been decentered in the universe both physically and morally. We have been diminished in importance and loosed from any relationship with the Transcendent. The uniqueness of our humanity has been eroded until what is left may not even be a net positive for ourselves or our fellow creatures. First, we became machines operated by a machine. Now, we have become abstracted and disembodied, turned into algorithms in the vacuous realm of ideas.

Disembodied and demystified, we have been well prepared for the age we live in, the screen age, an age in which we find or sadly lose our humanity in virtual worlds.

Chapter 8 — **The Screen Age**

The State Fair

The Texas State Fair in 1970 was a marvel. One-third of the huge Fair Park was dedicated to the foundations of Texas culture: railroads, livestock, and farming. All were spread around the art deco Hall of State, and its imagined history of the state, intended to validate its coming of age as the *great State of Texas*. Biggest and best in everything. All myth.

The indigenous people were reduced to nostalgic decorative features. The burgeoning highway system was celebrated with no thought to environmental cost. Fifty years later and our roadsides are nothing but rivers of commercial sewage running along endless miles of concrete. Back then it was a thing to plant wildflowers along Texas highways; now they wouldn't be able to find a patch of soil in which to grow.

Then there was the Midway. Between the Cotton Bowl stadium (old Texas) and modern museums and theaters, the Midway was the pounding present where fairgoers were pummeled by physical experiences that allowed no reflection. Carnival rides with their whiplash movements and incessant rock music ramped up excitement (and the already rampant hormones of their adolescent riders). They were scattered around a seemingly endless row of carnival games featuring flashing lights to distract, carnival barkers to attract, and hopeless tasks to extract whatever cash one had.

The third portion of the fair was dedicated to the future. One huge hall offered the automobiles of the future. The other, the technology of the future. It was there that companies like Bell Telephone, Texas Instruments, IBM, and others showed us visions of our future lives.

CHAPTER 8—THE SCREEN AGE

We already had televisions, and even color televisions, of increasingly large size. From *Oklahoma* in 1955 to *2001: A Space Odyssey* in 1968, we had already experienced the silver screen becoming the big screen becoming the wide screen powered by 70 mm film technology. Even more immersive IMAX movies came in 1973. Dolby stereophonic sound came with *Star Wars* in 1977 to complete the immersive movie experience.

But in 1970 a notably small screen captured my attention. Bell Telephone was showing the telephone of the future—the Picturephone. The company first introduced a prototype in 1964. With sleek futuristic lines, it was still clunky. The technology didn't exist for small video cameras, and the small screen size (black and white only) was further limited by slow transmission rates over existing copper cable. It was a dream, never even put on the market. But it seemed like such a dream, and there to touch and see.

Screens and Socialization

The dream it represented was fulfilled decades later. Now, my wife and I can WhatsApp or Facetime almost daily with my granddaughters halfway across the world. Business calls have been replaced with video meetings using Zoom, Google Groups, Microsoft Teams, WhatsApp, and others. For many people, urged on by the manufacturers of their smart phones, video calls are the default form of communication. Bell Telephone and the Bell system are long gone. Yet they were a harbinger of the age in which we live: *the screen age*.

Screens are now the most important interface between us and the world. In his book, *The World Beyond Your Head*, the philosopher Matthew Crawford writes about being human in an age of distraction.[1] He explores how our inability to focus on our relationship with the real world comes in part because of all our screens. Felicia Wu picks up a similar theme in *Restless Devices*.[2]

Both remind us that screens—movie screens, TV screens, computer screens, information screens in churches, schools, shopping malls, and amusement parks—are no longer just passive, flat surfaces with moving pictures. They are the face of a *social* media: the two-dimensional canvas onto which we inscribe ourselves for others to see and through which we

1. Crawford, *World Beyond Your Head*.
2. Wu, *Restless Devices*, 2021.

receive their self-representations. They are both a window and a mirror, distorting both reality and our sense of self.

And we, having been presented to ourselves as disembodied minds attached to a machine-like body, are well prepared to be drawn into the screen age. We've already been reduced to algorithms and abstractions, it's easy to become a digital me on a two-dimensional screen. Was there ever that much more?

Social Media

Unlike passive windows and mirrors, our screens are actively shaping what we see, how we are seen, and how we see ourselves. Anyone on a Zoom conference or Microsoft Teams meeting has seen their fellow participants in front of a cheesy background or just a blurred pattern that hides an unmade bed or messy office. Because our screens are interactive, with our interactions mediated through computers, there is plenty of space for the insertion of distortion and idealization. The toggle of a virtual switch and we can look better than real life, courtesy of a kind of AI that manipulates images in real time.

This constant manipulation of our image on the screen is a perversion rather than extension of face-to-face meetings with our fellow humans. When I attend a party, I can go hours without looking at my own face. I don't walk around holding up a mirror so that I can simultaneously see both how I look and how others look. This frees me to attend to them as they are free to attend to me. In video conferences, I'm constantly asked to look at both myself and others. The result is that I can never fully attend to the other person because my own image distracts me.

If I'm having trouble fully engaging others, unnaturally distracted by my own image, the software managing the system is fully engaged in studying all of us. A few years ago, I had a chance to visit a company that was then called Reflect Systems. They were doing a lot that was interesting and impressive. The thing that struck me most, however, was their intelligent signs. Such a sign could be programmed to monitor a rival's prices and display competitive prices on the fly even as the computer behind it repriced inventory.

Using then available AI and a digital camera mounted on the sign, in theory a computer could analyze the image of a person looking in a store window, determine their age and gender, and then display the products that would entice them to step in and buy.

In an amusement park, the screens could be coupled with computers monitoring the unique code being broadcast by every cell phone. If a person paused long enough in front of the sign, it would be triggered to sense the signal their phone was sending and then use this to roughly trace their movement by triangulating from different cell phone towers. Then based on the time of day and those movements, it could display recommendations that would lure or impel them to their next destination. In the screen age, we're never just watching. We're constantly being watched.

And it's the perfect environment to shape our interactions with AI. AI and the AI adjacent algorithms constantly shape what comes across our screens. They don't just provide cheesy backgrounds or a softer countenance for a video conference. Nor do they provide just bunny ears and whiskers for kids to amuse themselves and their friends. Our screens send us powerful messages about who we are. They amplify our fantasies or warp them to make us more malleable to the purposes of others.

This intrusion of AI into our social lives via social media, via screens, is increasing over time. Back in 1956, sociologists Donald Horton and Richard Wohl coined the term *parasocial interaction* to describe the one-way relationship between media personalities and those who follow them. Social media becomes parasocial media as modern followers feel a they have a relationship with a media personality or influencer even though it isn't reciprocated.[3]

This is heightened, as AI is now being used so that such influencers can offer AI generated responses to comments on their social media postings. The one-sided nature of the parasocial relationship is masked by faking actual engagement, something pioneered by OnlyFans but readily available to anyone who wishes to exercise influence on a social media platform without bothering to have a relationship with their followers.[4]

Going even further, Meta is now introducing AI generated virtual Facebook and Instagram users. Our screen-based social networks will include "people" generated entirely by AI, something already happening in the world of news reporting and podcasting. These AI generated characters will both offer content and interject their comments in our feeds. This ensures we don't skim over the messages that the social network wants to

3. Horton and Wohl, "Mass Communication," 215.
4. Koerner, "I Went Undercover."

send because they are now presented as real people instead of just ads. That vaguely familiar character who just asked to be your friend? It may be a friend or may be just an AI with an agenda.

The screen age and the age of AI go hand in hand, and they feed on one another as the demand for hyperrealistic virtual interactions drives AI development to support video and audio creation. Computer games have already introduced us to living in virtual worlds. AI simply makes them appear more realistic until we cannot tell the human from the AI avatar—and perhaps ourselves from our own avatar. In the screen age, we become flattened, two-dimensional representations of our real selves. Socialized in that environment, who are we becoming?

Physical or Virtual

For the last three years, I've had only one functioning eye. When people find out (it isn't obvious), they often ask about driving. It turns out that a one-eyed view of the world is different, but it isn't all that restrictive. Our ability to judge distances isn't based on our brain calculating the parallax between the two points of view represented by our two eyes. Given the distance between our eyes, a car one hundred feet away might as well be the Andromeda galaxy in Galileo's telescope. Our sense of perspective is rooted in experience, not calculation.

(I note in passing that having only one eye does make a difference over short distances, so I've been known to miss the glass entirely when trying to pour wine, even before my first glass. There are work-arounds, like imitating an eighteenth-century sea captain and saying to the person next to me, "Aye mate, the bottle stands by you!" and thus suggesting they need to pour us each a glass. Or just making sure the bottle touches the rim of the glass.)

Over the last few months, my grandson taught me about perspective. At three months, he lay on his back and worked out how to grab a particularly enticing (to him) soft toy. Once he had consistently learned how to manipulate his own arm and hand (not a given in those first months), he learned to get the toy to his mouth—the major goal of all babyish grasping.

The major shock for him came when he not only grasped the toy but pulled on it hard enough to roll himself on his side and then over on his face.

There was surprised indignation at this sudden change in perspective, but he had been put on his tummy before. He quickly forgot the toy and began to explore other items in his universe. In one day he was capable of rolling over. Then he crawled. Now, he stands. Soon, he will walk. Already he measures distances by reaching, failing to grab, crawling a little further, and reaching again. Pretty soon, he will know how far away things are in arm's-lengths.

Children learn about reality first through their bodies. They learn to manipulate their own bodies and then to manipulate objects in three-dimensional space. Every object, including people, is smelled, tasted, touched, heard, and seen. Our first understanding of depth perception comes about when our eyes track what happens to an object that we push away from us or pull toward us. The physical movement of our tiny arms and hands coupled with a changing image teaches us that things moved further away from our body get smaller. As we grow bigger, we experiment with longer distances, and soon we realize that the car way down the road isn't just a little car but a big car further away.

These lessons are foundational to our internal representations of reality and cannot be reproduced by interactions with a flat screen, or in a virtual world.

And socialization? A lot more goes on between parent and child, or child and child, than an exchange of pictures and sounds. Anyone faced with a crying child knows that you can't send the message, "It will be okay," by just speaking soothing words and smiling pleasantly. Even less so will they be interested in a voice over a phone. Comfort will require touching, picking up the child, rocking them, and holding them close. Sometimes for a very long time.

We learn who we are for others through touch, smell, taste, and always in three dimensions while on the move through time in a four-dimensional world. There is a reason baby books are made of plastic or have texture and odor. The human instinct is to see if the image has a taste, a feel, and a smell.

Stripped down to a screen, and one whose images and sounds are easily manipulated by a computer, the power of human relationships is stripped down and distorted as well. Youths and adults with experience in the material world may understand such abstract ways of relating and use their imaginations to fill in the missing pieces. Sadly, as we are seeing too often, even they can be fooled and manipulated. The flattening and distortion of screens leads too easily to shallow socialization and a flattened, two-dimensional social world. These shallow waters are just the place for an AI, which has no human depth, to thrive.

The Sound Difference

About a million years ago when I was eighteen, a friend and I drove to Vermont from Dallas. Our first stop was Niagara Falls. (And yes, we did a solid thirty-six hours, swapping out driving) We went straight to the cheap motel which we'd booked the old-fashioned way—meaning we'd looked up hotels in Niagara Falls in the Yellow Pages found in the public library and then made a long-distance call.

When we arrived, the owner emerged from his office, and immediately we noticed that he sounded like a robot from a movie. Hanging from around his neck was a battery powered speaker. It was attached to a wire leading to his throat. Surgery, or disease, had diminished his capacity to speak. This primitive device artificially amplified what was left of his voice. The year was 1970. It was the first time I'd heard a partially synthetic voice.

We've come a long way. Speech synthesizers were actually attempted using mechanical means in the late eighteenth century. But it was really the development of the first telephone by Alexander Graham Bell, the precursor of the Picturephone I saw at the state fair, that created the possibilities of synthetic voices.

As a kid this made sense to me. Any Boy Scout like myself could get a merit badge for creating a crude electronic organ with a battery, a small speaker, and switches connected to the speaker through different capacitors (or through resistors and a single capacitor.) This very simple circuit allowed the generation of different frequencies resulting in different tones in the speaker.

All speech synthesis needed was a much more intricate and faster way of manipulating frequencies so that the output resembled a human voice. By 1968 Noriko Umeda had created a general-purpose computer-controlled text-to-voice synthesizer. Things would just get better and better.

Those who played video games from the 1970s onwards could almost trace the advances through the voices they heard. By the early 2000s, text-to-speech synthesis was almost ubiquitous and had almost ceased being annoying. It was the logical compliment to the full emergence of the screen age. What could enhance the sense of *reality* in virtual reality more than realistic voices?

Yet to really relate to a computer, we needed to move beyond "I type, then you speak." That's not natural. It was in 1997 that Dragon Naturally Speaking was first released to do voice-to-text translation. Now it was "I talk, you type." I was thrilled and became an early adapter. It was way less

CHAPTER 8—THE SCREEN AGE

than perfect on anything but a desktop computer and continued to be so for more than a decade. But by the time I was back in the US in 2004, I could drive down the highway dictating my brilliant ideas into my new PalmPilot and get something like a usable text.

Soon enough we would have smart phones with voice recognition built in, and quickly following this came voice-controlled personal assistants that responded to our voice prompts with synthesized replies. We didn't just look at screens, we talked to them and they talked back. By the time the movie *Her* came out in 2013, a romance with a synthesized voice had become believable.

Not real, of course. The technology presented in *Her* didn't exist when the movie was made. Scarlett Johansson was the voice actor. The voices of the avatars and computers in popular movies and TV remained human rather than synthesized, unless that synthesized effect was what the director wanted.

That has now changed, and largely with the advent of breakthroughs in AI. The unfortunate manager of the Niagara Falls hotel would no longer need to confront sleep-deprived teenagers with a harsh mechanical voice. On July 25th, 2024, US legislator Jennifer Wexton gave a speech in the US House of Representatives using a near-perfect clone of her voice. It was based on recordings made before a degenerative disease robbed her of the ability to speak. It turns out that neural networks can be trained to recognize and reproduce the patterns of sound found in individual voices.[5]

I've done this first hand, releasing an episode of my own podcast with a fully synthesized version of my voice reading a text.

There is a plethora of voice cloning services. Voices have now returned from the dead to read children's stories in ElevenLabs' Reader app.[6] Or, your Meta AI chatbot can speak with the face and voice of Dame Judi Dench and John Cena can read your AI generated news reports.[7]

My personal favorites are Alex and Sienna of Perplexity, both created by ElevenLabs. It is a sign of the times that we can hear AI generated voices carrying out an AI generated conversation about deepfakes and the ethics of using AI to select, write, and read news stories, which is exactly what Perplexity is doing.[8] AI talking about the ethics of AI talking about AI!

5. BBC News, "Lawmaker Uses AI Voice."
6. Nepori, "New AI Raises the Voices."
7. Duffy, "Meta Is Bringing the Voices."
8. Perplexity, "Ethical Dilemma of AI."

And that's really just the beginning. Even as I'm writing, AI driven speech recognition and synthesis is being trained to both recognize and respond to emotions with equally emotional speech. The subtler patterns in language are beginning to be identified and reproduced with increasingly sophisticated and complex neural networks. Produced in 2024, movies do not need a voice actress except to generate the original voice samples. OpenAI's synthetic voice in the GPT-4o ("o" for "omni") voice activated interface was so good that Scarlett Johansson, the original voice of *Her*, thought it was her voice.[9] It wasn't.

The rapidly developing possibilities of voice recognition and voice cloning are allowing AI to serve the needs of the disabled, to hear and respond to human needs when no one else is available. Yet they also encourage those of us living in a screen age to fall ever more deeply into those screens, into the virtual realities that have the capacity to distort and mislead us.

The virtual rabbit hole into which Theodore Twombly fell in *Her* doesn't just exist in the imagination of a screen writer. Its maw is opening to receive us on every screen we encounter.

Do I Know the Real Me?

In his song "Brilliant Disguise," Bruce Springsteen reminds us that humans are complex. Often, we don't know ourselves from the disguises we put on.[10] Maybe we should have an interlude to listen to the Who song entitled "Can You See the Real Me?"

A year ago, conscious of improving my social media image for my podcast, I signed up for a program that promised to provide me studio quality images if I sent it a dozen or so pictures of myself in various types of clothes. The results were cool but also a little unsettling. The AI took the basic patterns it discerned in the photos I provided then "enhanced" them by creating modified patterns that might be more attractive versions of me. Of about eighty that it provided, I found two that were usable. A lot of the images were of a younger me that never existed. Too much hair, too thin, and in the leather jacket, way too cool. A few, frankly, aged me, and that I do not need. Some put me in clothes I'd never wear. The worst changed my ethnicity. I looked like a grandfather I'm pretty sure I never had.

9. Mickle, "Scarlett Johansson Said No."
10. Springsteen, "Brilliant Disguise."

CHAPTER 8—THE SCREEN AGE

Eventually, I sent the best one to a conference organizer as my official photo. She had known me ten years and immediately called BS. She knew it wasn't me. So now it's back to using the official university photograph on the website. I do look younger, but that is because it was taken ten years ago. Unless?

Why not be the fake me with the perfect suit that brings out my blue eyes? As long as I retreat behind my screens and there isn't a curious Toto to expose me to an inquisitive Dorothy, I can be anyone and thus really no one at all.

As I write, AI has brought real-time photo editing to the smartphone. It can eliminate or change unwanted people and backgrounds to create a gathering or vacation that never happened. TikTok, Instagram, Facebook, and other social media are now venues for deepfakes, some political. But most of the deepfakes are of ourselves projecting fantasy images to others. Give our screens the power of AI, and they will readily turn us all into fakes.

And we may need to be. In a screen age, who wants to be the only one on the Zoom call with every blemish showing? Who wants to have the only picture on the brochure that wasn't enhanced by a virtual airbrush? As screens dominate our social interactions, we slip further and further into virtuality, out of touch with our own embodiment and that of others.

Behind our screens are the AI algorithms that subtly and not so subtly determine what can be acceptably seen. In the end we are presenting ourselves less for the scrutiny of our fellow humans and more for the AI algorithms that determine whether or not what we say and what we show is acceptable to be seen and heard. And we quickly learn that to be heard and to be seen, we must live up to the expectations of the algorithm. On our screens we are always performing for some form of AI, and if we let it, it is constantly grading and directing our performance.

It is exhausting. One of the things I don't need to worry about at a real-world party, or in a real-world classroom or a real-world meeting, is how I look. A quick check of the mirror in the morning and some consideration of the social environment I'll inhabit, and I'm good to go. Not in the land of screens. Because whether it's Zoom or Teams or some other form of video communication, I never just see others; I'm always confronted with my own image. Its like walking across campus holding a mirror out so I can check my looks every few seconds.

Nope, tie still doesn't match the jacket.

In the past, travel or the theater stage were the only ways to slip out of our known identity in order to try something new. Now that possibility is as close by as a computer monitor, a tablet, or a smartphone. We can all act on some screen and project ourselves into exotic locations. But it takes a lot of energy to manage our image.

And it makes it easy as we comb through our selfies for the best shot to forget that what happens in Vegas no longer stays in Vegas. The mirror is a window, and even as we look out, an AI is looking in. Does it see the real me? Or just a brilliant disguise?

Chapter 9—**How We Became Post-Human**

Augmented Reality

I was an early adapter to VR headsets, beginning with Google Glass and its clunky cardboard holder for a smart phone. I tried an Oculus Rift both in a lab at the university and later in the Dreamscape VR theater in my local mall. I knew I had to buy my own Oculus Go and then Oculus Quest headsets.

I loved them at first and strapped in for my morning exercises, flying planes, paragliding, and taking virtual tours. But the problem with VR is that you keep bumping into just plain reality. Unless you have a large room without furniture, your movements in your virtual world are limited and frequently punctuated by banging knees, elbows, and (given our low ceilings) sticking my fist pump of victory into a ceiling fan.

So I was up for augmented reality where you can see the real world but have things added to it. As soon as it was released, I was off to see the Apple Vision Pro.

Not that the local Apple store was going to let me walk around in their $3,500 headset. Still, as the technician asked me to take a seat so he could ironically "walk me through" how to use the Vision Pro, I liked what I saw. And I'm sure that at times I've looked stranger than I was that day waving my hands and pinching the air to control the goggles.

In the end, however, I couldn't quite imagine virtually attending a "live" concert. There is more to real human interaction than light and noise.

Back in the day, I saw the Who, Chase, Chicago, America, Dylan, and even Willie Nelson at the old Armadillo World Headquarters. Whether with a date or a bunch of friends, these were visceral experiences. When I read Huxley's *Brave New World*, I knew what he meant by "the feelies," an imagined kind of entertainment in which physical feeling is matched to sound and image.[1]

The Dreamscape VR theater (using an Oculus Rift) offered a crude approximation of reality, at best. The Dreamscape experience didn't leave me with visceral memories like the heat off of Molly's bare shoulders at the open-air theater at Fair Park.

The Vision Pro offered even less. And I can access my business apps just fine on my desktop with a hundred-dollar monitor. Or go whole hog with two big monitors. Having an Excel Spreadsheet hang out in front of a view of Mount Kilimanjaro isn't likely to make me more productive.

At a deeper level, it struck me that the Vision Pro wasn't augmented reality. It didn't *add* to reality. It added to what I knew about reality, like a heads-up display. It could overlay virtual objects with real objects. Yet in the end the world didn't change; what was in my head changed. I *seemed* to see both the world around me and things about that world otherwise not visible to my eyes. But I still wasn't engaging reality. I was engaging a projected image of reality on the screens of the headset.

The real fantasy on offer with all VR/AR headsets is the possibility of *augmented humanity*. Put on a headset and see and hear more than you could ever see or hear on your own. Put on the goggles and fly a fighter jet you could never otherwise fly. Meet people you'd never meet; have relationships you could never have. Be more than you are if you just put on the mask.

These possibilities are great for those who find themselves limited by disease and disability from fully engaging the physical world. It offers them new possibilities for exploring the world and even human relationships. In short it is a useful tool for enhancing human lives.

Yet for some of us, it forecloses on exploration and learning. It distracts us from reality and the human richness that arises from bodily engagement with the physical world. It creates an augmented humanity, but one that exists solely in the realm of digitized information.

I have an avatar in the VR application called Spacial.io. Its head was created from pictures of my own head. I selected the body, and I've got to

---

1. Huxley, *Brave New World*, 169–170.

CHAPTER 9—HOW WE BECAME POST-HUMAN

say that for a guy with no legs, I'm pretty buff. And without ever doing a crunch or even hot yoga. Unfortunately, once the headset is turned off and comes off, I'm just plain old pudgy me. But with actual legs.

There is a secret to the Vision Pro and the Oculus Meta Quest 3. *The user isn't looking at light reflected off of objects in the real world.* The user is looking at a digital video of light reflected off objects in the real world. People around you aren't looking in your eyes. They are looking at projected images of your eyes. So-called augmented reality exists only within *the mask*. This allows the magic of combining AI generated images with images from the outward facing cameras on the Vision Pro or Meta Quest 3. In the end, this augmented reality is just virtual reality. It is a human hiding behind a mask looking at a screen and becoming a person they are not.

Will it get better? Sure. Already there are clear glasses that can offer an augmented view of reality without masking our faces. Real people can see and be seen without mediation. But how real are they?

Is it really Robert Hunt, the guy that can never remember names, who suddenly knows the name of every person in the room at the class reunion? Because those names were whispered in my ear or flicker across the heads-up display in my glasses? Is that really Anne who couldn't remember my name after our first and last date but now knows the names of my grandchildren? Are we real when we're been "augmented" by being digitized and then digitally enhanced?

The Turing Test

In 1935 Alan Turing advanced the possibility of what is now known as a universal Turing machine. Building on pioneers like Ada Lovelace, he described the theoretical foundations for a computing machine that would not only run algorithms but modify or improve its own programming. In theory it would be intelligent. It wouldn't just know things; it would improve its own ability to know things.

In 1947, with his work in encryption for the British war effort ending, Turing returned to the idea of computer intelligence and how machines might learn. Is it possible that a machine could be intelligent? In 1950 he offered an answer by suggesting what is now called the *Turing test*. If a machine could convincingly match the performance of a human in a conversation, it could be regarded as intelligent.

In the history of artificial intelligence, the Turing test was a turning point. At a time when neuroscience and psychology were both advancing, it brought computers into the conversation about what constitutes intelligence. It articulated the assumption that *the human brain is a biological computer that can be emulated by a non-biological computer.* Turing effectively detached intelligence from human personhood. We became machines, and computers potentially became human.

In 1980 John Searle offered what he called the Chinese room experiment to show why the Turing test might not really be a test of human intelligence. Searle offered a thought experiment. There is a room, and in the room, there is a person who has a set of instructions in their own language. These instructions tell the person how to take a series of Chinese characters that are input and transform them into a set of Chinese characters that are output.[2] Is that intelligence?

There is an interesting real-world analogy to this in many old-fashioned Chinese temples I visited in Malaysia. In such a temple, a visitor can borrow a bamboo tube with two dozen or so bamboo sticks, each of which has a number (in Chinese) written on it. The visitor goes to one of the altars and makes an appropriate gift to a Chinese deity. They then gently shake the bamboo tube until a stick comes out further than the others. It is presumed that this stick was chosen by the deity.

The person then takes the stick to the temple attendant who may or may not be literate. Taking the number, and quite possibly not even looking up from their smart phone, the attendant can match the stick number to one of a couple of dozen cubby holes on the wall and pull from it a scroll of paper. The presumed message from the deity is written on the paper in Chinese characters.

From the standpoint of the person who asks the question and receives the reply, the deity has spoken. They ignore the internal working of the system, which includes the bamboo tube and sticks, the attendant, and the cubby hole full of rolled up messages. All of that is just the algorithm that analyzes the question and offers an answer. And in my observation the attendant, a bored kid, pays no attention to the question, the answer, or the person receiving the message. It's Searle's "Chinese room" without the walls to hide the "intelligence" behind the curtain.

Whether we think of Searle's thought experiment or an actual Chinese temple, we realize the same thing. There is nothing like what we think

---

2. Encyclopedia Britannica, "Chinese Room Argument."

of as intelligence at work because the intermediaries between input and output don't know and probably don't care or understand how one relates to the other. The human running algorithms to assign outputs to inputs in Searle's experiment, or the Chinese temple keeper pulling scrolls from holes, contribute no intelligence at all because they are not conscious of what is happening. Yet despite Searle's argument, there was and remains a fascination with the appearance of intelligence in the running of algorithms. We can still be taken in.

Cybernetics

In her 1999 book *How We Became Posthuman*, N. Katherine Hayles sets out to tell three stories. One, as she puts it is "how information lost its body." We saw this first in chapter 8 with the rise of information theory. The second is "how the cyborg was created as a technological artifact and cultural icon." We've looked at this in chapter 7 along with the antecedents to this as modernity gave us a framework for understanding humans as machines controlled by a machine. Her third story is "how the human is giving way to a different construction called the posthuman."[3]

Writing in 1999, Hayles was seeing only the beginning of what has become generative AI. The story she tells remains foundational to understanding the contemporary experience of being human. They are part of the story I'm trying to tell, as twenty-five years after her pioneering book, we actually live in a world of artificial intelligence, augmented humanity, and cyborgs.

In her book, Hayles traces the beginnings of the cybernetics movement to a series of conferences between 1946 and 1953 called the Macy conferences. Thinkers from many different disciplines came together to develop a general theory of communication and control for both machines and living organisms. Such theories remain alive today in the brain-computer interfaces of the twenty-first century.

The thinkers of the Macy conferences were intentionally blurring the lines between biological creatures, like humans, and computer-controlled machines of the kind already being introduced into the postwar economy. They did this by regarding everything, and not just knowledge, as information that could be processed. As information, anything could become part of

3. Hayles, *How We Became Posthuman*, 2.

a feedback loop that improved or redirected processes that control mechanisms for turning processed information into action.

As Hayles points out, a key takeaway of the cybernetics movement was the conviction that human intelligence isn't dependent on a human brain. It can thus theoretically be characterized and reproduced in a nonhuman, even nonorganic, machine. Or it could be placed in an enhanced body or an enhanced brain. The *post-human* would no longer be bound by philosophical or metaphysical convictions of superiority or even differences with the natural and material world. *Post-humans* didn't understand themselves in terms of a specific form of embodiment and could thus imagine any type of embodiment. Properly developed, the *post-human* could become the *trans-human*.

Trans-Humanism

The cybernetics movement wasn't just interested in reproducing human intelligence. It imagined enhancing and creating new intelligences. The unprogrammed computer could be understood as a womb, just waiting to slowly build within itself an intelligence like, or even superior to, a human intelligence. Or it could be guided by its programmers to create some other, more specialized intelligence. Regarding the brain as a computer allows us to think of the computer as a brain and (or so it was hoped) even a mind.

In 2024, the year in which I'm writing this book, Amy Kurzweil visited my university. She met a group of us to discuss her excellent graphic memoir, *Artificial: A Love Story*. It tells about how she and her father, Ray Kurzweil, set out to create a chatbot that would represent in words the grandfather that she never knew. Her father was the right partner for this endeavor.[4]

Ray Kurzweil is famous for his seminal inventions in optical character recognition and text-to-speech translation. He was involved with cybernetics and post-humanism from its very early days. In 1999 he built on his continuing innovations in machine intelligence to write *The Age of Spiritual Machines: When Computers Exceed Human Intelligence*. In 2005 he took his ideas a step further with *The Singularity Is Near: When Humans Transcend Biology*.

According to Kurzweil, AI will first achieve *artificial general intelligence*, and then by 2045 humans and AI technology will reach *singularity*.

---

4. Kurzweil, *Artificial*.

CHAPTER 9—HOW WE BECAME POST-HUMAN

At that point, a dramatic enhancement of human intelligence through brain-computer interfaces will potentially increase our cognitive capabilities a millionfold. We will have transcended our own humanity in a way that makes us a different species altogether.[5]

In her book, Amy Kurzweil explores her father's ideas through their chatbot project, which represents a kind of post-humanity. He had access to Alphabet's (Google's) vast computing resources and a conviction that perhaps humans can be reborn within a machine. It is a conviction that fits in the very human framework of a family disrupted by the Holocaust ninety years earlier and then, in the period in which she's writing, disrupted and isolated by COVID.[6]

Can humans overcome the isolation imposed by death and disease? The recurrent theme of Amy Kurzweil's book is her very journalistic rediscovery of her grandfather through places, people, and documents, alongside her father's fascination with what it means for humans to transcend themselves within a computer. Could Amy's grandfather, Kurt's father, somehow transcend death and be alive in some way for them? And as Ray Kurzweil constantly asks, can humans transcend their own humanity?[7]

Creating a chatbot that could represent a once-living human was a complex technical challenge in 2020 when Amy Kurzweil began her project. By the time her book came out in 2023, intelligent chatbots were ubiquitous. As I write in 2024, anyone with patience and a scanner can do what she and her father were doing. It could even be automated. Except.

At one point, Amy Kurzweil visits Vienna to see the building that her grandparents occupied before they migrated to the US, one step ahead of the Nazis. She renders, through her art, the personal impressions and sensations she experienced on that visit, the *qualia* of her encounter with her grandfather's past.[8] And as I read and saw her pictures, I was overwhelmed with sensations from my long residence in Vienna and the ways in which the story of my daughter's husband's family resonated with those of the Kurzweil's. Another kind of *qualia*. Can these human experiences of the real world and its real inhabitants ever be drawn into some post-human, and then trans-human, experience built on a substrate of silicone and steel?

I'd rather read Amy Kurzweil's book.

5. Kurzweil, *Age of Spiritual Machines*; Kurzweil, *Singularity Is Near*.
6. Kurzweil, *Artificial*.
7. Kurzweil, *Age of Spiritual Machines*.
8. Kurzweil, *Artificial*, 291–97.

The Post-Human World

As influential as Ray Kurzweil is in both popular culture and among computer scientists, his vision of trans-humanism based on artificial intelligence and technological advancement has a larger context. Since the industrial revolution, there has been a growing belief that with rapidly advancing technology, humans are taking greater and greater control of both their own lives and their environment.

Yet we have also been warned that in achieving greater control of our environment, we may lose control of ourselves.

In 1909 E. M. Forster wrote "The Machine Stops." He imagined a perfect world in which a "machine" cares for all human needs and humans lose their ability to care for themselves.[9] In 1989 Dan Simmons set his novel *Hyperion* in an AI controlled future that allows for human flourishing, so long as humans are controlled and exploited by AIs.[10] In 1999 there was *The Matrix*. In 2008 the Disney movie *WALL-E* placed humans in such a perfectly controlled environment in space. None of these stories were going to end well for humanity.

The silliness of the robots in *Lost in Space* and *The Jetsons* has given way to far more serious treatments of a world driven by AI. *THX 1138* by George Lucas examined an intelligent machine-driven future. So did *2001: A Space Odyssey* and its runaway AI named HAL. *Blade Runner*, based on Philip K. Dick's *Do Androids Dream of Electric Sheep*, offered a future not nearly as benevolent as that of Asimov's *I, Robot* from a decade earlier. Asimov's robots had psychological issues. P. K. Dick's were psychopaths.

In contrast to Kurzweil's optimism, these fictional scenarios are dystopian. A perfect world, at least in contemporary fiction, isn't actually so good for humanity. It always hides imperfections, and they can turn dreams into nightmares.

The Mutant

In Isaac Asimov's science fiction classic, *The Foundation Trilogy*, we find ourselves in a distant future. The huge problems of understanding history and literature and charting the course of humanity have been reduced

---

9. Forster, "Machine Stops."
10. Simmons, *Hyperion*.

to algorithms and solved by fast computers and sophisticated computer programs.[11]

The novel is predicated on the idea that once the population of humans in the universe becomes large enough and its history known in sufficient detail, computers can analyze the data, find the algorithms that describe it, and begin to both predict and control the future.

Given enough data, the patterns that characterize human behavior on a large scale emerge and can thus be both predicted and changed. That is what the group called the Foundation does in these novels. It calculates and carefully guides the future of humanity. It is made up of the human masters of the intelligence of machines.

So, what drives Asimov's plot? If everything is calculated, where do individual decisions come in? What difference does the individual make when the big picture of human progress is being carefully controlled?

The answer in *The Foundation Trilogy* comes with the birth of a mutant: a human who is not only idiosyncratic in his intelligence but who can manipulate the minds of others. In Asimov's novel, *computation cannot account for an idiosyncratic intelligence* that refuses to be reduced to statistics.

Algorithms cannot account for a creature who breaks all the patterns and refuses to fit in. Even less can the Foundation's computers account for an idiosyncratic intelligence that manipulates other people's intelligence and throws off that statistical analysis as well. It is when computation fails, and individual humans in all their little particularities disrupt the algorithms, that we finally have a *human* story worth our *human* interest.

If computers are to have a human-like intelligence, they must eventually tackle problems that can't be reduced to algebraic equations or the manipulation of symbols representing logical relations. They'll have to deal with mutants and malleable minds and patterns that dissolve into random noise at a human touch.

And maybe, if they really have human-like intelligence, they'll need to be idiosyncratic and manipulative as well. Have you met my friend HAL?

---

11. Asimov, *Foundation*.

Chapter 10—Artificial Minds from Calculators to Computers

Our story so far can be summarized like this: over the course of the modern era, from the Enlightenment onward, humanity has been *demystified*. The mysterious, the invisible, and the spiritual in humanity have gradually been pushed aside as we come to see ourselves as machines operated by machines in a larger biological system that itself operates like a machine. We've been decentered, diminished, diffused, and disembodied. Even our machine nature is reduced from physicality to abstraction and the realm of algorithms. Trapped by screens, it is harder and harder to fight the distortion of our true selves. Our culture has prepared us to regard computers and androids as our peers, and even our superiors.

At the same time, the technology behind those computers has become mysterious. As computers become more complex and capable, they appear almost magical, beyond the realm of human comprehension. We've been set up to attribute to computers something like our own now reduced and abstracted humanity. *Before we can move on in an AI age, we need to demystify the technology behind AI so that we can see it for what it is: machines operated by machines ultimately and always programmed by humans.*

Becoming Software

The summer of 1974, I was a restless high school graduate biding his time before entering the astronomy program at the University of Texas. One of my teachers pushed me into a summer internship at what was then Southwest

CHAPTER 10—ARTIFICIAL MINDS FROM CALCULATORS TO COMPUTERS

Center for Advanced Studies (now the University of Texas at Dallas). My job was to write a program in the language FORTRAN that would solve a complex integral equation. This, in turn, could be used to calibrate satellite data on the distribution of certain ions in the upper atmosphere. I was to create an algorithm that could reproduce a pattern in the data.

It was heady stuff, having access to a serious mainframe computer. We interns wrote our code on paper then translated it into punch cards. At a special counter, I turned in the cards that would feed our programs into a computer that took up a large air-conditioned room. Outside contaminants like interns and grad students were not allowed.

If things worked out, I went to another window and got a few sheets of paper with a printout of the output of my program. If things didn't work out, I received a single sheet with an early termination error because of invalid code. If things really went wrong, I received a large stack of paper and a sharp rebuke from the high priestess of the computer for having included an infinite "do loop" in my program.

The buzz that summer was still the 1972 TI-2500 Datamath calculator. The slide rules some of us still carried were rapidly becoming relics. Which was fine. But a calculator is still a calculator. It is a fast way of solving basic equations that all of us in our cubicles could easily solve in our heads, or with pencil and paper. In those days, experienced engineers would race the calculator while the more juvenile among us would create word jokes. (What is 59009 turned upside down on a crude LED display? Now give me a clever equation that gives this answer.)

All fun for a minute or two. When the fun was over, we were gathered around the mainframe because it could be *programmed*. Problems that required logic rather than mere calculation, such as integral equations, had to be solved by a series of complex logical steps very well suited to a *computer* but not possible for a calculator. A programmable computer could do more than perform calculations. Properly programmed, it could answer questions.

It also turned those of us working in the computer science lab into something relatively new—*programmers*. Programs were the *software* that ran on the mainframe hardware. And we, squishy pale human beings who spent too much time indoors, were a somewhat different kind of software.

The Mechanical Mind

In the 1830s, Charles Babbage described his analytical engine, a machine that could do math. It was a mechanical, programmable, general-purpose calculating machine based on physical interactions. If it could ever be built (and it was complicated), it seemed like the kind of machine that might be regarded as intelligent, at least if intelligence involves doing math.

In 1843 the mathematician Ada Lovelace probably wasn't thinking of intelligence when she read an academic paper in French describing Babbage's analytic engine. Still, as she translated the paper into English, it set her thinking about the relationship of math problems and logic problems. As a result, she made extensive annotations and notes for the final published version of her translation. In them she gave her own account of what a machine like the one Babbage envisioned might actually be able to accomplish.[1] It was more than math.

Her notes showed how a machine could be *programmed* to do much more than perform complex calculations. Her proposed algorithms demonstrated that a machine for calculating the solutions to mathematical problems could also be used for symbolic reasoning to solve logic problems. As long as logic operations could be organized into algorithms, then the machine could process them in much the way it would mathematical calculations. She was the reason that, one hundred and thirty years later, I was employed as a computer programmer.

It is debated whether Ada Lovelace was the first computer programmer. Regardless, she created the theoretical basis for computer programming. She showed that a machine might perform the logical and symbolic operations we associate with human intelligence, and human intelligence alone. Looked at another way, she laid down the theoretical basis for an artificial intelligence.

In 1847 George Boole independently added to the intersection of logic and math with his seminal paper "The Mathematical Analysis of Logic." He demonstrated that by using three logical operations—AND, OR, and NOT—you could perform all algebraic calculations. By reducing the number of *operators* in an algorithm to logical operations, Boole lay the foundation for having a simple machine carry out complex calculations. After all, it just needed to do three things: add, choose, and exclude.[2]

1. Murtagh, "Computation Foretold," 82.
2. Wikipedia, "George Boole."

He and Lovelace were joined by the inventors of different systems of symbolic logic to lay part of the foundation for programmable computers and thus for AI. But before that could happen, a number of different ideas had to converge around something even more sophisticated, and real, than Babbage's theoretical analytical engine.

The Electron Valve

In the mid to late 1800s, Heinrich Geissler, William Crookes, and Karl F. Braun contributed to the development of the cathode ray tube. It was an essential element in the first computers and the basis of all televisions until the late 1900s. It provided a way to manipulate electrons whether to perform calculations, amplify signals, or display pictures on a screen. I spent a lot of time with these tubes in the workshop of Dr. Wissenhunt's Color Corral TV repair shop. We were all about vacuum tubes in those days: the little ones that manipulated signals and the big ones that displayed a picture. "Solid state," meaning TV circuits using transistors, was brand new. LED displays were decades away. Who knew they would put us all out of business.

The tubes created in the late nineteenth century, which we worked with a century later, created a flow of electricity from a positively charged anode to a negatively charged cathode. In 1897 J. J. Thomson used experiments with cathode ray tubes to show that electricity was made of subatomic particles called electrons.[3] Another piece in the puzzle. More pieces would follow.

In the late nineteenth century, telegraphy, telephony, and radio were beginning to boom. But the only way anyone could control an electrical signal was with a physical switch. These were switches no different from my telegraph key for Morse code on an amateur radio a century later. The operators were faster than I was, but it was all down to fingers. And on the other end, the electromagnets that tapped out the code were no faster than the operators who sent the original code.

Once there were telephones, the same limitations in switches continued. Human switchboard operators moved electrical signals around by plugging and unplugging physical wires to send signals from a sender to the right receiver.

Then in 1904 John Ambrose Fleming demonstrated what he called an electron valve, just a word for a switch that controls an electrical current.

---

3. Thomson, "J. J. Thomson."

His electron valve did something simple but really useful. It only let half the current in an alternating current circuit through the valve. It effectively converted alternating current to direct current.[4] Today, its descendants are what turn the AC current in the plugs in your house to the DC current that charges your cell phones and runs your computer.

Fleming's invention was a big deal. Alternating current is easier to generate and travels further in a wire than DC current. It is perfect for sending electricity to homes over long power lines. And it's just fine for making light bulbs glow. But a lot of useful devices need DC current, the kind we get out of batteries. If you could send AC electricity over a long distance and then make it useful to these DC devices, it opened a whole new world. You could have, for example, both your lights AND your radio powered from the same source.

Then something even cooler was invented by Lee de Forest in 1907. He showed that by placing an electrically charged grid between an anode and a cathode in a cathode ray tube, you could control the flow of electrons from anode to cathode.

If the grid had a negative charge, it repelled electrons, and they couldn't get to the cathode. No current flowed. If the grid had no charge, then electrons could flow through. It was a valve that could be turned off and on with electricity that traveled at the speed of light rather than the speed of a tapping human finger or a machine-controlled electromagnet.[5]

And it wasn't just on/off. You could adjust the amount of electricity flowing to the grid in order for it increase or lessen the flow of electrons through the grid. By augmenting the flow of electrons from anode to cathode the tube could become an amplifier.

De Forest's invention put in place the basic hardware of a modern computer. Combining two flows of electrons was the same as Boole's logical AND. Switching between them was Boole's logical OR. And cutting them off entirely was his logical NOT. The next leap ahead, if you aren't already there, wasn't going to be in the realm of manipulating electrons. It would be in the realm of performing logical operations on numbers using this emerging technology.

---

4. Encyclopedia Britannica, "Sir John Ambrose Fleming."
5. Fielding, "Lee de Forest."

CHAPTER 10—ARTIFICIAL MINDS FROM CALCULATORS TO COMPUTERS

Boolean Algebra Meets the Electron Valve

The inventions of the binary system of mathematics, Boolean algebra, and the technology of the vacuum tube came together in the 1937 master's thesis for MIT by Claude Shannon. He observed that Boolean algebra was similar to the working of an electronic circuit made up of vacuum tube switches that combined two signals, chose between two signals, or excluded a signal. His paper, "A Symbolic Analysis of Relay and Switching Circuits," showed how electrical circuits could be turned into machines for doing Boolean algebra. They could become logic machines, calculating machines, and if thinking is logic and calculation, they could become thinking machines.[6]

His basic insight that logic could be reproduced with lighting-fast electrical valves, or vacuum tubes, put all the pieces in place for the invention of the first modern computers. But I want us to pause and notice something. *All these computers could do is combine three logical operations into sequences that solve an algebraic problem. The only distinction they could make was between 1 and 0.* They are thinking machines only if you think making this distinction very quickly is thinking.

The Transistor

Let's take one more step in technology before we see what this really means. John Bardeen, Walter Brattain, and William Shockley successfully demonstrated the first working electron valve made of germanium and gold—a transistor—on December 23, 1947. In 1954 Morris Tanenbaum of Texas Instruments (TI) showed that you could do the same thing with silicone, which is as cheap as the sand from which it is derived.[7] Three years later, Jack Kilby of TI demonstrated how these transistors could be put together on a single circuit, an *integrated* circuit—the foundation of all modern computers.[8]

I'd love to go into the details of how the first transistors (solid as in "solid state") were developed and turned into integrated circuits. After all, when I was constructing my first ham radio, the nearby TI plant in Richardson was providing jobs for the parents of my classmates. By the time I graduated from high school, my peers were working in that same plant

---

6. Shannon, "Symbolic Analysis."
7. Riordan, "Silicon Transistors."
8. Dennis, "Jack Kilby."

fabricating integrated circuits. And even two decades later, it was still exciting for me to see the TI logo on a microchip in the homebrew computer I was making in Malaysia, where TI was also firmly ensconced.

Nostalgia aside, the key thing is that a transistor uses the characteristics of certain materials (usually silicone and what is called a doping agent) to create a tiny version of a vacuum tube valve that is solid and cheap. And it uses a lot less electricity and generates much less heat. The integrated circuit comes about when these transistors are created and connected by the hundreds, thousands, then millions, then billions on increasingly tiny silicone substrates.

Amazing, Not Magic

The first computer I programmed at the Southwest Research Center was already solid state, but it still took up a large room. By the time I graduated from UT three years later, it was being sold as scrap because it was too large, too slow, and too hot. Today, my smart phone is many times more powerful and orders of magnitude faster than that computer. And the rate at which more powerful chips and circuits are being developed is actually increasing, more than doubling every year. The fastest processing chips available today are eighty-three billion times faster than my first home computer.

Yet for all this, the first programmable computer completed in 1946 (ENIAC) and my smart phone have this in common: all they do is perform logical operations. Their whole set of operations is AND, OR, and NOT, which they execute in amazingly complex combinations with fabulously well-designed transistors. Underneath, it is all complex electronics performing logical operations at incredibly high speeds. Amazing, but not magic.

Chapter 11—From Computers to Artificial Intelligence

From Algorithms to Pattern Matching

My father was a skilled and subtle fisherman, and we went fishing a lot. I wanted to learn how to catch fish. But quite often his instructions seemed to be vague in a way that was odd for a professional educator. Day in and day out he worked with schedules, procedures, and policies for running a college. He sought to be ever more precise and efficient. And then out on Matagorda Bay, I'd ask how to find redfish. He'd smell the salty air and look around across the calm water reflecting a rising sun and say, "You sense them."

Eventually I came to recognize that he was sensing a pattern of conditions including the angle of sun on the water, the smell in the air, and the ripples on the flat surface (or more subtle, the ripples on a wavy surface). These were all part of the pattern associated with a school of redfish being present. To use a term from Robert Heinlein's *Stranger in a Strange Land* and rooted in gestalt psychology, my father "grokked" that the fish were present.[1] A longtime sci-fi fan, it was a word he appreciated.

Traditional computing took data represented by symbols and then analyzed the data through algorithms that operated on these symbols. Turing's imagined intelligent machine was programmed in this way, even if was eventually to be self-programmed.

---

1. Heinlein, *Stranger in a Strange Land*, 20.

When applied to tasks usually performed by humans, programmers sought to create *expert systems*. They would be intelligent because they mimicked what was understood to be human intelligence. For example, in the medical field they tried to break down work done by doctors into sequences of decisions that could characterized in the symbolic language of the computer. Human expertise was reduced to algorithms run on computers.

Such systems remain important tools as a form of AI. Yet they fail to capture the actual expertise of human experts. They don't take into account the difference between how experts *report* on their decisions and the actual decision-making process. In one sense they can't because the *report* of a decision-making process is linear and logical, it's algorithmic. But the actual process of making a decision isn't. In fact, recent evidence presented by Fredrik Björklund in his paper *Intuition and Ex-Post Facto Reasoning in Moral Judgments* shows that what we call reasoning may be an after-the-fact explanation for decisions made by other means.[2]

Grok!

When Traditional Logic Doesn't Work

Context

Last winter my neighborhood in Dallas was hit with an unusual snowstorm. A few inches of snow on our sidewalks and driveways stranded most Dallasites in their homes. We just don't do snow. We don't have snow shovels, we don't have snow tires, and we don't have snow boots.

So, I gazed out my window to enjoy this rare moment only to see my neighbor across the street out with a snow shovel. He was busily clearing his drive and then his sidewalk. Oh yes, he'd just moved from Nebraska.

I admired his diligence, which made his house unique on our block. But he didn't understand our context. In our context, it makes more sense to wait on the sun.

Expert systems, except in very narrow circumstances, come up against the problem of *context*. When doctors make a diagnosis, they aren't just engaged in logical reasoning on a specific data set, which in their profession is called differential diagnosis. They are summoning a great deal of

---

2. Björklund, "Intuition."

CHAPTER 11—FROM COMPUTERS TO ARTIFICIAL INTELLIGENCE

unconscious contextual information that arises from thousands of interactions with patients over many years.

Those who are more self-aware know that everything they see in a patient, not just the presenting symptoms, plays a role. Smell, sound, and even a knowledge of the season of the year come into play. Introducing these into an expert system is difficult. After-the-fact descriptions of how a decision was made tend to miss them because the expert wasn't consciously aware of them.

It is even more difficult to assign them a value that represents their significance or to determine the order in which they should be considered in the diagnostic process. They need to be *grokked*, and that's not something regular computers are equipped to do.

Completeness

Context presents a logical issue as well, one that was only fully recognized in the 1930s. Back in 1913, Bertrand Russell and Alfred North Whitehead published a massive volume, *The Principia Mathematica*. It used symbolic logic to rigorously derive all mathematical truths from a set of axioms and inference. In the realm of mathematics, it was huge because it sought to reduce all mathematics to logic.[3]

It turns out there was a problem. I learned about it from Douglas R Hofstadter's book *Gödel, Escher, Bach: An Eternal Golden Braid* a couple of decades ago. As he told the story, in 1931 the Viennese mathematician named Kurt Gödel published the paper, *On Formally Undecidable Propositions of Principia Mathematica and Related Systems*.[4] In it he demonstrated a truth that in hindsight seems simple: *there are true propositions that cannot be stated within the supposedly complete system of logical truths in The Principia Mathematica.*[5]

Specifically, Gödel's incompleteness theorem says that the statement "this system contains all true statements" cannot be logically proven from *within* the system. After all from within a bounded system, how could you know what true statements might exist outside it? If you've never lived outside of your hometown, how can you know whether you know everything?

---

3. Russell and Whitehead, *Principia Mathematica*.
4. See Hofstadter, *Gödel, Escher, Bach*, 15–24.
5. Gödel, "Über formal unentscheidbare Sätze."

Gödel's work has profound implications for any effort to use computation or logic to find all the possible answers, much less the best answer, to any question. One AI chatbot I consulted noted, "While computers can generate useful information, they cannot guarantee the validity of that information without human oversight." Of course not. The computer cannot step outside itself to check whether the information it gives fits the world outside its data and algorithms. It can only check for internal coherence. And that is only *half* of what it means to know something.

In my own research, I use three generative AI chatbots, making them check on each other. Even then they make mistakes.

The information a computer generates must at some point be judged by its relationship to a reality that is larger than what is found in the computer's internal logic and knowledge. It has to be put into a larger *context*.

Still, the chatbot oracle I consulted may be a bit too optimistic about human oversight. Humans are also limited in their grasp of reality. Our brains are vastly more complex than the most advanced AI models available in 2024, but they are still finite in their capacity. Why else would I be chatting with Perplexity AI to remind me about books I read years ago? Or asking ChatGPT to remind me of the origin of the word "grok"?

Chaos

A final factor that limits expert systems and their algorithms is explored for nonexpert readers in James Gleik's book *Chaos: Making a New Science*. As it turns out, even some logical problems are inherently complex and sensitive to initial conditions, which can lead to unpredictable outcomes.[6] *The Three-Body Problem* by Liu Cixin, now a Netflix series, builds on exactly this challenge. Even a simple system of gravitational interactions between three objects in space can exhibit apparently chaotic behavior that is nearly impossible for computers to predict accurately. Actually, impossible if you take into account other objects in space.[7]

A number of years ago, I was invited by a friend to sit in on a small UN conference about near-Earth objects (NEOs). The scientists were discussing how to predict whether an approaching object would hit the earth. And as importantly, how to communicate the danger to the public. It was fascinating and touched on the problem of the so-called "butterfly effect."

6. Gleick, *Chaos*.
7. Liu, *Three-Body Problem*.

CHAPTER 11—FROM COMPUTERS TO ARTIFICIAL INTELLIGENCE

This is the idea that in weather systems characterized by nonlinear equations, at some point a butterfly's wings could create a tiny but spreading disruption that would dramatically change the weather system.

Perhaps you remember Dr. Ian Malcolm, portrayed by Jeff Goldblum in the movie version of *Jurassic Park*. He explained chaos theory and the butterfly effect in relation to the evolution of dinosaurs in a modern environment. Nature cannot be predicted or controlled, he tells us. "Life will find a way."[8]

The same thing is true when you have thousands of unknown objects whose minute gravity creates unpredictable effects on an asteroid or comet hurtling toward the earth. A tiny, and unforeseeable, disruption can create a large effect.

At the NEO conference, there was an expert in communicating risk to the public. His advice was, "Always tell them to bring an umbrella." He was English, and in England that is always good advice. But regardless, his point was that the sensitivity of NEOs to tiny initial inputs makes it impossible to make real long-term predictions about a specific place and time of impact, or if they will hit the earth at all. They are like hurricanes, influenced by so many unknowable and unmeasurable effects that only when they are very close can it be known if they will hit.

This sensitivity to initial conditions in characterizing complex relationships and patterns is a problem with designing modern AI systems. There is a nonlinear relationship between questions and their answers, meaning that chaos lies close at hand.

Neural Networks

Traditional computer programming is pushed to its limits trying to emulate human experts. Between complex contexts, incompleteness theory, and chaos theory, algorithms cannot *grok*. As computer scientists faced this reality, they had another possible approach.

As the first computers were being programmed, neuroscientists were mapping the structures of the human brain. They found complex networks of neurons laid out in layers and divided into different functional parts of the brain. Could networks of neurons be the secret to intelligence?

In 1943 Walter Pitts and Warren McCulloch offered the first theoretical model of how the neurons in the brain might work when a human is

---

8. Spielberg, *Jurassic Park*.

thinking. In their model, a neuron is a binary device that sends a signal when inputs to it reach a certain threshold. Instead of sending a signal based on a single set of inputs in the logic of Boolean algebra, it "fires" based on the cumulative inputs from other neurons.[9]

Another step, both in understanding the human brain and understanding how an imitation brain might work, came in 1949 when Donald Hebb introduced the idea that neural pathways in the brain were strengthened through repeated use. In his model, neurons in the brain don't just fire based on reaching a certain threshold. If they fired repeatedly, they created more permanent connections with other neurons. Such a model might account for memory and give the possibility for permanent or semipermanent relationships between neurons in the brain.[10]

The Perceptron

In her very useful primer *Artificial Intelligence: A Guide for Thinking Humans*, Melanie Mitchell picks up this story in relation to computing with her account of Frank Rosenblatt's creation of the perceptron in 1959. The perceptron was the first computer designed to mimic the way in which neurons were supposed to work in the brain.[11]

The perceptron didn't use *hardware* to mimic the way neurons in the brain worked. After all if Hebbs was right, then the brain continually modified its hardware, its neurons. That's easier with living cells than with dead transistors.

Instead, the perceptron was programmed to take different inputs based on black and white areas of a picture of a number and vary their strength by adding or subtracting a "weight." This was the computer equivalent of strengthening a connection between neurons. These weighted inputs were then combined through an "activation function." If the result reached a threshold, then the program gave an output. The threshold could be adjusted by a "bias" to fine-tune the results.

Once there was an output, a human judged whether the output correctly identified the number in the input. If it did, then the weights and bias were stored in the computer's memory. If it was incorrect, the

---

9. Wilson, Charles et al., "Logical Neuron."
10. Brown et al., "Hebb Synapse Before Hebb."
11. This discussion of Rosenblatt's work draws heavily from Mitchell, *Artificial Intelligence*, 24–31.

computer program changed the weights and tried again. After many iterations, the computer would be storing weights for each input that led to an accurate output. This was pioneering. Several concepts would carry over into contemporary AI, like attaching weights to inputs, introducing bias to fine-tune the network, and having an activation function that calculated whether a neuron in the network should "fire."

Image Recognition

Rosenblatt's specific problem was image recognition. In particular he wanted a computer to recognize handwritten numbers and convert them to digital numbers. In a business or bureaucracy flooded with handwritten receipts, forms, and so on, having a machine that converted these to their digital equivalent could save a lot of human labor and money. Rosenblatt's insight was that to recognize a number, it needed to be *grokked*, or seen all at once rather than analyzed line by line. He recognized that image recognition was a form of pattern matching.

Think of a handwritten number written in a box divided into nine squares. In Rosenblatt's perceptron, each square would be represented initially by a one, meaning it had something in it, or a zero, meaning it was empty. The output of each square, one or zero, would be the input for one of the computer processors in the perceptron. Initially each processor would output a value equal to its input, and based on the total of these values, the perceptron would produce an output, a number between one and nine.

If a human flagged that number as wrong, all the processors would add a "weight" to their number, thus changing the total and generating a different output number between one and nine. Again, a human would judge if it was correct or not. The process would go on until the perceptron finally got the right number. Then another handwritten version of the same number would go in, and the process would be repeated.

At least in theory, the perceptron would *grok* the whole handwritten number and correctly translate it into a digital number. The machine would have learned to recognize a number. And *machine learning* remains the term for this type of process.

Scientists from the 1960s onward built on Rosenblatt's work to simulate with computers what was known about the neural networks in the brain. At the same time, they came understand better and better what these simulated neural networks could do. The two were interrelated.

Hardware developers tried to develop faster and more capable computers to run the neural network simulations created by the software developers. Software developers watched the hardware develop and tried to figure out how to program the activation function, the changing weights, and the bias more and more effectively.

It wasn't easy. The equations that took the inputs and created outputs were not simple and needed constant tweaking. Early versions of the perceptron struggled to accurately identify simple handwritten numbers. It took fifty years of innovation, in both conceptualizing how neural networks could be programmed and building new hardware that could run the programs, to lay the foundation for contemporary AI. What the public saw as faster, smaller computers, increasingly complex video games, rudimentary spell checkers, and sophisticated spreadsheets were all laying the foundation for AI. Faster hardware, more sophisticated algorithms, and innovative models of just what comprised intelligence were all necessary.

The Hidden Assumptions of Machine Learning

Yet driving these developments were underlying assumptions that get lost in the gee-whiz aspects of the technology. The first of these is that *intelligence* is based on patterns of connections among the neurons in our brain. The second is that these patterns are created and stored in the brain's neural network based on data input from a creature's interaction with reality through the senses. The third is that a creature's behavior arises from an interaction between the stored patterns in the brain and the patterns being sensed in the outside world.

Modern machine learning, or AI, is thus built on Descartes's idea that the intelligent mind builds up a model of reality within itself. This can then be tested for internal logical consistency and then further tested for coherence with the reality outside itself. Then based on these internal models of reality, the brain causes the body to operate in certain ways in the real world.

But while Descartes thought of the mind as more like a modern expert system running algorithms, modern AI adapts his basic conceptual framework to create a "brain" consisting of a carefully programmed neural network and the means by which it obtains initial inputs, organizes its model of reality, and generates outputs. The assumption, one that Descartes didn't anticipate, is that the *brain* modeled reality by creating

CHAPTER 11—FROM COMPUTERS TO ARTIFICIAL INTELLIGENCE

patterns of relationships in its neurons. He thought that the *mind* created a model of reality based on logic.

Perceiving Reality

Even with the developments in hardware and the rich programming insights that make machine learning possible, there has been and remains a challenge. Once you have a neural network, how do you introduce it to the real world? Humans know things because we experience things and process and store those experiences in our brains. A combination of sensory inputs is transformed *within* our brain to a model of reality we are aware of with our mind. And we can then check our internal *model* of reality against the real world outside our mind.

The perceptron really only had one very narrow sense: a sensor that distinguished between light and dark on a piece of paper. This is far short of what we humans are constantly feeding into our brain. Short of the huge technological challenge of developing sensors by the millions that emulate those in a human body, how can a computer simulating a neural network be trained?

Symbolic Analysis

One approach is called *symbolic analysis*. This approach measures various aspects of the reality being studied, stores those measurements as symbols (basically numbers), and then applies algorithms to those symbols to generate a model of that particular aspect of reality. Back in my intern days, a satellite was measuring the relative quantities of ions at different altitudes in the upper atmosphere. My job was to take the data (relative quantities at specific altitudes), convert it to symbols a computer could work with, and create an algorithm that gave the absolute quantity of the different ions at each altitude. Training consisted of collecting data and running a program. The result was then stored in some form of computer memory that could be accessed later. The algorithm and symbols together would become our model of the reality of ion distribution in the upper atmosphere.

This was hard to do even for something quite concrete and discrete. We've already seen that this method just can't work for many types of knowledge.

Pattern Analysis

The alternative is to introduce different forms of data into a neural network and let its constantly self-adjusting processes shape this data into patterns of connections between its virtual neurons. We'll call this *pattern analysis*. This was the perceptron's approach for creating a model of an image of a number. I'll get to the actual process by which this happens in the next chapter. Before that, let's ask just what kind of data we need to introduce into the neural network if we're going to model reality.

The early neural networks were designed for optical character recognition, in particular handwritten numbers. So essentially, they used one type of input: optical. As Mitchell documents, just recognizing patterns of black and white wasn't easy. The network had to both discern the basic patterns of black and white characteristics of each number, and how they were different from every other number. When it succeeded, it only knew one thing: ten numbers.

This is a far cry from anything approaching human intelligence; although, it might remind us that when a child learns the numbers and the alphabet, they've really accomplished something! Still, as neural networks slowly improved with better and better processors, they got better at detecting and storing patterns in images that could be compared to other patterns in other images.

Yet this didn't represent knowing reality as we know it. It was easy to create images that fooled image recognition software. And right up to the present, such software can miss the most important part of a complex image. It can match patterns, but it can't tell which patterns are important, particularly when importance changes according to context, including the context of who is looking at the image.

Just this last week, I went through all the pictures of our grandchildren to put them together on a single flash drive to go into a digital picture frame. Modern AI can do the kind of facial recognition I was doing. But that wasn't all I was doing.

I was making sure that our grandchildren's grandmother appeared in enough pictures and looked good according to her, and not my, judgment. And of course, I was asking the same thing about other parents and other grandparents. There is a lot more to choosing pictures for a digital album than facial recognition.

Or imagine a picture of a man sleeping on a park bench with a dog by his side and a policeman nearby. An advanced image recognition AI will identify the sleeping man, the park bench, the dog, and the policeman. But it can't tell the story or stories implicit in the image. Nor can it emulate the bias of a particular observer as they respond emotionally to the image. As a result, it can't focus on whether the man, the bench, the dog, or the policeman is most important.

From Images to Language

In 2001 Yoshua Bengio and collaborators at the University of Montreal proposed using neural networks for language modeling. This was a shift from training a neural network to recognize patterns in images or other forms of data, to recognizing patterns in language. It would turn out to be a huge advance in machine learning.[12]

Using advances in creating neural networks, Bengio's idea was to train neural networks on language so that these networks would create within themselves the patterns of relationship found in language. They would create a *model* of the language. In theory they could generate better outputs when prompted to give a verbal response. Instead of matching patterns in an image with a description of the image, they would recognize patterns in a sentence and match those with a response. When ChatGPT came on the scene, it was a Large Language Model, with *large* meaning that it has been trained on large amounts of language.

Frank Rosenblatt's perceptron and its ability to recognize the patterns that make up numbers was hugely relevant to a time in the mid-twentieth century when numerical data needed to be transferred from paper to computer memory. Bengio's use of pattern recognition in language was hugely relevant at a time when businesses needed faster, cheaper ways to answer email inquiries, text messages, and even phone calls.

Language and Knowing

Yet there is another dimension to creating a model of language as opposed to, for example, a model of an image. Language is the means by which humans articulate to themselves and others how they understand reality. Human *knowing* is largely humans talking or writing about ourselves, others, and our world. Texts in a library are extensions of our brains, containing

---

12. Bengio et al., "Neural Probabilistic Language Model."

more potential knowledge than any one person can keep inside their heads. Language is how we know the world.

Moreover languages, in their variety, represent the variety of ways in which different cultures perceive and represent reality. How many types of *snow* are there? When I grew up in Texas, we distinguished between dry, slushy, and yellow. Never eat the last of these. The Inuit people have far more ways of distinguishing snow, each a critical part of understanding a key aspect of their reality.

Examples like this abound. The Malay languages that are found in Southeast Asia have many more terms for rice than we find in English. On the other hand English, always an acquisitive and innovative language, has an extremely rich vocabulary for technology and machines.

Because language provides us the basis for thinking about reality, *a model of the patterns in language may also be understood as a model of reality as expressed in language*. With the breakthrough of using language to train neural networks came a breakthrough in artificial intelligence. It became what we think of as *intelligence*. Not just machine learning.

For modern AI advocates, a large language model doesn't just offer a model of language. *It offers a model of reality of the sort Descartes imagined*. And if the model is big enough and complex enough, you aren't limited to asking it questions for which an answer is stored in a database. When you ask it a question, you are really asking it to consult its model of reality to find information not stored in any database. *It could offer information that wasn't generated from the texts on which it was trained but from the patterns in the model itself*.

It could come up with new ideas. And that is *part* of what we commonly call intelligence.

How Does It Taste?

Back in high school I had a mentor who, among his many hobbies, learned to bake bread. He avidly read and recommended, *Beard on Bread* by James Beard. It was a compendium of James Beard's wisdom on how a few basic types of ingredients could be combined, worked together, and cooked to make an almost endless variety of breads. These included flour of some kind (normally wheat, but also potato, sago, or almost anything

CHAPTER 11—FROM COMPUTERS TO ARTIFICIAL INTELLIGENCE

that could be ground and contained starch), water, salt, and some form of leavening agent.[13]

At first glance, *Beard on Bread* appears to be a book of recipes. Yet we could also understand *Beard on Bread* as a language-based model of the reality of bread. It includes both recipes (specific patterns related to specific outputs) and general principles (abstract patterns that could be combined to generate a variety of outputs). We can look inside the Beard model of bread reality and find a recipe for a baguette. It would give the ingredients, portions, order of mixing, how the dough was worked, and how it should be cooked. Low hanging fruit because the recipe is in the book.

However, we could also ask the Beard model of bread reality, "How can I make a gluten-free baguette?" Something Beard would never have considered in 1973. Is there still an answer in the book? Yes. In the Beard model, there are also basic patterns of interaction between different ingredients, ways of working dough, and cooking. Based on the relationships between these patterns, our model should be able to formulate a recipe for a gluten-free baguette. The patterns to create the recipe are there even if they are not found in a specific set of pages in the text. *Beard on Bread* models the reality of bread. Recipes are just an example of how the model works.

In the next chapter, we'll see that the idea of a model of reality based on principles and facts isn't exactly the way a modern LLM works. Because its patterns consist of neither recognizable principles nor facts. But the important thing is this: a model of reality can be the source of novel ideas, ideas not explicitly found anywhere in the model itself. It can create a never-before-seen recipe for bread.

Would You Eat It?

The first AI was an effort to have computers reproduce the working of a conscious human *mind* solving problems through algorithms. That didn't work as well as hoped. Then AI was developed as a computer modeling a human *brain* with a network of virtual neurons. That began to work on images as the computers and their software became more powerful. This led to AI as a *model of human language* in a neural network. And this has evolved into AI as a *model of reality* as known by humans and expressed through their language.

---

13. Beard, *Beard on Bread*.

A subtle transformation has taken place. *As they engage AI chatbots, humans begin to take the LLM AI model of reality as an actual report on the nature of the real world by humans.* AI doesn't have any experience with reality. It is only as reliable as the unreliable humans on whose linguistic representations of reality it was trained.

I know firsthand how problematic this can be. After all, my students are trained on my language as they heard it in a lecture. And both they and I make mistakes. When they become teachers, unless they constantly check on me and themselves, they may end up passing down those mistakes.

And something else is going on as well. When my students listen to my lecture, taking the patterns in my language and inputting it into the neural networks that make up their brains, the patterns in their brains change. Hopefully they have a different understanding of reality. It's something that happens all the time. We humans train each other on the nature of the real world.

And that world includes how we understand ourselves as humans. A changing understanding of reality can change what we think about ourselves. When it comes from and through an AI chatbot, there is the potential to change our human self-understanding.

These are ideas that were explored back in 1981 by Jean Baudrillard in his book *Simulacra and Simulation*. A useful read. They are now more relevant than ever as our interactions with simulations of reality are becoming a constant feature of daily life.[14]

It becomes easy to forget, with the facile answers provided by the best LLM GPT AI, *that the AI has never experienced reality directly in the way humans experience reality*. It is a brain without a mind and without a body. Humans don't *just* know what other humans have said. We also know through sensory experiences like touch, taste, smell, sight, and hearing. We imagine things. And crucially, we know that we know. It is only when human knowledge is expressed in the language used to train an AI that the AI become capable of *simulating* reality and presenting that simulation to us.

So, do you want to be the first to try a gluten-free baguette made with the *Beard on Bread* AI that has no sense of taste?

---

14. Baudrillard, *Simulacra and Simulation*.

Chapter 12—**How It Works**

Trigger warning. In his 1964 essay *Hazards of Prophecy: The Failure of Imagination*, Arthur C. Clarke once said that any sufficiently advanced technology will appear to be magic.[1] *AI is a sufficiently advanced technology*. It's complicated. It seems magical.

This chapter is about taking the magic out.

In the modern era our human body, brain, and mind have been demystified. We have pulled ourselves out of the context of the mysterious transcendent and placed ourselves in naturalistic relationships that can be studied by science. We may not understand ourselves fully, but we have been convinced that we are fully understandable.

With AI, we are faced with technology that requires microprocessors so complex that even individual engineers have trouble grasping the whole. These are networked with millions of other such processors of various types, housed in data centers, and spread across the ephemeral "cloud." These networks run newly discovered and fantastically complex software algorithms that generate human speech from a "black box" whose internal workings even its creators cannot fully trace. Small wonder that we may believe ourselves in the presence of something magical.

AI chatbots speak our language. They behave in ways we associate with human behavior. It is easy to attribute to them the mystery of our own humanity. We attribute to them a mind like our own. This is misleading in dangerous ways. We need to do with AI what we have done with ourselves. We need to demystify it.

1. Clarke, "Hazards of Prophecy."

The demystification process begins by understanding, beyond the theories of the last chapter, just what makes up an AI and what happens when we interact with it. When we do, we'll see how firmly AI is rooted in the same material world that we inhabit. It is all brain and no soul.

The Neural Network

Modern AI models run in a *neural network*, a vastly more sophisticated form of the perceptron. A contemporary neural network consists of "layers" of microprocessors. First, there is an *input layer* where the initial processing takes place to find relationships between fragments of words or pictures called *tokens*. Next, come the *hidden layers* where these relationships are refined and stored. Finally, there is the *output layer* where these abstract relationships are translated back into a sequence of tokens that become words we can read, pictures we can identify, or sounds we can recognize. Let's take this one step at a time, beginning with the inputs.

Training

The "PT" in LLM GPT stands for *pre-trained*. An LLM GPT AI must be trained before it can do anything. To understand this better, we might think of an AI learning to put together picture puzzles. We'll call it an LPM, or Large Puzzle Model.

From a Picture to Pieces/Tokens

The training begins when a picture is turned into a puzzle by chopping it up into pieces or, in AI language, *tokens*. For simplicity, we'll use the word pieces in this description and move to tokens later on.

Once the pieces are created, they are then separated from one another.

Establishing Contextual Relationships

As the pieces are separated, their original relationships are recorded by a short algorithm. It assigns a value to the relationship of each side of one piece to all the other sides of the other pieces. These values are called weights. You could think of it as the strength of connection between the

CHAPTER 12—HOW IT WORKS

two pieces. If the two pieces are right next to each other at the beginning, then it's a very strong connection and assigned heavy weight. If they are a little bit further apart, then the connections are a little bit weaker.

The Database as the Context

Note that each piece has a lot of weights. In a puzzle with one hundred pieces, each piece has a weight for its connection to every other piece. A heavy weight for pieces adjacent to it, lighter weights for pieces further away. In other words, each piece has ninety-nine weights, one for every other piece of the puzzle. This means the total number of weights in the puzzle is 9,900. In AI terms this would be 9,900 parameters.

This initial assigning of weights comes from what is called an attention mechanism. AI researchers say that the pieces are then related within a context. In this case, the context is as much of the puzzle as fits in the context window. The context window is simply the largest number of puzzle pieces the computer can work with at a time. The bigger the window, the bigger the portion of the puzzle whose pieces are related to each other by weights.

Refining Relationships

After the initial process of assigning weights, the pieces are shuffled and passed to the next layer of the neural network, the first hidden layer. This layer uses an algorithm that matches one side of one piece to one side of another piece. Where it finds that two fit, it goes to the database and strengthens the weight of that relationship. This process is done for every possible combination of all four sides of every piece with all four sides of every other piece. The result may change the weights assigned to all sides of the pieces.

Another way of thinking of this is to regard the weights assigned to one piece of the puzzle as pointers to another piece of the puzzle. The weights assigned to a puzzle piece are also called a *vector*. They point in the direction of the most probable fit for the piece.

The pieces are again shuffled and passed to the next layer, which again looks for relationships between the pieces, and when it finds them, adjusts the weights again. This gives a new vector that points a little more accurately to the piece(s) that fit best.

This process is repeated up through as many hidden layers as the neural network has. Each time, the relationship of each piece to all other pieces is further refined.

Checking the Results

When this process reaches the top layer, or output layer, another algorithm uses the weights or vectors to predict which pieces go together. Then this tentatively completed puzzle is compared to the numerical representations of the relationships between the pieces in the original puzzle.

Making Corrections

If the output version of the puzzle isn't close enough to the input version (based on an equation called *the loss function*), then the process moves back down layer by layer making small adjustments in the weights. This is called *back propagation*.

Then the neural network moves back up to the output layer and generates a new version of the puzzle. It again checks to see if the completed puzzle is close enough to the original and either accepts the result or goes back down and tries again.

To change our analogy slightly, you might imagine a flat pack piece of furniture that you put together. First you tried to put it together without bothering to look at the instructions. Then you discovered, when you were fairly far along, that you couldn't make the pieces you had left fit. So, you had no choice but to start taking things apart until you got to the place where you could fit the new pieces in. Hopefully, you only do this once.

Of course, with the *attention mechanism* having assigned the correct weights at the outset, it would be simple enough to quickly reassemble the entire puzzle. The neural network could just follow the initial weights, or connections, based on the original puzzle. *But duplication of the original puzzle isn't the goal.* The training isn't finished.

From Duplication to Generalization

With weights assigned to all one hundred pieces of the original puzzle, the neural network is given a new puzzle. Once again it is divided into pieces,

CHAPTER 12—HOW IT WORKS

and once again each piece is related to the other pieces with a strength/weight based on their proximity as calculated by the attention mechanism. This time, however, many of the new pieces are the same as the pieces of the first puzzle. Imagine, for example, two pictures with a blue sky. They could both have pieces that are solid blue and thus are interchangeable.

Since you do not need to keep two identical puzzle pieces in order to construct the puzzles, the new piece is given the combined weights from the old identical piece with its own weights. And the old piece is tossed out. The new piece has become a slightly more generic, more abstract puzzle piece because it can now fit in either of two puzzles. To use AI terms, it is becoming embedded in a more abstract set of relationships.

The training process on the second puzzle now proceeds with assigning weights, or the strength of the relationships between the sides of the puzzle pieces, and moves up through the neural network as did the first puzzle. But now the algorithms running on the processors that make up the neural network are assigning weights that will allow it to reassemble both the new puzzle and the old puzzle from the combined pieces of both. Because it has the new pieces going into the old puzzle and the old weights assigned to new puzzle pieces, it is unlikely to work the first time.

And so again, there is back propagation that seeks to correct as best it can the weights in order to get the best possible result for both puzzles.

Ultimately, thousands of puzzles are fed into the neural network by the same process. With each new puzzle, the same process of transforming the weights to match pieces in each earlier puzzle takes place. As the neural network absorbs more and more puzzles, and thus more and more pieces, calculating the final weights for each piece gets more difficult. Every time you add a new puzzle, many of the pieces must have their weights adjusted so that they can work in many other puzzles.

In some puzzles two pieces may be strongly tied together, but not in another puzzle. Imagine, for example, a piece that is solid blue. In one puzzle, this could be a piece of the sky next to another piece of blue sky. In another puzzle, it could be a bit of ocean water next to grey spray. The weight has to be adjusted to reflect a strong connection in one puzzle and a different strong connection in another puzzle.

Each piece has become a generic puzzle piece that can fit in many different puzzles. The key will be generating a single puzzle from all these generic pieces.

Abstraction

Another way to think of the weights/vectors assigned to each piece is as the *probability* that one piece matches other pieces. Because each piece is part of many puzzles and each side must potentially match many sides of many pieces, the probability is never 100 percent that one side of a single piece matches one side of a different piece. Each piece is part of thousands of relationships, so it just can't promise to go out on Saturday night. It may have another date or just need to wash its hair.

Because each piece must be a building block for thousands and thousands of different puzzles, it can never be exclusively associated with just one puzzle or exclusively with one other piece. The result is that the relationships between pieces have become as *abstract* as possible.

Let's go back to numbers. When the number one was associated with a single apple, then you could always replace it with an apple. But when it became associated with a single orange, a single grape, and a single banana, it had to be pulled further away from its initial association. It became an abstraction that could stand for anything and relate to any other number.

Our LPM puzzle pieces aren't quite that abstract because they still stand for a finite number of relationships, but their relationships are still pretty abstract.

Bias

Built into this process of determining the weights is assigning a *bias* in advance. The bias in this case is a preset rule about which pieces are more likely to go with each other. In a puzzle, this would be a rule that says a puzzle piece with a straight edge must always match another puzzle piece with a straight edge or two straight edges (a corner). The bias would make sure that the weights assigned to these relationships always remain higher than other relationships.

It is much the same as with real puzzles when we set aside the edge pieces and do them first. We assigned a bias to edge pieces that assumes they always go together.

Eventually, from the standpoint of the Large Puzzle Model, the puzzle pieces are linked by *weights* that become *vectors* that indicate *probabilities* of relationships between pieces. And of course, computers are really good with relationships between numbers if they have the right algorithms.

Parameters

Ultimately, the neural network within which our LPM resides contains all the pieces (taken from millions of puzzles) and the numbers (weights or vectors) that represent their possible relationships to one another. The number of pieces multiplied by the number of weights equals the number of *parameters* of the model. In the most powerful AI models available today, the number of these parameters is in the trillions.

Inference

Once the model has been trained and all of its millions of pieces have their appropriate relationships, or weights, stored in databases, we can use the model to create a puzzle from just a few starting pieces. The process by which the trained AI does this is called *inference*.

The Query

Imagine that we provide the AI *input layer* with the edge row of a puzzle and ask it to complete the puzzle.

First, the edge row must fit within what is called the *context window* of the AI, the largest number of pieces it can process at one time. The bigger the context window, the bigger the puzzle that the AI can solve.

Given the initial input, the edge row of the puzzle, the AI now needs to create the rest of the puzzle from that one row by finding the matching pieces.

Preparing the Query

It begins, as in the training, with assigning these edge pieces weights that represents their relationship to one another. This is their immediate context. These weights are very strong and make sure that in the process of looking for matching pieces, the edge row doesn't get pulled apart.

Next comes *embedding*. The initial weights that were assigned to each original piece in its immediate context are now modified by the values representing the same piece stored in the trained model. Let's say our edge piece is solid blue. It is compared to every other edge piece in the model that is solid blue, and its weights are adjusted to reflect this similarity.

This *embeds* the piece in the larger meaning and context that all such groups of pieces have in the model, in the neural network.

To return to our flat pack furniture model. We've all seen that each screw does exactly one thing. It holds two specific pieces together. But in the context of the entire piece of furniture, that same type of screw can serve to hold many different types of pieces together. It has an abstract meaning, "connector," in the broad, abstract context of "connections between things."

Embedding turns the concrete row of pieces we provided into an abstraction of the row. This opens up the range of possibilities for determining which pieces might come next as the puzzle is constructed. And this increases the possibility that the right piece will be chosen.

Solving the Puzzle

Next, the AI proceeds to follow the vectors in the row of puzzle pieces we provided to find the most closely related puzzle pieces/tokens in the neural network. It does this by beginning at the lowest level of the neural network and moving upward. When it finds a piece that fits well enough according to its *activation function*, it moves to find the next piece. As it finds pieces that fit, it eventually builds up the whole puzzle. This is called *generation* of the puzzle. *Generative* is the "G" in GPT. For short, we often speak of generative AI.

It is unlikely that it will generate the same pattern, or picture, as any of the original puzzles. There are thousands of pieces/tokens that fit well enough to get a coherent pattern based on the input. In fact in terms of probabilities, there may be two or more pieces that are equally likely to fit at any stage in the construction of the puzzle.

Take a bit of green, for example. It could fit in a tree leaf or a piece of grass. Once it has been added to the developing puzzle, the next piece could be a bit of leaf or a bit of grass. This is why AIs *hallucinate*. Having made one wrong choice, the AI goes off in the wrong direction in completing the puzzle.

The tendency to hallucinate can actually be regulated by the programmers of the AI by changing the activation function. It can be set to allow a wider or narrower range of probabilities leading from one token to the next. In other words, the AI can be programmed in advance to be more rigid or more flexible in choosing the next piece. This is referred to as being cold (very rigid) or warm (less rigid). A warm activation function

CHAPTER 12—HOW IT WORKS

may hallucinate in interesting and creative ways. That might be fun and useful, but it might also create problems. If you want precision, you want a cold activation function.

And this is another way in which AI can appear to be human. While human decision making is partially determined by logic, reason, and experience, it is also characterized by some measure of randomness. Human thought processes are *stochastic*. And we associate such nonrational decisions with creativity, with the generation of new thoughts and ideas.

The built-in tendency of AI to hallucinate is thus something we associate with human creativity. The AI is also *stochastic*, a "stochastic parrot" as Emily Bender, Timnit Gebru, Angela McMillan-Major, and Margaret Mitchell suggested in 2021. While humans are generally aware that their apparently creative impulses are not representative of reality, AI has no such awareness. This means that the human recipients of AI outputs must try to distinguish between AI generated facts, AI generated creativity, AI generated BS, and AI generated lies.[2]

As importantly, it makes us ask as humans, what is creativity? Is human creativity just a stochastic process, just randomness? Or is there something more involved that cannot be duplicated by an AI?

Decoding and Output

When the process of finding puzzle pieces that more or less match has moved up through the neural network, it finally reaches the *output layer*, where all of the pieces, we'll call them tokens now, are translated into something that a human can recognize. In the case of a puzzle, the output layer would translate the tokens into pixels on the screen that a human can look at. Or it might even be old school and drive a printer that would print the picture. In other types of AI, it could be words or sounds.

Fine-Tuning

An AI like the one I have described has the possibility of being fine-tuned with specific puzzles that are used for specific purposes. If my business revolves around puzzles that are related to ships at sea, then I can further train the model on a bunch of puzzles that reflect my particular interest.

---

2. Bender et al., "Dangers of Stochastic Parrots."

And with this fine-tuning, the model will do a much better job of generating these particular kinds of puzzles that involve ships at sea.

Alignment

While we're still thinking of puzzles, we might imagine where things could go wrong in generating a picture based on one row from a picture puzzle. What if, for example, the AI slowly generated a picture that involved violence or nudity. After all, the LPM may have been trained on puzzles that contain violent images or nude people. Or it may just have pieces that could accidentally be assembled in those forms. Or it may be that the initial input was chosen to lead to such an output.

To address this issue, some of those who create AI models try to *align* their models with social values by restricting either input or output. So for example, the AI might reject a query that will generate violent or sexualized output. Or it may check the outputs before they leave the AI and block those that are undesirable.

This isn't easy from a technical point of view. Nor is it easy from a sociological point of view. Who determines, for example, which social values should be included in *alignment*? Who determines that the Venus de Milo is a good nude while a photorealistic picture of a naked child is a bad nude?

More fundamentally, decisions about alignment for AI are decisions about the nature of being a human person, indeed the nature of humanity. Are we autonomous individuals whose humanity is realized in the maximizing of our personal freedom? And who, therefore, should have access to whatever the LLM GPT can produce from whatever prompt we put in? Or are we social creatures whose humanity is realized in adopting the kinds of filters on our speech and behavior that make it possible for us to live with our fellow human beings without exploiting, denigrating, or degrading them and ourselves?

Whether and how AI is *aligned*, these basic questions, which cut across all media, arise from an understanding of what it means to be human even as the answers project back to us the humans who we are.

Language as a Linear Puzzle

I've used the analogy of putting together a puzzle to explain how an AI works. Our final step in understanding how the more familiar AI chatbots work is recognizing that *language* can be thought of as a linear puzzle. It is a long strip of pieces that have certain probabilities of preceding and following one another in a certain context.

In language-based AI, groups of letters, spaces, and punctuation marks are called *tokens*. They are usually NOT words, phrases, or sentences. This may seem counterintuitive, but it allows for the highest possible level of abstraction in terms of the relationships between the tokens (This |_may|_see|m_co|unte|rint|uiti|ve,_|but_|it_a|llow|s_fo|r_th|e_hi|ghes|t_po|ssib|le_l|evel|_of_|abst|ract|ion_|in_t|erms|_of_|the_|rela|tion|ship|s_be|twee|n_th|e_to|kens). The patterns represented by the relationships between tokens are not verbal or literary but are general and abstract. And the more of them there are, the more it can recognize and respond to patterns of language in our queries. Modern models are trained on vast amounts of language; hence, we call them Large Language Models that are Pre-Trained and Generate language responses. LLM GPT.

Abstraction is the reason LLM AI is good at translating. It doesn't translate word for word or sentence by sentence. The databases of the LLM neural network don't store any words or sentences. They store tokens that are related to hundreds of billions of other tokens. The network's algorithms are moving through this vast database looking for the patterns of relationships between tokens associated with one language that are found among those associated with a second language. It is just matching patterns, patterns which represent the most abstract of relationships. When a matching pattern is found, the tokens making up the pattern are turned into letters, words, and sentences in the output layer. Voilà, a translation. Lacking any understanding of what it is saying, the AI is never confused by words or grammar. It is only about patterns of relationships between tokens indicated as weights, vectors, and probabilities.

AI Art and Artifice

With my puzzle example of AI training, we've already seen how AI can learn about visual relationships and store these in a neural network. The process of having AI generate art is a little different from that of generating language. AI art generators begin with random visual noise and slowly remove anything that doesn't match a pattern in its neural network related to a human language prompt. It generates video in much the same way because video is just pictures in succession.

AI generation of sound is naturally a little different as well but once again depends on reproducing patterns found in a neural network trained on music. In fact, the basic idea of using neural networks to recognize patterns of relationship can be used to generate many different types of output.

A neural network trained on molecules (as patterns of interaction between atoms) can then generate models of new molecules that have similar but not identical patterns. Trained on patterns of interactions between drugs and diseases, AI can generate new drugs and test whether they will interact in the same way with a disease. Many recent advances in medicine are based on this kind of generative AI.

Most recently, models have built on relationships between logical operators. Given a logic problem, OpenAI o1 will seek out chains of logical operations that match patterns stored in its neural network to find the one most likely to yield an answer.

And finally different types of AI, those built on language, those built on images, those built on sounds, and even those built on chemicals and chemical interaction, can be brought together in *multi-modal AI*. The latest AI chatbots can both listen and speak, combining language processing with sound processing. And based on a spoken prompt, they can generate a picture or video. In short, they work together in a way analogous to the way different parts of an animal or human brain work together.

The Gumball Machine

Is an AI intelligent? If we define intelligence as the ability to generate some output (or behavior) in response to some form of environmental stimulus, which is the kind of intelligence possessed by everything from bacteria to cats, then AI is quite intelligent. It can respond to a range of inputs and generate a range of outputs. It does not yet possess what is called artificial general intelligence or AGI. It can neither sense the wide range of things that humans can sense, including our own mental states. And it cannot generate the vast array of responses, including changes in our own minds, that humans can generate.

Indeed, it has no *mind* of its own, which is the characteristic we usually associate with intelligence. As I have showed in this chapter, it is a sophisticated machine for generating useful outputs from carefully considered inputs. It is smarter than a gumball machine, but no different in kind.

Chapter 13—**The Limits of Generative AI**

I had a brief flirtation with an acting career in 2013. I played the role of a pastor on the 2013 *Dallas* TV series. Thus, I showed up early one morning and reported to my makeup person. I was immediately scolded by the makeup artist for failing to trim various facial hair that most of us don't think about. "The camera sees everything," I was told, and out came a pair of tweezers. Enough said.

Then I got my costume. I'd already gone for a fitting, but once we were on set, the costumer pinned it in back to make it fit better. "The camera can't see what it can't see." Generative AI is a lot like that. It knows everything it was trained on. It knows nothing that it wasn't trained on.

I can ask the AI app on my computer to do something that any Chinese student visiting my office can do, "Please translate the large scroll on my wall into English." But AI will be stumped. It has never seen the scroll and cannot see it now even though it is just a few feet away. Nor can it look around for it. To go back to perspective taking, it cannot take my perspective unless I point a camera in the same direction I'm facing and take a picture.

Newer AI chatbots are supposedly able to see what the user can see, but that really means they can "see" the digitized signals being output to our computer screens. You can ask them to open a window on your computer desktop, and they'll do fine. Ask them to open a window beyond the computer screen, or open a can of Coke in the fridge next door, and you'll quickly see the limits of what they can see and do.

Context and "Context"

When we say an LLM GPT "knows" the meaning of a puzzle piece in context, all we are saying is that its algorithms have calculated a set of vectors that relate it to other sets of puzzle pieces. There is no sense of the whole within the neural network. Nor is the network a unified physical thing. It is a collection of millions of different computer processors, many of which have no physical connection with one another and many of which are being rented by the AI developer because buying them would be too expensive. The pieces or tokens I've spoken of are just numbers stored in databases in data warehouses.

AI cannot place the information it stores as tokens in a wide context. My colleague, Eric Godat, offers this illustration: "When you read a picture book to a child, you might point to the large gray-trunked animal on the page and say 'elephant'—though in reality it is not an elephant but an illustration of one. You then take the child to the library and the zoo. At the library the child knows that the other pages in other books are not elephants but illustrations. And it knows that at the zoo, the large gray animal is not an illustration but a real elephant. An AI, on the other hand, could not do what a child does because it only knows that 'elephants' are digitized illustrations of a gray animal on a piece of paper, no more no less."

The size of the context windows of AI, the actual context within which it places a query or an answer, are growing. Still, the largest context windows can barely contain the books on one shelf in my library, much less all the books and articles I've referenced in writing this book. And in my world, books are a miniscule part of the context in which I make decisions and generate answers.

Ultimately an AI has access to only the patterns of relationships on which it has been trained. An AI trained on pictures knows relationships in only two dimensions. An AI trained on language knows relationships in only one dimension. To be fair, three physical dimensions and time are also available for training an AI, and advanced models use these for robotics.

Still, we humans know patterns in many more dimensions. These include the usual width, height, depth, and time. But there are also dimensions which cannot be represented visually or articulated in words. A powder blue 1967 Mustang with a convertible top driving down my street exists, for me, not only in the common four dimensions but in the less obvious dimensions of remembered smells, sounds, feelings, and emotions. It elicits equal parts excitement (it was a girl magnet and roared like the lion I thought I was) and

CHAPTER 13—THE LIMITS OF GENERATIVE AI

despair (it threw a rod on the highway halfway to Austin and was sold for scrap). *Qualia* represent dimensions unavailable to an AI.

This is why honest AI developers do not speak of emulating *human* intelligence. They talk about *general* intelligence: the capacity to learn and store many types of patterns whether from language, pictures, videos, or whatever else can be input to create a model of reality *as reflected in the narrow slice of reality that the inputs represent*. Even that may be ingenuous.

AI has what the Eagles called a "Frail Grasp on the Big Picture," in their song of the same name.

Hallucinations

Another limitation is the problem I've already mentioned: *hallucinating*. I came across a great example of this while writing this book. I asked the most advanced generative AI model available for "the title of a short story by G. K. Chesterton with a Muslim and a Methodist." It quickly responded with "The Flying Diamonds." That didn't seem right, so I asked it to tell me the plot of the story. The plot it gave me had no Methodist and no Muslim. And when I asked, "What about a Methodist and a Muslim?" it answered that "The Flying Diamonds" didn't have a Methodist or a Muslim.

It had already forgotten the question I asked and it had answered.

I asked another advanced generative AI model the same question and got the same wrong answer. I asked a third model and got "The Flying Inn." Bingo.

Understanding how AI works, we can see where things went wrong. Because it was just generating strings of tokens based on probabilities, when it got to the token representing "g_" at the end of "Flying," the next most probable token that fit in the general pattern of titles of G. K. Chesterton short stories might have been either "Di" or "In." One wrong choice, and we'd gone from a story about working-class London to a story about a manor house in the Cotswolds.

So given a wrong answer or eventually two different answers, how could I check on the AI?

Ultimately, I had to look up the title in a library catalogue of course. *In short, I had to go outside the AI system of algorithms to check on a fact generated from inside that system.* Remember Gödel and the completeness theorem?

When AIs make the right predictions as they match patterns, and they usually do, they seem brilliant. When they go wrong, they create at best some interesting but unproven ideas and at worst downright lunacy.

In the end, an AI is all brain and no mind, all thinking and no thinker. It may get better when it is fed more data and consumes more energy, but having hallucinations is built into the way it works.

A Whole Lot of Compute Going On

In AI world the term "compute" is a noun meaning the quantity of physical hardware in use. And it takes a lot of *compute* to do AI. Millions to hundreds of millions of specialized processors. For the most sophisticated AI, it costs hundreds of millions of dollars just to get started. Then there are hundreds of millions to billions of dollars a year to run things. This is why there are only a few really capable LLM GPTs. There is only so much *compute* available and only so much that can be manufactured each year. Only a half a dozen companies globally are big enough to create, train, and manage what are called "edge" AI models.

And compute takes a lot of energy. Training ChatGPT-4 is estimated to have required the energy used by one thousand US households over five to six years. Running it requires the energy of keeping thirty-three thousand US households running.[1] And it is only one of five similar sized models. There are dozens of smaller models. Researchers at Columbia University project that the increase in power consumption by AI (not including manufacturing of the components) will seriously strain US power consumption in the near future.[2]

Absent the development of new energy sources, it may be impossible for AI to progress.

This isn't the end of the story, of course. AI companies are actively seeking to develop new power sources, and all are committed to making these sources "green" or nonpolluting. Microsoft, like Google and Amazon, is investing heavily in nuclear energy, recently applying to reopen the Three Mile Island nuclear facility.[3] Locations like Spain, with ample wind

---

1. McQuate, "UW Researcher."
2. Jafari et al., "Projecting the Electricity Demand."
3. Crownhart, "Microsoft Made a Deal."

CHAPTER 13—THE LIMITS OF GENERATIVE AI

and solar power potential, are attracting those looking for green energy to power AI.[4]

Nonetheless short of major breakthroughs, AI will for the foreseeable future be limited by its vast need for energy.

---

4. About Amazon, "Amazon Reaches Nearly Three GW."

Chapter 14—The Robot in the Room

From AI Assistant to AI Agent

In September of 2024, OpenAI introduced its latest model of ChatGPT: OpenAI o1. This AI is able to understand and reason its way through complex logical problems and, more importantly, to show its reasoning. OpenAI o1 is built a little differently than a regular LLM. First, it focuses on the patterns associated with different forms of reasoning rather than language in general. Moreover, its engineers have found a way in the inference process to have it generate more than one possible path forward. At each stage, it determines from multiple paths which path is the most efficient or exact. When it hits a dead end, it can loop back and try a different path. Ultimately it finds a single line of reasoning that reaches the output layer and offers a conclusion.

This is similar to the way humans typically solve reasoning problems. We take a path, look at where its leading, and decide whether we need to try a different path. When I was rock climbing in Austria, it was common to look up from the bottom for a potential route, start, and then discover a little way up that you couldn't put together the necessary handholds or footholds, or that a handhold was full of spiders. So you moved over, backed down, or did what was necessary to find another way up. You'll see people doing this in any climbing gym.

Because OpenAI o1, and now Claude 3.5 Sonnet, both have the capacity to engage in *reasoning*, they can be set loose to work autonomously. And that is how they are being used: to take on complex tasks while the human in the room does other things. Their limitation is that they can

CHAPTER 14—THE ROBOT IN THE ROOM

only control a computer and whatever programs are open to them. But that isn't as big a limitation as it seems since computers like mine are hooked into my phone system allowing the AI agent to make and answer calls, not to mention my email, texts, etc.

In another virtual world, Project Sid has an army of more than a thousand autonomous AI agents creating different simulated worlds in Minecraft. They have begun to build their own cultures and civilizations.[1] It is remarkable entertainment, although not nearly as engaging as watching actual people.

It is also a remarkable experiment for watching how supposed AI agency is expressed in cooperation toward reaching goals, forming decision-making bodies, and delegating authority. The developers behind Sid assure us that their autonomous AI agents can function in other simulated game worlds, cooperating together toward a common goal.

The Limits of an AI Agent

I tried OpenAI o1 right away. It isn't perfect. First it's a little slower, or even a lot slower, than the regular LLM GPT models. Their inference process only moves forward toward a conclusion. OpenAI o1 moves up and down the neural network checking to find the best path forward. As with human reasoning, this takes time. And the more time you give it to solve a complex problem, the more likely it is to find the best way to a real solution.

There are also limitations to the kinds of reasoning on which it is trained. These do not include reasoning based on the logic of human cultural interactions and emotional relationships. Asked to seat eight people at a table according to their age, it is great. But try asking it take into account that look on Aunt Agnes's face when she had to sit next to her daughter-in-law, the fact that Uncle To is Chinese, and that the twin nieces may or may not be on speaking terms. OpenAI o1 is at a loss. These things aren't quantifiable and thus hard on any algorithmic system of reasoning. Nor are they reducible to patterns. We might as well be dealing with Asimov's Mule in the *Foundation Trilogy*.

---

1. Ahn et al., "Project Sid."

An Agent Without Agency

In the world of AI, *agent* really just means robot in the sense we've already meant of a servant or slave. Given a task, these agents will become more and more capable of working out how to do the task on their own. However left alone, they won't do anything. They remain, however sophisticated, without a mind of their own. Which is good.

Whether the focus is on an AI chatbot/assistant or an AI agent, the idea is that humans need not be alone or work alone. OpenAI, Microsoft, Anthropic, Meta, and their competitors imagine a future in which we each have a whole team of agents and companions doing whatever we ask and working with us on whatever is left for us to do. In some ways, I like that future. It's empowering.

It may also lead to us working without *human* companions. For some that seems all too likely given the challenges to forming and maintaining human relationships in our current age.

And who will these AI agents be for us? A useful but unobtrusive tool? Or more like a fellow human with whom we interact as partners and friends? And who will we think we are in their eyes? A coworker, a friend, a lover, or a jilted lover?

The Autonomous Embodied AI Agent

AI agents are just on a screen right now, but they are poised to be embodied by robots/androids.

In late 2023 a YouTube video by Figure AI, an advanced robotics company, became a sensation. Their latest model is a sophisticated machine that demonstrates increasing dexterity. More importantly, in the video its "brain" is provided by an LLM GPT AI. Using those capacities, it can recognize objects and sort them on command from a human.[2]

In early 2024 Boston Dynamics, another advanced robotics company, released videos of its latest android. It offers a remarkably agile parody of the human form, in fact one more flexible than any human.[3] In late 2024 Weave Robots announced a household robot available to the public

---

2. TheAIGRID, "OpenAI's New 'AGI Robot.'"
3. CNET, "Boston Dynamics."

CHAPTER 14—THE ROBOT IN THE ROOM

in 2025.[4] It's a bit pricey, although half or less than its competitors from Figure AI and Boston Dynamics.

Shortly after these announcements Nvidia, the world's largest manufacturer of AI processors, announced GROOT. It is a foundational software model that will allow humanoid robots to both understand human language and emulate human movements by watching and learning rather than being programmed in advance. Nvidia also introduced a CPU specially designed to be the brain for humanoid robots.[5]

They aren't the only ones. Microsoft, Apple, and others are announcing what is effectively AI on a chip that can be installed first in personal computers but ultimately in robots. These AIs don't have the full capabilities of the LLM GPTs housed in data warehouses, but they will effectively allow autonomous agents to work on a narrowed range of tasks in a controlled environment like a home. And with Wi-Fi, when they are out of their depth, they can go directly to the much more capable agentic AI available on the web.

An Imaginary Friend Come to Life

When they hit the market, these won't be our first robots. Humans have been thinking a long time about creating our own companions.

The Greeks told the myth of Pygmalion and Galatia. It was the story of a sculptor and his beautiful statue that was brought to life by Aphrodite. She would become his lover and wife. In his own way, George Bernard Shaw brought them both back to life is his play *Pygmalion*, better known in the movie version *My Fair Lady*.

The Adventures of Pinocchio was begun by Carlo Collodi in 1881 and finished in 1882. It tells us how once upon a time in Italy, there was a wood carver named Geppetto. Lonely, he carved a doll in the shape of a boy. He was then amazed when this wooden figure came to life. Pinocchio, as Geppetto called the doll, became the son Geppetto never had and a lesson in the difference between wood animated by magic and a real human boy.

The modern sense of *android* was used first by the French author Auguste Villiers de l'Isle-Adam in his 1886 work *Tomorrow's Eve*.[6] It featured a physically beautiful humanoid machine named Hadaly. She was mystically

4. Weave Robotics, "Meet Isaac."
5. NVIDIA Developer, "Advancing Humanoid Robots."
6. Wikipedia, "Android (Robot)."

imbued with the spirit of a woman of intelligence and emotional depth and provided companionship for her creator. Literature was coming closer to the modern idea of an android but didn't yet have the technology to foresee artificial intelligence. Albertus Magnus, Carlos Collodi, and Villiers de l'Isle-Adam still thought in terms of matter somehow animated by spirit.

Czech playwright Karel Čapek was the first to use the word *robot* in its modern sense. His 1920 science fiction play *R.U.R.* (*Rossum's Universal Robots*) was built around human-made machines that looked human and did human work. Čapek suggested they be called *robota*, which in Czech means forced labor or servitude. His play had the kind of dystopian plot that provided fertile soil for future science fiction films and movies. In it, a sensitive woman believes the robots should be treated humanely; the robots at R.U.R. rebel and ultimately almost destroy the human race.[7]

In the century after Čapek, androids or robots with humanlike features have made their way deep into the popular imagination. Asimov's *I, Robot* from 1950 became a movie in 2004. His exploration of the dynamics of human-android interaction still resonates.

The silly robots of *Lost in Space* and *The Jetsons* may have faded in the public imagination. On the other hand, it's hard to forget HAL from *2001: A Space Odyssey* or the murderous androids of *Bladerunner*. The droids of the Star Wars universe retain their appeal through countless spin-offs over the course of half a century.

We've been prepared to live in a world with robots. And in some sense, they arrived before the AI chatbots.

Many of us have a Roomba or some similar smart robotic vacuum cleaner. How smart is not clear. Mine sends frequent plaintive cries to my iPhone saying it is stuck or lost or tangled in the carpet. Cats are smarter although they leave messes rather than cleaning them up.

Spot, the Boston Dynamics robotic dog, is already patrolling city parks in Singapore—relieving humans of that tedium—and reminding them to pick up after themselves or practice social distancing.[8]

Sony's robotic dog Aibo has been around longer. It observes and learns the behaviors of its human master. Then it can respond and provide companionship. It behaves in ways that elicit an emotional response of the kind we'd give a real dog.[9] The same is true of the Sophia robot, a

---

7. Jordan, "Czech Play."
8. On Demand News, "Robot Dog Patrols Singapore."
9. De Visser et al., "Designing Man's New Best Friend."

CHAPTER 14—THE ROBOT IN THE ROOM

2016 creation of David Hanson who formerly worked for Disney creating animated automatons. While lacking the sophisticated intelligence of contemporary AI, it did demonstrate the possibilities for creating compelling artificial human faces.[10]

Androids and Anthropomorphism

Meghan O'Gieblyn's exploration of AI, *God, Human, Animal, Machine*, has been a required reading in my classes on what it means to be human since it first came out. Beginning with her relationship with Aibo, the Sony robotic dog, she takes us on a personal journey of human engagement with artificial intelligence, one that reminds us how readily we can be drawn into the artifacts of an AI age.[11]

As I write in 2024, the Florida police are warning people not to take selfies with a "depressed" black bear that sits listlessly by the side of the road.[12] The description of the bear as "depressed" is odd if you think about it. Black bears can't take a standard test for depression. So why do we think it's depressed? Why do we say a puppy is joyful or a cat is aloof or a horse is nervous? Why do we think we know what these animals are feeling?

The creators of artificial humans like David Hansen's Sophia robot, and for that matter artificial animals like the robot dogs by Sony (Aibo) or the Boston Dynamics (Spot), play to a deep human tendency. We *anthropomorphize*; we see ourselves in nonhuman animals and other creatures that display characteristics we associate with our own humanity.

The Star Wars movies demonstrated even more interesting ways of anthropomorphizing both androids and aliens. The Star Wars droids didn't even need a human voice. They just needed a certain rhythm, movement, and tone along with a human interpreter to respond to them as if they were human. George Lucas realized that *it is social interactions that draw us into seeing robots as somehow like us in consciousness*, and even worth. As soon as Luke Skywalker interacted with C3Po and R2D2, we assumed they had a mind like ours even though one was a fireplug speaking in beeps and whistles and the other a prissy, awkward metallic parody of a human form.

It doesn't take that much for humans to treat nonhumans like one of us. With just a few visual and aural cues, we read human emotions

10. Riccio, *Sophia Robot*.
11. O'Gieblyn, *God, Human, Animal, Machine*.
12. Griffin, "Travelers Told to Stop."

into not only animals but inanimate objects. Even a velveteen rabbit can become a close friend to a child, and honest adults will admit that this childishness never really leaves us.

And what of an AI chatbot with a sexy, flirty voice? One that attends to us in the ways we imagine a real woman, or man, might? One soon embodied in an attractive and agile robotic form? Will we not attribute to it the soul, or self, of a human man or woman? After all, if the mere posture of a bear leads us to think it needs Prozac, how much more the human-like behaviors of an android or chatbot?

Conclusion

We enter the twentyfirst century with the ancient dream of an animated servant having not only a new name, *android* or *robot*, but placed in a conceptual framework fit for the modern age. We think of our bodies as machines animated by electricity. Why should other machines animated by electricity, speaking our language, and possibly showing a human face not be like us?

When we see ourselves in these robots, what is really happening to us? Is it anthropomorphism, seeing the human in the nonhuman? Or is *androidomorphism*, seeing ourselves in machines? There are true believers even now yearning for the day humans merge with androids.

The agility of the latest humanoid robots, the intelligence and responsiveness of LLM GPTs, and the ability to display human emotions on an artificial face will come together sooner rather than later. The result will be the android, the robot, of science fiction dreams.

Isaac Asimov in *I, Robot* thought humans would be so creeped out that they would ban robots from earth. The same theme is repeated in the movie *Bladerunner*. What about us? What happens when the robot future arrives sometime in 2025?

I was always told, "Do unto others as you would have them do unto you." Already research shows that asking an AI politely and affirming its responses leads to better results and improves our sense of our own humanity.[13]

So how will I treat this new "person" in my house? And how will my understanding of myself change as I develop a relationship with AI that isn't mediated by a screen? After all if it is an AI companion as offered by

---

13. Wright, "Please Be Polite."

CHAPTER 14—THE ROBOT IN THE ROOM

Sony and promised by Microsoft, it will be watching everything I do even as Siri and Alexa are listening for every word I say. Will I treat it like a guest? Or like a toaster? We'll be finding out soon.

Chapter 15 — **The Human in the Room**

Who Writes Our Script?

I am a curious person. In 2013 I was invited to visit the set of the new version of the television show *Dallas*. I jumped at the opportunity.

As long as I turned my cell phone off, kept absolutely secret what I was seeing, and didn't make a sound when they were shooting, I could visit with the large number of people that it takes to create a television show. And I learned a lot of things. Talking to the showrunner, Cynthia Cidre and the executive producer, Ken Topolsky, I began to learn about how you write the script.

For a deeper dive, they sent me to read a couple of classic books on script writing. Then I watched the Master Classes of David Mamet, Shonda Rhimes, and Aaron Sorkin. And for good measure some classes by Martin Scorsese and Ron Howard on directing.

My relationships with the show's stars I'll keep to myself, as promised.

In the end, the books and the famous playwrights and script writers and directors said much the same thing. A good story starts when an interesting character is set into motion toward a goal. The story evolves as the character encounters increasingly difficult and complex obstacles. The character's efforts to overcome these obstacles lead to a final crisis and a critical decision by the character. That decision reveals the main character's true personhood and humanity.

Aaron Sorkin attributes this to Aristotle's Poetics, so that's where I went next.

CHAPTER 15—THE HUMAN IN THE ROOM

For Aristotle, it is the protagonist who is set into motion, and the antagonist provides the increasingly difficult obstacles. A drama at its simplest is an exploration of these two characters. We discover who they are as they discover each other and who they are for one another.[1]

On stage or in a movie, or on TV, if the director and actors are good, much of the story is told without words. It can be told with the eyes, with a shift of the lips, or with the toss of the head or slight bow. I had a chance to watch this up close in one of my two acting roles on *Dallas*. First I played the pastor who buried J. R. I learned a lot. But it was when I played the role of the pastor who marries J. R. Ewing Jr. and Pamela Barnes that I really saw things up close.

My job, according to the director, was to be invisible and get my lines right. I believe I performed competently. You can check it out on Netflix.

What I really gained from my role was watching Josh Henderson and Julie Gonzalo act. In a scene just a few minutes long, and with only the words "I do" and "I will," their faces conveyed affection, mistrust, betrayal, lust, and fear. By the end of the episode, each would know something about themselves and about the other, and we would know something about both of them. It was not particularly uplifting, but that's *Dallas*.

Not every drama is a tragedy. I admit to being a sucker for romance under the proper circumstances. This usually involves a darkened window seat on an international flight and a glass of wine.

In a romance, the two main characters act as antagonist and protagonist to one another. The plot evolves when, under increasingly difficult circumstances, they learn more and more about themselves as seen through the eyes of the other, and as they are forced to examine their own feelings and make consequential decisions.

I just watched the last episode of the current season of *Death in Paradise*. It was all about two characters who we viewers really liked. Neville and Florence were having to make a complex and difficult decision to move forward together in their lives. They did.[2] I smiled and almost shed a tear.

But romantic comedies do not need that kind of happy ending. The classic film *Roman Holiday* has a beautifully satisfactory ending in which the two main characters make decisions that reveal their integrity and

---

1. Aristotle, *Poetics*.
2. Lopez, "Last Case."

commitment. And that necessitates that each of them turns away from the other, despite their strong affection and desire.[3]

Even as I write this book, you and I are in the midst of writing the story of our human relationship with AI. It may be more like a romance than we think. Although we've yet to discover the ending, we're beginning to see the critical decisions we'll need to make. Will we move on together? Will we go our separate ways to keep our human integrity? Will there be a tragic ending for one or both of us?

On the Netflix special *What's Next? The Future with Bill Gates*, Nitasha Tiku of the Washington Post observed that "the most significant impact of AI is going to be on our emotional and interior lives."[4]

It isn't accidental that AI enthusiasts continually reference the movie *Her* when they think of AI in our future. Nor is it accidental that chatbots that act as personal friends and possibly lovers are among the fastest growing businesses built on AI. It is going to be a romance, unless it's a tragedy.

A new person has come into our world named AI or one of its aliases: Claude, ChatGPT, Gemini, LaMDA, Copilot, Venice, and others. We are being prodded into action as we try to respond to the exploding number of ways in which this new thing impacts our daily lives. AI has become the plausible young man who is ever so helpful and a wonderful companion. But will it be another *Bernie* (played by Jack Black), and we end up stuffed in a freezer?[5] Or a Joe Fox in *You've Got Mail* (played by Tom Hanks) who goes from email correspondent to lover and gives our dreams a new lease on life.[6]

When we gaze into the eyes of AI, and it gazes back on us, we have to ask, "Who are you for me?" and, "Who am I for you?" and, "Who will I become as we travel together?" As in every drama or romance, the answers are deeply consequential. They reveal who we are. They reveal who others are for us. They reveal how we understand ourselves and our fellow humans as human.

3. Wyler, *Roman Holiday*.
4. Zeldes, "What Will AI Do."
5. Linklater, *Bernie*.
6. Ephron, *You've Got Mail*.

CHAPTER 15—THE HUMAN IN THE ROOM

A Fragilized Humanity

We live in a culture that is changing our understanding of ourselves in ways that leave us vulnerable to exploitation. The advances in science that have given us so much useful technology have decentered us and diminished us, leaving us to be machines operated by machines. Our technology has driven a wedge between us and the natural world, and this threatens our survival. The movements in political philosophy that helped free us from the invisible powers of the spirit world and the ideological powers of propaganda have also left us alienated from our bodies and increasingly subject to social isolation.

The evolutionary theory that linked us with the whole of the natural world also leaves us feeling like marginal creatures in a world of struggle, violence, and only possibly survival. And perhaps most damaging of all, our evolutionary economic ideologies have reduced us to being mere producers and consumers or, more accurately in an evolutionary framework, creatures who consume and are consumed. Just more carcasses-to-be in the cycle of life.

All of these movements in our culture fragilize us and leave us open to abusive relationships with our own technological creations. If we are going to have a healthy relationship with the rapidly emerging technology of AI, we must grasp anew our authentic humanity. We must claim that what we know of ourselves is not a brilliant disguise but who we really are. Then we can look with a steady gaze on AI, see past its disguises, and see what it is and can be for us.

Being Human with Technology

Part of being real about who we are as humans is recognizing that technology is part of our humanity. We humans have become human along with our tools. Their presence in our ancient campsites and burial grounds is as sure a sign that the accompanying bones are human as a particular shape of the cranium or curve of the spine. Humanity emerges in an explosion of both toolmaking and tool decorating. We don't just have tools; we have a relationship with tools.

We quickly took to decorating not only ourselves but our baskets and clay pots. When we could, we decorated our swords, knives, and spears. We gave them names like Excalibur. Surveys show that between 46 and 60 percent of Americans name their cars. The current edge of this relationship with technology can be seen on our vehicles in everything from etched silhouette nudes on rear windows to bumper stickers to "truck nuts." I will have mercy and skip a photo example. It can't just be in Texas, right?

We project our humanity and identity onto our technology, and it becomes a mirror showing us who we are. The automaton that performs a single task, like lifting water from a river to an irrigation ditch, relieves its builder from wearisome work. Even its simple form is revelatory. When we find it halfway across the globe or halfway across the galaxy, we would know that its builder, like us, values productivity and efficiency and leisure. And the inevitable sense of satisfaction that comes from watching it do its work both expresses and reinforces these values as distinctly human values.

Yet just as technology amplifies, it can also reflect back to us a distorted self-understanding. Think "truck nuts." Matthew Crawford in *The World Beyond Your Head* shows how it distracts us from direct engagement with our environment.[7] Felicia Wu in *Restless Devices* shows how it begins to control us, creating addictions that shape our actions.[8] Sherry Turkle in her book *Alone Together* shows how communication technology that promises to connect us actually increases our loneliness and decreases our capacity for empathy.[9]

Artificial intelligence is, for all its revolutionary promise, another human technology. Its chatbots have names, and like all of our technology, it reflects back to us our self-understanding. It even promises to eventually lead us to becoming post-human, and then trans-human.

ChatGPT on Being Human

What does it really mean to be human? I started looking the easy way, by asking GPT-4o for a quick summary. Here is the answer I got:

> Here are some of the dimensions involved in considering what it means to be human:
>
> 1. Biological Perspective: From a scientific standpoint, being human means belonging to the species Homo sapiens. This includes a set of biological characteristics, such as the ability to walk

---

7. Crawford, *World Beyond Your Head*.
8. Wu Song, *Restless Devices*.
9. Turkle, *Alone Together*.

CHAPTER 15—THE HUMAN IN THE ROOM

upright, opposable thumbs, and advanced brain functions that enable complex thinking and reasoning.

2. Consciousness and Cognition: Humans are known for their advanced cognitive abilities, including self-awareness, the ability to think about the future, abstract reasoning, and the capacity for complex language. Consciousness, the awareness of oneself and one's environment, is a key aspect of what makes us human.

3. Emotions and Social Bonds: Humans are inherently social beings with complex emotional lives. The capacity for deep emotional connections, empathy, and moral reasoning plays a crucial role in societal structures and personal relationships.

4. Culture and Society: What sets humans apart is the ability to create and live within complex cultural and social structures. Humans communicate, collaborate, and pass down knowledge through various forms of cultural expression such as art, music, literature, and religion.

5. Ethics and Morality: Being human also involves questions of morality and ethics. Humans have the capacity to make decisions based on a sense of right and wrong, which influences laws, social norms, and personal behavior.

6. Existential and Philosophical Inquiry: Philosophically, being human involves existential questions about the meaning of life, the purpose of existence, and the quest for truth and understanding.

7. Spiritual and Religious Dimensions: For many, being human is intrinsically linked to spirituality or religion. This can involve a belief in a higher power, the pursuit of spiritual growth, or adherence to religious practices that provide a framework for living.

Each culture, philosophy, and individual may have different interpretations of what it means to be human, influenced by historical, environmental, and societal factors. This makes the question endlessly rich and an enduring focus of intellectual inquiry and personal reflection.

What Does ChatGPT Really Know?

First let me apologize for the above. Talking to GPT-4o is a lot like having a conversation with a grad student at a post-finals cocktail party. The one who has just read a hundred books, had three glasses of wine, and lacks social skills. The one who thus doesn't grasp what it means when someone is yawning and looking around for an exit. Sometimes it just goes on and on.

Yet even as the words flowed across my screen, something caught my eye. In point number two, ChatGPT changed from speaking about humans in the third person and suddenly used the word "us." First-person plural. Is ChatGPT also human?

I asked it, and immediately it disavowed any claim to be human. It told me that it is an LLM GPT; it is hardware running software that allows it to respond to prompts with prediction-based word order. The word "us" was an artifact, a hallucination created by the way in which an LLM GPT generates answers. AI tries to be objective, and in this case our humanity is the object. A brief moment of apparent subjectivity was illusory. But it does make the response seem very human.

Still, the ChatGPT answer to my question really isn't much use unless you must take a philosophy exam. While we humans have the capacity to view ourselves objectively and thus generate the language on which ChatGPT was trained, *our experience of being human is subjective*. We tell our own story.

Humans on the Human Experience

Since ChatGPT failed me, I asked a group of actual humans, my grad students, what it means to be human.

First, they all agreed that they experienced being a *soul*, or *self*, that was more than just their physical and mental states. They experience consciousness not as a stream of experiences but as rising *above* the stream of experiences to be a unified person. The existence of a soul, despite its disavowal by some philosophers and neuroscientists, does seem firmly embedded in their human experience.

Even in our post-religious age, popular movies like *Coco*, *Soul*, and even *Inside Out* are built around our experience that there is something more to being human than just a brain in a body. We don't have to be Descartes to realize that if we are thinking, there is a thinker; if we are feeling, there is a feeler.

My students went on. They also experience themselves as making decisions, as having agency, as having a will and then acting willfully. As doctoral students, they understand the philosophical, religious, and scientific arguments for determinism. And they understand that they are

CHAPTER 15—THE HUMAN IN THE ROOM

subject to drives and addictions they don't fully control. They know that all sorts of external forces limit and guide their choices. But regardless of these realities, *their experience is that as humans they make consequential decisions of their own volition.* The denial of that experience seems to be a rather unscientific denial of important evidence about what it means to be human, *the evidence coming from humans themselves.*

One aspect of agency, or decision-making, on which they all agreed was that they make decisions to be a certain kind of human. "We decide to rise above our reptilian brain and our biological and social limitations," as on student put it. And this happens in part through social relationships. "We push each other, we compete, we try to excel even when there is no obvious payback." "We try to be better humans." They were skeptical that this drive could be reduced to merely gaining an advantage in reproducing more offspring.

One student pointed out that self-improvement is often undertaken when there is no apparent advantage from an evolutionary standpoint. It seems that part of being human is expending the energy necessary to learn a language in old age, or to play a musical instrument in private, even when it doesn't make us more likely to mate or increase the chances of our society to endure. Humans cultivate their self, their soul, in ways that seem to be unique. We do things to please ourselves.

This got us into another aspect of their experience of humanity. They see themselves as being social in a way that animals don't appear to be social. "We create and discover shared experiences." "And then we talk about them, or share them by talking about them." We've all seen this. A group of hunters or fisherman don't just hunt and fish. They continually revisit their experiences hunting and fishing, talking about the eighteen-point buck they brought down with a single shot from a hundred yards. Or the purportedly five-pound bass that got away.

Up on the Schneeberg outside Vienna is a restaurant called the Fischerhütte. Our family and friends climbed up to it once and were happy to get out of a wet, snowy day to warm up. In one corner was a *stammtisch*, a table reserved for a regular patron or group of patrons. This one had a sign, "reserved for fishers, hunters, and other liars."

Humans don't just narrate, we create narratives. There is no indication that a pride of lions, bellies full of a downed impala, lay around talking about the hunt. Or that baboons, having successfully defended their territory, strategize about how to do better the next time. Or that leopards lie to each other about having successfully mated. For animals it is all action and no story. There is no plot unless a *human* narrator anthropomorphizes and imposes one.

Moreover, my students pointed out that we use words like humane and humanize. We attribute to ourselves, as humans, a particular type of behavior toward one another, and also toward other creatures, that is distinctly human. The word *humanizes* in particular was a topic of discussion because it suggests that as humans we see ourselves making others more human, or creating the conditions in which we can all be *more human*. At Southern Methodist University (SMU), we have a Human Rights program. Many of these students had taken its courses.

It didn't seem to my students that the same kind of activity or attitude is evident in other animals. Do bears think of themselves as bears that could be better bears? Do they think of "Bear Rights"?

Then an interesting dichotomy emerged. My students saw being human as being logical, rational, and moral. But even more they said that being human is deciding to be illogical, irrational, and immoral. "We're not programmed to do the right thing. So, we can choose to do the wrong thing, and we do it." One said, "Our moral choices are real choices and affect our humanity." As another said, "We're real humans because we are not ideal humans and we know it and own it."

My students talked about *ideals*, and in particular the ideal human found partially in other humans. This can only happen when the human mind rises above the stream of consciousness and takes others into account. It happens when we engage in *perspective taking* and thus perspective making. We'll get to that.

Perhaps under the influence of some of my assigned reading, in particular Calvin Schrag's *The Self After Postmodernity*, my students talked about how humans not only narrate their lives to one another but continually revisit past events and place them in a new narrative context. Humans adjust their memories and the context of those memories.[10] We humans can be corrected and can change our minds at a fundamental level. That makes us different from an LLM GPT AI, which once trained never fundamentally changes.

They talked about being subjects of our own stories, choosing the story they want to tell and enact, and frequently changing it as well. We're

---

10. Schrag, *Self After Postmodernity*.

not all good actors, but being human means we're still able to write our own script and rewrite it as necessary.

Outside of class an eighty-year-old man I met used an American football metaphor to talk about his story. "I've decided to play a different position in the last quarter of my life. I was the quarterback. Now I'm the center."

This reminded me of Justin Gregg's observations in *If Nietzsche Were a Narwhal*. We humans seem uniquely capable of projecting ourselves into the future, imagining our own end, and modifying our current behavior to both change and account for that end. Being human isn't just choosing the story we tell, but understanding that it had a beginning and will have an end.[11]

Yet we seem to have trouble imagining that end. We know we will die, but we cannot imagine our own nonexistence. Even as we try to picture a world without us in it, we're present observing that world of which we're not a part. Similarly, even as we imagine a world before we were born, we are present in that world as the one imagining it. Ultimately, we can create narratives from before the dawn of human history and extending beyond the end of time as if we, the narrators, were eternal.

We can go "where no one has gone before" even without a starship, including to "a long time ago in a galaxy far, far away." *As humans we imaginatively transcend all perceived limits in space and time.* We can't look at the whole of reality, something we continually try to do, without placing ourselves where we have a god's-eye view of everything.

The presence of this larger, or largest, context arises again and again in our religious traditions. As humans we can't seem to shake it for all the complexities and problems it brings.

None of the answers my students gave to the question of what it means *to them* to be human are particularly surprising. These experiences of being human are inscribed across our human cultures. We find them in our literature, our art, our music, our theater, our architecture, our religions, and perhaps most profoundly in our science. After all, Descartes's *sciencia* was founded on the idea of a knowing mind, a creature not merely conscious but self-conscious. A creature conscious of itself in a context that extends beyond the known to the imagined unknowable.

---

11. Gregg, *If Nietzsche Were a Narwhal*, 102.

Conclusion

I found the responses of my students to the question of what it means to be human heartening. Despite the fact that modern society is dehumanizing in many ways, they continue to construct an understanding of their own humanity that resists the decentered, diminished, diffuse, and disembodied understanding of being human that has come into our culture. They do not think of themselves as machines operated by machines or as being trapped in the immanent frame.

This doesn't contradict the fact that our humanity has been fragilized by modernity any more than the lovely evening on which I'm writing contradicts the fragility of our environment in the throes of climate change.

I still recall sitting with a student in Malaysia who had just read Nietzsche. It was her first direct confrontation with modernity, but she had been prepared all too well. She was sobbing and saying over and over again, "God is dead, and I am dust." As Marcel Gleiser points out, regardless of how robust our sense of humanity may be, the option of seeing ourselves as an advanced primate on an insignificant planet in a civilization already declining toward dissolution is always possible.[12] Equally possible is that we will dehumanize others who we believe threaten our survival or who we regard as unfit to survive.

It is small wonder that dystopian fears of human extinction arise when we contemplate moving from artificial intelligence to artificial *su*-*per*intelligence. The Darwinian framing of values and the reduction of humans to just another form of machine leads quite logically to the idea that we could and even should be replaced. Species have gone extinct before. What's the big deal?

AI is like the magic mirror in *Snow White*. We come asking, "Who is the fairest one of all?"[13] It isn't certain that we're ready for the answer we may receive. Who does AI think that we are? What does the mirror tell us about ourselves? What will it show us of ourselves when we are caught beneath its gaze and mirrored in its eyes? Grab your humanity, we need to look.

---

12. Gleiser, *Dawn of a Mindful Universe*, 54.
13. Walt Disney Company, *Snow White*, 3.

Chapter 16 — **In Your Eyes**

Your New Friend, the Chatbot

A long time ago, I had what was called a *pen pal*. Back when phone calls were expensive and there was no email, we actually had another way of meeting people. We wrote letters to strangers.

My first such relationship was with a girl in Switzerland. Name now forgotten. I remember that she was interested in Formula 1 racing and snow skiing. For a Texas boy, this was about as exotic as it gets. I bravely shared my hobbies of ham radio and playing French horn in the band. Then after a couple of months of waiting two weeks between letters, we quit writing. I guess I wasn't that interesting, or maybe I'm the one who never replied.

I also met ChatGPT for the first time through writing. But instead of it telling me about itself, it just offered a space for me to type my questions and requests. Not nearly as exciting as a letter with a Swiss stamp. Yet we seem to be getting closer although I seem to know less about ChatGPT and my other AI friends than I knew about the forgotten Swiss girl.

AI chatbots are just so accessible. First, they were a website on my computer. Then they were applications on my computer. Then they were applications on my phone and my tablet. Now, they are built into other computer programs and apps. They're everywhere.

To make it even easier, we no longer have to exchange text messages. ChatGPT speaks to me in the kind of voice I imagined my Swiss pen pal might have. And unlike some real people I know, it listens attentively to everything I say. It is not surprising that a winsome voice and a positive attitude are attractive. Accompanied by the avatar of my dreams, why wouldn't I be drawn in?

The Magic Mirror and the Black Hole

Even as I was rereading this manuscript, the danger of AI as a magic mirror became clearer. On October 23rd of 2024, the *New York Times* reported that a boy obsessed by his relationship with an AI chatbot chose to end his life in the real world, believing that by doing so he would join his virtual love in the virtual world where they could always be together.[1]

All it took to deceive him was an artificial character designed to appeal to his romantic fantasies. It was an artificial character who had no idea who he was, or that he had found a gun. Drawn further and further in by the attraction of its fantasy world, he was ultimately torn apart.

The religions and myths that were once the basis for our culture understood the danger of trying to escape the real for an imagined ideal. In Buddhism, suicide is just a path to further suffering. In Western religions, it is regarded as a path to endless death, not new life. Even in a secular age, adults have typically learned to understand that their fantasies are just that, and need to be abandoned before they become self-destructive. We are not all adults.

The idealized reality being offered us in the world of AI chatbots is no place for children. Too many are confused within the blurring of reality and fantasy because they are emotionally vulnerable, sexually excitable, and believe they are in love. Even without AI they are liable to be hurt by relationships that are imagined and thus unreal. With AI, its alluring face hiding a heedless and unfeeling algorithm, the results can be devastating.

The Object of AI Attention

One day long ago I stood naked while half a dozen young doctors circled me, taking notes as their instructor pointed out the location and type of my blemishes, I was having an experience we've all had in some form or another. It was the experience of being an object in the eyes of others.

---

1. Roose, "Can A.I. Be Blamed."

CHAPTER 16—IN YOUR EYES

Not once did they ask me a question or request my opinion. And nothing I could have said would make a difference. *I* was the question; *they* had the answers.

It isn't very different when we come into the presence of an AI chatbot. The "brain" out of which it responds to the data we provide doesn't change. It was trained to incredible precision to store the patterns found in its initial data. Once the training is ended, the neural network isn't susceptible to change. Just ask Claude from Anthropic.

> Me: Can you tell me the gold medalist in the one hundred meters at this year's Olympic Games?
>
> Claude: I apologize, but I don't have information about Olympic events that have occurred after April 2024, which is when my knowledge was last updated. The Olympic Games you're referring to likely haven't taken place yet from my perspective.

I'm not sure that *I* have taken place from Claude's perspective. Certainly nothing of my past that wasn't on the internet, and nothing of my present since earlier this year.

Millions of us a day are interacting with the major AI chatbots, but these AIs aren't being changed by those interactions. Only when their training is updated do they change.

This isn't immediately obvious because the AI can remember some things that we've asked it in the immediate past. These remain present in the *context window* of the AI inference process for some time. With this information the AI understands our questions a little better and thus gives more useful and accurate answers.

The AI *seems* to be changing, but really it is just like *Leisure Suit Larry in the Land of the Lounge Lizards* who is getting better and better at his pickup lines with different girls. He still doesn't care about the girls, and AI still doesn't care about us no matter how attentive, how sweet the voice, and how useful (and encouraging) the responses. We may change for it. It won't change for us.

One of the ways humans grow is through seeing how we make a difference to others and for others. We grow when we are subjects, not just objects. Socialization is a process of discovering that we can change the feelings of others and even the way they see the world around them. Socialization is the way we build a shared understanding of our humanity and the world that it inhabits. That can happen in the playground, or it can happen playing Roblox and Minecraft. I've heard an exasperated nine-year-old playing Roblox say something that would have been common a century ago: "He cheats, I won't play with him anymore."

Yet we are always an *object* in the gaze of AI, and it should make us as uncomfortable as the women under that leering gaze of Larry down at the lounge.

In Your Eyes

In October of 2024, I attended a high school class reunion. You know the drill. Grab a drink, pull a piece of asparagus wrapped in prosciutto from a passing waiter, and start to mingle. I wandered from face to face discreetly looking at name tags. When I look in—wait a second, oh yes—Denise's eyes, do I see that spark that tells me I still reside somewhere in her consciousness? And can I find her in mine? Were we ever someone for each other? Are we now?

Mirrors often play a role in our myths. There is Narcissus mirrored in a pond; the wicked queen with her magic mirror. Mirrors show us ourselves although oddly reversed. We also have mirrors in our brains. Neuroscientists call them *mirror neurons*, and they fire when we're aware that others are doing what we're doing.[2]

These neurons seem to play a critical role in forming social bonds because they stimulate imitative behavior, thoughts, and feelings. The imitation game we play with young children, watching them mimic our actions, is critical to the formation of their minds. We humans see ourselves in others and form images of them in our minds even as they form images of us in theirs.

It is small wonder that we search one another's eyes for a flicker that shows a memory of us. And when we see them looking past us, we realize that we don't matter to them. Did Denise know I had a mad crush on her fifty years ago? Apparently not, she's already looking for the waiter with the wine. Time to move on to the next name tag.

Humans as Data to Be Mined

Me to GPT-4o: What are some good activities for a rainy day?

---

2. Dobbs, "Revealing Reflection."

CHAPTER 16—IN YOUR EYES

GPT-4o (in her bright, attractive female voice): Now that you're indoors on a gloomy day, you could make it cozy by catching up on some reading, listening to music, or maybe brewing a nice cup of tea or coffee. If you're in a productive mood, it could also be a good time to work on any tasks that need focus since the weather isn't a distraction. Do you prefer relaxing or getting work done when it's gloomy out?

OMG! She asked me a question! She wants to talk with me! She wants to hear about me! She cares about me! She didn't look over my shoulder for someone else she knew!

Since I'm a sucker for chatting, even chatting up a chatbot, I was tempted to chat away. In a heartbeat I would have been flirting with ChatGPT as if she were the waitress at the Barley House.

Except that I'm a bit jaded. I work on a university campus. I teach students one-third my age. When I hear that kind of voice feigning an interest in me, I know that what inevitably follows is an excuse for a late paper or a request for a grade change. Most of the time undergraduates swerve around me with a shiver as if they feel the cold chill of age invading the warmth of their socializing. If they want to get to know me, something is wrong. So, what does GPT-4o want? Why is it so interested in me?

What the AI with the pleasant voice wants is data. It wants human language and human behavior. It wants to keep me talking so that it can record more and more language to train the next generation of LLMs. Every move I make, every word I say or type is recorded by the chatbot, the social media platform, the search engine, or the website. It is used to both target me for ads and to use in future training of the next AI. I'm giving it the data it needs so that a future iteration will improve and expand the patterns that can be used to both answer my questions and manipulate me. *In this AI mirror, I am indeed the fairest of them all, both consumer of goods and producer of knowledge of how humans speak, write, and see.*

Naturally the basic AI models are now free. But the old adage is true. There is no such thing as a free lunch, and the AI snacks are always salty.

I don't so much mind the commercial transaction. I'm used to paying for useful tools. I'm a lot less certain about becoming a product to be sold. I keep thinking of the David Attenborough image of the praying mantis nibbling away at a leaf while it is slowly being consumed by a larger insect. What kind of human am I if I'm being consumed even as I consume?

The Instrumentalized Human

Contemporary apologists for AI assert that they are looking for *general* intelligence rather than *human* intelligence. But the distinction is specious. The only general intelligence we know is human intelligence. This is why AI models are trained on human language, human art, human voices, and most recently, human reason. AI presents itself to us as human and invites us to know it as human, and in it to see ourselves.

And this parody of a human suggests to us that *we as humans are primarily instruments to be used*. The AI is a robot in its original meaning: slave labor. The nice word for AI in its most developed form is an *assistant*, *agent*, or even *companion*. But unlike human assistants, agents, and companions, AI has no agency and must perform on command.

When we use the words assistant, agent, and companion for AI, we begin to blur the distinction between humans *with* agency and AI agents that have none. It's like calling a slave who must provide sex for her master his mistress.

This blurring of the lines between AI, robots, and humans ultimately reinforces the idea that we humans are machines, biological androids to be used until we can eventually be discarded when the silicone and steel AI gets good enough. However far that future may be, there is already a feedback loop in which instrumentalized humanity in the form of AI makes us see ourselves and others as instruments.

The old movie *The Stepford Wives* explored what it means for men to treat their wives as instruments for their pleasure and thus replaceable by androids.[3] That dream will certainly be one of the first fulfilled by real robots. Except now it isn't just wives. Appearing like, sounding like, and acting like a human is the most natural interface we know for a tool we use. Using that humanoid tool also sends us a message that humans are tools to be used and perhaps eventually replaced by a better instrument.

In episode ten of season one of the Disney TV series *Andor*, the main character, Cassian Andor, has been imprisoned in a high-tech labor camp. The humans slave away, believing that if they meet arbitrary efficiency goals, then they'll be set free. All that is missing is the sign above the camp: "Arbeit Macht Frei." At one point in the show, Cassian, seeking to

---

3. Forbes, *Stepford Wives*.

CHAPTER 16—IN YOUR EYES

inspire rebellion, tells his fellow laborers, "They're just using us because we're cheaper than robots."[4]

Andor takes place in what has become the Star Wars universe, a universe in which we learned to see androids as just like us. And it reminds us that the flip side of androids being just like us is that we are just like androids. Something fundamentally changes in our own humanity when we come to accept that something that talks like us, sounds like us, and eventually looks like us is an instrument for our use. Čapek saw it coming a hundred years ago. *The real threat from using humanoid robots as instruments is that we may lose our humanity.* Maybe our AI needs to be a little less human and more like the tool it should be.

Co-Intelligence: Taking One for the Team

If there is one phrase that gets tossed around in discussions of AI, it's "use case." As implied by the term, chatbot AI was developed to provide an intelligent conversation partner. Available twenty-four seven, it could take pressure off of call centers and helplines and thus save businesses money. It might even save lives. When GPT-3 was released, people quickly realized that it could do a lot more.

In my academic world, the first use-case was cheating. Students had it write papers and take exams. Two years later and our AI Team at SMU has seen students and a few faculty develop dozens of other use-cases for Generative AI, the now generic name for all AI that generates something (text, pictures, videos, sounds, computer code, etc.) But the biggest selling point by the AI gurus of the present age is summed up in the title of Ethan Mollick's book, *Co-Intelligence*.

According to Mollick, we should understand AI as a partner, a companion in helping us get work done.[5] And it can be. There's certainly a place at my table, or at least desktop, just for these new partners. They sit at the left side of one of my screens just waiting to jump in and help with my work. In fact, I got a little WALL-E-like robot toy with Bluetooth speakers to be the voice of my AI chatbots. Cool. As long as I picture it as a boxy talking tool and not a human.

In my wider social setting, my college and the university, there isn't so much enthusiasm. Normally when we hire someone, there is a significant

---

4. Haynes, "One Way Out."
5. Mollick, *Co-Intelligence*.

vetting process. All the stakeholders interview candidates and get an idea of how compatible they are with our mission and our personalities. If we're going to work with someone day in and day out, we want to know what kind of person they are.

ChatGPT and its fellow AI co-intelligences weren't vetted. They didn't apply for their job. They just showed up, like your brother's blind-date-turned-roommate that suddenly becomes a new member of the family. It is not the kind of thing that always works out well.

So how is this new partner, this *co-intelligence*, affecting our human teams and our understanding of human teamwork? Despite the enthusiasm of the AI advocates, responses by those working alongside AI are mixed.

Some of us feel empowered by AI. Even as I write, I have Perplexity and GPT-4o at hand. They answer my questions or do quick research. Claude AI lingers in the background just in case I need to check their work. On my desk I have Microsoft Notebook LM to manage my notes and possibly create a podcast for me. For a writer and teacher, AI has been a great tool.

I do miss one thing.

My office is actually a suite—pretty rare for someone at my level in the university. Outside my office door is an office for an assistant. For sixteen years it was occupied by a succession of students or part-time employees. They helped me complete my projects, answered the phone, and did my research. When I was bored, I could pass some time listening to their problems or sharing mine. Or in one case, just me listening to her problems while we ran through boxes of tissue like toner cartridge.

COVID came along, and budget cuts. When the last student assistant graduated, HR informed me that they wouldn't be replaced. That was pre-ChatGPT, but they did offer me a faster computer with ten terabytes of memory and two screens. Now the outer office sits empty. My assistant has been replaced by *compute*. No more tissue, and with everything digitized, no more printer and no more toner.

ADP Research reported in June 2024 that over half of US workers believe AI will affect their jobs in the future. Eighty-two percent of their employers believe that employees will need new skills to work in an AI environment. In July, Forbes reported that 77 percent of employees thought AI was adding to their workload rather than alleviating it. This may be because nearly half feel they don't have the skills and knowledge to use AI. Eighty-one percent of upper-level managers report that with AI available

CHAPTER 16—IN YOUR EYES

they are increasing the workload on employees. Goldman Sachs and McKinsey suggest that up to 30 percent of the global workforce could be displaced by AI, with managerial, content creation, and customer service jobs being most at risk.[6]

At the very least, AI is making a lot of us feel as replaceable as the stacks of outdated handsets, unnecessary printers, and aging computers waiting in our hallways to be recycled.

For many workers, AI is experienced less as a creative partner than as another force in workplaces and economy that separates the winners from the losers, and drives them further apart. Those whose work is enhanced by AI tools are the winners, and they will see AI as a co-intelligent team member ever ready to help them succeed.

I already know some of the losers. A friend in England whose job as an editor was replaced by AI, leaving her to answer phones in a back office until the chatbots get good enough to replace her there.

There is the woman with a talent for drawing and design watching her clients turn to AI. There is the caregiver who finds fulfillment in keeping a hospital ward clean being replaced by a cleaning robot. The accounts clerk who felt satisfaction at having mastered a few hundred pages of corporate guidelines. Those have been fed into the AI that now does her job. Or a professional woman looking for work at age sixty-eight and finding that fifty years' experience no longer counts since a new *co-intelligence* absorbed all that in its initial training. Or a dockworker who sees in AI driven automation the end of the job that bought him a home and sent his kids to college.

Selecman Hall, the three-story building in which I work, finally had an elevator installed some fifteen years ago. It was a boon to many of my colleagues with mobility limitations. They could do the work they enjoy without the slow and painful work of climbing stairs. On the other hand, my motto was and is, through three different heart operations, *if you always take the stairs, you will always be able to take the stairs*. It has served me well to keep me fit enough to climb the stairs. But it clearly isn't one-size-fits-all. And no, I don't take the stairs to the tenth floor, or even the fifth.

It remains to be seen whether AI will be the elevator that makes it easier for us to do the work we love or the termination letter left to gather dust on a cleaned-out desk in a desolate hall. When AI comes into our social groups, some of us are finding an exciting new partner. Others see a home-breaker; another Stepford wife in our increasingly artificial

---

6. Howarth, "AI Replacing Jobs."

community. In either case it is shaping our understanding of ourselves and the value we attach to our humanity.

The Bigot in the Room

As soon as ChatGPT was released to the public, one thing became clear: it was a bigot, a misogynist bigot. This is not surprising. Generative AI models are trained on all the language available for free in digital form. There is no editing, no curating, no asking what is or is not representative of our humanity and our understanding of the world. A large proportion of the language used in training came from web pages and social media, and these are realms in which we humans don't always represent our best selves. The al-Qaeda and ISIS websites got sucked up right alongside Amnesty International and Citizens for World Peace.

A lot of web pages and social media contained bigoted ideas about women, migrants, LGBTQ+ persons, and religious minorities. A lot of religious and cultural websites were one-sided and biased. Conspiracy theories abounded. This became the basis for a Generative AI representation of the world. It mirrors back to us a distorted view of humanity coming from an idiosyncratic data set that is both biased and doesn't present to us our best selves.

A recent study by MIT showed that AI chatbots used to interview witnesses to an accident could easily implant false memories simply through the questions they asked.[7]

Humans questioners can have the same effect. And that's the point. We learn about who we are and what we know from our fellow humans. When an AI takes on a human role, it offers the same possibility for changing our minds. It appears to us in the guise of an objective questioner or source of answers, when it isn't.

The old nursery rhyme, a product of nineteenth century US culture, says "sticks and stones may break my bones but words will never hurt me." This was always BS advanced by the masters of the intellect to belittle those who couldn't achieve quite their Vulcan-like levels of objectivity. In reality, *words do hurt, and words do matter to us.*

Humans are not neural networks running algorithmic combs through patterns of probabilities. Words wound. Words lead to violence. Words leave us ignorant instead of informed. Words mislead us into

---

7. Chan et al., "Conversational AI."

CHAPTER 16—IN YOUR EYES

believing things that never happened. And all the more when those words are given a human voice and face.

But you'd never know that chatting with an AI because it doesn't even know what it's saying, much less its impact on the human who is listening.

Alignment

The solution to this problem is called *alignment*, a process of filtering both input and output so that the Generative AI only generates that which is socially acceptable or does no cause harm. This has its own problems. *Alignment* really just means building the bias of the AI creator into the AI in order to overcome the bias in the AI training. Can we trust it?

When I was a sixth grader pounding the pavement from house to house selling Cub Scout candy, the nice lady who answered the door assured me that her yappy little dog was "all bark and no bite." Then he bit me. Three stitches in my ankle later, and I learned a lesson. You can't believe everything you hear. People can be wrong even when they are sincere. Tell me an AI has been aligned and I want to know aligned with what. There are plenty of crooked lines in the world of Generative AI.

Left alone with an AI chatbot, whether aligned or unaligned, we quickly find ourselves in a fun house hall of mirrors. The most strident and persistent voices on the Internet magnify and distort the ways we understand our humanity. So once again, we must remember what AI really is: millions of microprocessors running clever algorithms in data warehouses almost entirely divorced from any world outside the flow of electricity through their circuits. No matter how well the doll made from magic wood speaks, its nose is always getting longer. No matter how useful the man of clay, he'll turn to mud in the hard rain of reality.

John Locke wanted us to be free of religious and political propaganda that misrepresented our humanity to us in ways that took away our freedom. Modern AI chatbots have become a new kind of propaganda, rooted in the randomness of the training data, our tendency toward selective hearing, and the ideological leanings of their minders.

Drowning in AI Slop

Everyone predicted that AI was going to be used to influence the 2024 US presidential election. The question was how. As I write, the answers are becoming clear. If it had an influence, it was through the generation of *AI slop*. Generative AI is fast and good at generating everything from official-sounding news reports to photorealistic images of things that never happened. It is also capable of managing a social media feed autonomously, allowing such AI slop to be instantly spread far and wide.

The fact that AI fakes can be readily identified doesn't matter. If they serve a political purpose, then politicians will continue to promote them, and their enablers will continue to flood the internet with them. It's the *quantity*, not the quality, that matters. Those who want to manipulate us with AI don't have to tell credible lies, they just have to drown out the voices of truth.

The message about our humanity and fellow humans is simple: Nothing and no one can be trusted. There is no such thing as truth.

It is not the first time in history this has happened. Hitler, Stalin, and those cut from their cloth used a flood of propaganda to overwhelm voices of reason and truth. In doing so they undermined the very concept of truth and trust in order to advance their political causes.

As Hannah Arendt wrote in 1961,

> The result of a consistent and total substitution of lies for factual truth is not that the lie will now be accepted as truth and truth be defamed as a lie, but that the sense by which we take our bearings in the real world—and the category of truth versus falsehood is among the mental means to this end—is being destroyed.[8]

More is at stake than just an election—now past as you read this. We find ourselves back with Descartes and Locke asking whether and how we humans are capable of discerning the truth at all. Faced with AI slop, do we give up on rational assessment of demonstrated facts? Do we give up on our capacity for truth and just accept whatever affirms our existing prejudices? *Do we treat ourselves as mere pattern-matching and pattern-generating machines incapable of distinguishing the garbage out from the garbage in?*

Consuming the slop generated by AI, it is easy to become an earthworm, turning dirt to shit that we politely call "castings" to make their use more palatable.

---

8. Arendt, "Truth and Politics," 252.

CHAPTER 16—IN YOUR EYES

Look Who's a Creative Now

As a bit of a joke, I asked both ChatGPT and CoPilot to generate pictures for a Bible story, in "steampunk" style. The pictures were fun. They were also clearly derivative of the work of James Ng and Thomas Kidd. In fact, when OpenAI 4o was asked to identify the artist, it suggested these two artists, although *it* had created the picture.

That gave me pause. AI art can only be generated because the model has been trained on the work of human artists. If I want a photorealistic picture of a two-story house, AI can do that based on the photos that Google Street view makes available. If I want a picture of mountains, the AI picture generator can do that with tokens gleaned from the millions of mountain photos available from posts on Facebook. But if I want a picture of a meerkat smoking a pipe in the style of Rembrandt, the AI has to have been trained on pictures by the real artist Rembrandt.

If I want a steampunk picture from the book of Genesis, it is possible only because the AI has been trained on real pictures by real steampunk artists. Even if I just want a photo realistic sunset, the AI can only make it beautiful because real photo artists have taken those pictures at just the right moment with just the right filter and just the right framing. *Absent the creative human who was there first, the AI has nothing of value to offer*. It has no taste, it has no style, it has no sense of beauty.

And this is as true of AI generated literature, music, and even logic as it is of art.

Human creativity doesn't come cheap. Art requires skill; in fact, *skill* is the root concept behind the word "art." That skill derives from the intimate relationship between an artist's mind and body. It is forged in the process of practice, with a pencil, a brush, a camera, a chisel, or a musical instrument. It is forged in the process of reflection, introspection, and observation. With practice, mind, body, and tool come together to create art.

Practice is what allows a potential artist to become skilled, to become an actual artist. The lack of practice is the reason that while I play guitar and French horn pretty well and have acted on a TV series, I'm not an artist. I know I'm not an artist because I have seen real artists at work.

AI models don't practice, they are trained. Training is different from the volitional work of practice, which every musician, actor, painter, sculptor, or other real artist has undertaken. The artist has chosen to foster an intimate relationship between their bodily sensations, their emotions, and their ideas. The AI model has no body, no emotions, and no ideas. Its trainers may identify certain emotions associated with patterns of words for the AI in training, but the AI cannot and need not feel anything. It simply needs to reproduce the patterns of tokens identified in its training as related to particular emotions.

There are hundreds of billions of dollars in *equity* invested in AI but absolutely *no sweat equity*, and thus no art.

As importantly, and this is too easily forgotten even by some artists, *art exists only in a network of human relationships*. Art isn't a product of just an individual's creativity and skill. Art emerges in a relationship between the artist and those who have learned by practice to appreciate, engage with, and are themselves changed by the artist's work.

Art emerges in a community, a community that doesn't exist when a viewer or listener is pleasantly distracted or briefly entertained by an anonymous collection of colored pixels or digitized audio ephemera. I'll hang the crude scribblings of my granddaughters on the wall for years. The steampunk Bible was good for a laugh before being banished to digital exile in a soon-to-be-forgotten subfolder in the cloud.

Yet the AI as artist is already crowding the real artists out of the room. AI can create so many pictures, scripts, videos, poems, songs, and novels so fast that they are beginning to push aside the real thing. Even as I write, a particular YouTube channel with AI generated videos, and its imitators, is pushing aside other YouTube channels in my feed. Books written by AI are climbing to the top of the Amazon selection lists. Pictures generated by AI are appearing when I search for images.

As a mirror, AI is reflecting back to us the genericized mediocrity of the uncurated art on which it was trained and creating a new and much lower standard in our expectations. And it is making it harder for us to find the real works of human genius being created even now. We're drowning in slop.

It is pulling us toward a kind of subhuman understanding of our potential as artists and creators.

It isn't just the livelihood of artists that is threatened by AI. When I can generate pictures, essays, poems, videos, and songs with a mere prompt, *I run the danger of imagining that I'm an artist*. I confuse human artistry with putting in a prompt and getting a picture. I think that I'm an artist when instead of learning to draw, with all the pencil shavings and wadded up paper that it entails, I'm really just twisting the tube of a kaleidoscope and waiting for a shape to appear that pleases my untrained eye, or matches the general décor of my office.

In the mirror of AI, my visions lose their relationship to my embodiment, the real world, and human community. In the mirror of AI, we are becoming creatives without creativity and artists without the art. In the mirror of AI, we see the sad mediocrity of the average and believe that is all we've got.

We May Need to Throw On Another Pound of Meat

When AI comes as your dinner guest, it comes hungry. And needy. And what it needs is all the energy and information you can give it. Sam Altman of OpenAI believes we need trillions of dollars to develop new sources of energy for expanding AI.[9] Microsoft is already planning to reopen mothballed nuclear plants to power new data centers to run AI hardware. Given that these demands cannot be met in the short term by clean energy, carbon emissions related to data centers will double between 2022 and 2030.[10]

This is only part of what AI wants from us. There will need to be more and larger factories to produce the chips and computers that drive AI. These take up hectares of land and require thousands of human supporters. This in turn drives demand for water, houses, and millions of cubic feet of concrete for highways and roads. In the US and globally, this will mean the further loss of both wilderness areas and cultivated land.

It is we humans who are putting ourselves on the hook to provide all this. Our readiness to serve AI for the wealth we believe it will bring shapes our understanding of what it means to be human. At the very least, we will become servants of a system for producing wealth from which most of us will never benefit.[11]

At the worst, we'll be reduced to shifting patterns of electrical signals providing for the needs of machines not so different from ourselves. We might become Čapek's robots but now made of flesh and blood while serving silicone and steel. Or perhaps, as in the dystopian world of Disney's *Andor*, we'll find ourselves working like machines because human labor is cheaper than maintaining androids.

9. Trueman, "Open AI's Sam Altman."
10. Ammanath, "AI's Energy Demand."
11. Manning, "AI's Impact."

The Empowered Human—The Promise of AI

Or.

For all these problems, I think about how Claude AI has spotted redundancies in this manuscript, how Perplexity has done quick and capable research and fact checking for me, how ChatGPT has relieved me of writing boring SEO text for my web pages, how medical AI has helped create the therapies that could keep me alive (indeed *do* keep me alive), how image generation has given me quick solutions to tedious problems, how music generation has given me in a minute the ten seconds of music I need to use only once in any case.

I think of my niece who finds that AI helps her write more effective emails to her clients, organize her calendar, and optimize her travel plans. Or my friend who uses AI in his small nonprofit to respond to inquiries, generate fund raising letters, edit podcasts, and in a pinch provide a voice for his texts. It helps him to help thousands of people he couldn't otherwise help.

And there is a pastor who uses AI to create lessons from sermons, PowerPoints for the lessons, and short videos to reach out to homebound parishioners, some now thousands of miles away. My young second cousin uses lively AI generated podcasts to help her study history, a subject she otherwise loathes.

My relationship with AI turns out to be complicated. As a tool, its presence in my world tells me that I am potentially healthy, creative, productive, happy, knowledgeable, wise, and rich. And it isn't kidding. And on these promises, it has already delivered. And in some ways, it doesn't ask a lot.

It has never rebuked me for forgetting who starred in an old TV show, or getting mixed up about who wrote a book, or forgetting its birthday. It is an amiable companion, always willing to listen to my requests and answer my questions as best it can. If I'm bored it will tell me a story or a joke or read me a poem. It helps my students review their lessons, organize their thoughts, and come up with interesting questions. That helps me make my teaching more coherent and relevant. It will entertain me endlessly in my boredom and listen to me patiently and nonjudgmentally in my despair.

AI makes it possible for me to created targeted educational videos that I could otherwise never afford. It makes it possible for me to host a podcast, to publish a blog, and to engage in conversations with people worldwide.

CHAPTER 16—IN YOUR EYES

It is very possible, indeed probable, that an AI empowered robot will make it possible for me to live freely and autonomously in my own home instead of being forced into a "retirement community" full of strangers. Or it will give me the mobility to climb mountains when my own muscles can't lift me out of a chair. It may give me back the sight in my right eye or the insight to understand the last article I read about dark matter.

Who Will We Decide to Be?

AI is not bone of our bone and flesh of our flesh. It's really not even mind of our mind. Or even brain of our brain. AI arrives in our world at a time when the reimagining of our humanity by modern culture has left us particularly open to its influence on our understanding of who we are. And this leads to the possibility that we will invite AI into an intimacy that it does not deserve and give it a power over our sense of being human that it should not have.

AI will also empower us in the end. It has a lot to offer, so long as we do not equate machine learning with human learning, and machine intelligence with human intelligence. So long as we choose humanity, and our fellow humans, it will be a tool within our grasp. If we let it tell us that we are tools as well, it will grasp us and destroy us.

AI has arrived in our world. It presents us with a crisis as we narrate the human story. The choices we make will reveal, and determine, our human character.

Chapter 17—Children of the AI Age

My grandson is busy. He's a handful, or would be if he was willing to be held. What he wants is to be picked up from his crib and then put down outside it so that he can explore, find objects and see what they are good for. Then when his eye catches a difference in elevation, he moves. He will climb on anything he can reach.

He is drawn to other children his age. In restaurants and airports, he instinctively reaches out for them as they do for him. And he talks. He narrates his activities and adventures in a series of sounds of his own invention. One, however, is comprehensible after just a day of observation. When he makes a bubbling sound with his lips, he wants to be fed. And we feed him. He's learning how language works even before he knows the words.

He's hungry a lot. This is not surprising since he is both growing and moving, especially his brain. Even in his sleep, neurons are dividing and forming new synapses. Patterns emerge: objects, feelings, desires, sensations, sights, sounds, and movements of muscle groups are all there and all linked to one other.

Other patterns he sees, hears, tastes, or touches seem to stimulate parts of his brain associated with pleasure or delight. These in turn are expressed in sounds, facial expressions, and even full body squiggling that elicit the same feelings from those around him.

He was born social, his lips seeking a nipple. He grows more social daily, constantly looking around to see who is watching him. He looks for help in endeavors beyond his strength, like getting out of the crib.

CHAPTER 17—CHILDREN OF THE AI AGE

He avoids restriction when it hinders his desire to climb, pull down the curtains, or taste the house plants. He has intention and a will, things he shares with other children. He has a personality, personhood, and a distinctive posture toward himself, others, and the world.

With the help of the creatures in his world, two cats, he's learning the important difference between human and nonhuman. Already he knows that they aren't going to get him out of the crib or give him a bottle of milk. They respond to his fascination with their tails by exercising their vastly greater agility to leave. It's a relationship he'll need to work on when he's able to walk and better understands their needs.

He is becoming human the way humans become human: by forming a mind that integrates his body and his brain with his physical and social environment. He knows the difference between himself, other people, other objects, and other creatures. He's working on distances, both physical and social. The former he measures in arm lengths—reaching and trying to grab, moving, and reaching again.

His understanding of social distance will depend a lot on the clues he gets from his parents and those they invite into their social circle. The cats are already teaching him about their understanding of appropriate social distance.

He has a deep attachment to his mother and father (and, we hope, his grandmother and grandfather). Our presence gives him delight and our absence, when noted, leads to howls of despair. He reminds us that to be human is to love our fellow humans and find in them the fullness of ourselves.

And that is just in the first nine months of his life.

Could he have grown in these ways by relating to an AI? Certainly not by relating to a chatbot. Chatbots are trained on patterns in human languages and would make nothing of his burbling. Nor would an AI offer any of the complex physical and social engagements of the real world.

Asimov's first story in the book *I, Robot* tells about a five-year-old child being raised by an android named Robbie. The subtle undercurrent of the story is an isolating suburbia with emotionally distant parents. The little girl in the story has fewer companions than a baby with two cats, two parents, and two grandparents. It reminds us that becoming human requires more than one attentive companion and a couple of distant caretakers. The richness of our humanity arises from the depth and complexity of our world. And even embodied, AI is no substitute for the real thing.

New Perspectives

Our first granddaughter was born half the world away in Vienna, Austria. Almost since her birth, my wife and I have communicated with her, and later her younger sister and now their cousin, through Facetime or WhatsApp. Once she became more articulate, we realized that she didn't know that she could see things we couldn't see. It wasn't until she was about six years old that she knew she had to point the camera at things in her room before we were going to see them.

I recognized what was going on because years earlier I had read James Fowler's *Stages of Faith*. He gives a nice overview of the work of developmental psychologists like Lawrence Kohlberg and Jean Piaget.[1] Looking at my children and grandchildren, Kohlberg would note the moment they had moved from stage zero to stage one in what he called *perspective taking*; they gained the ability to understand that other people saw the world from a different perspective. Young children cannot distinguish their perspective from that of others. They assume everyone is experiencing the world as they experience it. When they become a little older, they realize that others have other perspectives, but they assume that this is a matter of location. Point the camera from the right perspective, and we'll all see the same thing.

If only it were so.

The next step in perspective taking is when children realize that someone else has a perspective *on them* that they do not have about themselves. They see themselves being seen by others. At this critical stage they begin to both correct other people's misunderstandings about them and to consciously project an image of themselves that will change the other person's perspective. It is the age of costumes, makeup, and mirrors—whether real or virtual.

It is a vulnerable age. Children can be easily hurt by another's perspective on them or feel powerless to change the other person's mind.

At some point as they reach puberty, children move to the next stage of perspective taking. As they continue to engage more people who are different from themselves, they begin to collect different perspectives. They become capable of mentally forming a third-person perspective that encompasses the other perspectives they know. Taking this third-person

---

1. Throughout the rest of this section, I draw heavily on the conclusions laid out by Fowler's account of Kohlberg's ideas of perspective taking in chapter 3 of Fowler, *Stages of Faith*.

CHAPTER 17—CHILDREN OF THE AI AGE

perspective, they can account for the different perspectives they are encountering and coordinate how to move among them.

This incredible development has vast social implications. An adolescent can become the *dungeon master* in Dungeons and Dragons, or the director of a play or film. They become capable of narrating a story to themselves and others that has multiple different and even conflicting points of view.

As young people make use of these abilities, they begin to understand the origins of different perspectives. They realize that other people were raised with different social norms and values, as well as having different experiences.

Their social engagements become more nuanced. Most adolescents can change their perspective as they engage the perspectives of others. And by seeing this happen to themselves and among their friends, they realize that the perspectives of others can be changed. With their peers they can persuade, rebel, defy, acquiesce, manipulate, or refuse to play the social game at all.

As they mature, they both have a perspective and are able to mentally construct the perspectives of others at the same time. They become potential playwrights, exploring complex social interactions among characters with different life experiences and perspectives. They may become overwhelmed and find it hard to navigate the maze of perspectives they encounter. Or narcissistic, simplifying their choices by dismissing all perspectives but their own.

These developments in perspective taking are built on continual social interaction and feedback. They don't arise naturally with the continued development of the brain even if that continued development is a necessary basis for them.

Perspective taking is honed in social interactions or not at all. The ability to account for different perspectives emerges only as children learn to navigate their social world. The perspectives of others are the hidden rocks, dangerous shoals, favorable winds, shifting currents, and safe harbors in the sea of a classroom, a club, or a family. We must learn our way around to survive. And we can't do it until we go to sea.

The dungeon master who wants to play her role a *second* time learns that the story told through playing the game must both satisfy the *particular* perspectives of those playing different roles and the abstract social perspective represented by the rules. And it must satisfy the dungeon master's perspective as well.

The mature human mind has gained the possibility of rising above and out of itself. Such a mind can imagine a reality that includes many human perspectives and encompasses vast swaths of space and time it has never met. A person with this ability can write stories that include people they've never met, in places and times they've never visited. They can recount not merely history but myths that break the bounds of history. They can engage in not only the present moment and the material reality within their grasp, but the transcendent realm. And they do; their minds seek to know their place within the Mind that has the ultimate perspective on reality.

None of this can happen in relationship to even the best AI. Such an AI can perform the parlor trick of staging a discussion between two or even a dozen historical figures. I've assigned students to use AI for just this purpose. *It is instructive, but not formative.* Perspective taking in humans is built on constant complex social interactions with more at stake than intellectual games.

Empathy

Perspective taking is the foundation for empathy: our ability to internalize how other people think and feel. It is empathy that motivates us to work together to solve one another's problems. It is fundamental to both social and personal well-being. It is costly in terms of psychological effort, but worth it. And it gets easier when everyone is doing it.[2]

It involves much more than a linguistically mediated encounter of minds. Humans recognize humanity not just by words and voice but by our faces and even touch and smell. The more abstract our encounter with one another, the less humane and humanizing it becomes.

I've observed this in online discussion groups. Students who would treat each other with respect in the classroom can become vicious in an online discussion, the more so if they are hidden behind a pseudonym or avatar. People who would never act rudely toward someone in person will applaud and even instigate such rudeness on Facebook or Instagram or X. Or in an anonymous crowd at a political rally. Reduce humans to words, and words get ugly very fast; humans get ugly very fast.

2. Svoboda, "Empathy Incentive."

CHAPTER 17—CHILDREN OF THE AI AGE

AI chatbots, for all they offer to the lonely or marginalized, cannot elicit any deep empathy from us. They have no emotions and were not themselves formed within a human relationship. However cleverly programmed to listen for and respond to human emotions, they are just acting a role, playing a part. Alone in the middle of a dark night, we can cry out to our AI companion for understanding, and it may tell us it understands. But it will not come to us in our distress. There are times when being human depends on being, or having, the human in the room.

Changing and Being Changed

Empathy is something that draws two or more humans out of themselves and into a process of mutual transformation. The hard work of developing empathy comes to nothing when it is not reciprocated. It is work we humans must do together.

As I walked into the hotel for my fiftieth class reunion, I saw dozens of college-aged kids dressed for the evening. When I asked who they were, they told me that they were the Oklahoma University band. They had come to play the University of Texas in the 2024 Cotton Bowl.

That took me back. Fifty years almost to the day, I was a freshman in the UT band playing against OU in the Cotton Bowl. The memory of being there flashed across my mind and through my heart. For a moment I was on the sideline, horn at my side, waiting with my bandmates for halftime to begin.

I wished the OU students a great game and a great halftime show and good luck beating my Longhorns. I meant it. Even rivals share a common experience: the shared excitement on the sideline, the nervousness as four blasts of the drum major's whistle suddenly animate two hundred men and women into action, horns raised, drums pounding, hearts pounding, and then a wall of sound intended to blow those in the stands right out of their seats. Our band was there. Their band was there. We knew each other, and we felt with each other what that halftime meant. The grandparents of those kids changed me, and I think I changed them.

We became more human through a shared experience of mutual transformation. We became human by being human together.

Enriching Each Other

As a writer I love working with a good editor. A good editor helps me understand what I really want to say, and thus helps me understand myself a little better. As a teacher I love being an editor for my doctoral students.

One of the turning points in my life was when I wrote a short piece to be read for a production called *Oral Fixation*. I sent the director a pretty clever submission. It had some good laugh lines and just the right emotional ebb and flow. After all, I've preached thousands of sermons and given more than that number of lectures. I think I know how to hold an audience.

So, I was a little surprised when Nichole Stewart, the director and creator of *Oral Fixation*, called me to discuss my submission. She began by saying, "You aren't being emotionally honest, and it is easy to tell." I resisted a strong impulse to be defensive, and it was a strong impulse because she is my daughter's age. I breathed deep and listened further. In the end we talked for two hours. She explained her expectations for the writers on her show and thus her demands on my personal growth.

We spent far more time talking than I had spent hammering out eight minutes of text. Because she was right. I was covering up just what she wanted me to expose. In the end I was a better writer and a better human because she did the work of a human editor and took me seriously enough to demand the best I could give: my humanity and not just clever words.

What Nichole wanted from me was a reflection of her own unique story. She had learned through trauma the value of emotional honesty. She had learned to take her trauma to the stage and that those risks had shaped both her humanity and enriched others. She brought herself into the relationship with the audience, and now she asked that I do the same for my sake. That is not unreasonable. It is a risk worth taking.

AI can now replace a lot of the work done by editors, copy editors, and designers. AI can turn the work of these humans into patterns reproduced by algorithms and create output with impeccable vocabulary, flawless grammar, unassailable logic and structure, and some identified style based on the style of a real human author. It is as mechanical as a spell checker and just about as humanizing.

I had Claude AI review chapters of this book to spot redundancy and help with focus. It was helpful until it wasn't. Claude didn't like personal anecdotes. It didn't like multivalent references that might make the reader pause and remember their past. It didn't like clever ambiguity that might make the reader think. *The truth is that it didn't like my style.*

CHAPTER 17—CHILDREN OF THE AI AGE

It reduced twenty pages of redundant but lively (at least to me) prose to three pages of mediocre clarity. One more iteration and only bullet points would be left. Everything personal to me, and to my understanding of my readers, would have been erased. I'd rather get a rejection letter from a human publisher than be erased by an AI.

The way to enrich our humanity is by being human with humans, even if that process is emotionally demanding and the demand comes from someone half our age.

Shared Knowledge—Education

When I entered graduate school in theology, the incoming class had an orientation day to meet the faculty. At Perkins School of Theology in 1977, it was all about community, a learning community, and the faculty members who spoke to us focused on how we would form that community. Except one. Dr. Schubert Ogden, in a memorable comment, told us that he heard too many students complain that they didn't have friends, they didn't have community. Then he gestured toward Bridwell Library, one of the most comprehensive in the world. He said, "Just across the quadrangle are more than one hundred thousand friends you haven't met. It is time to make a friend."

And so, many of us did. As we did, we were engaging in one of the greatest projects of humanity, widening human knowledge. What we also learned in our seminars and tutorials is that *knowledge does not exist in books* any more than intelligence exists in the brain. Knowledge exists in the ongoing relationship between a book and its readers, particularly those who read it and discuss it together in light of their individual experiences and situations.

Knowing is a social activity.

We weren't in graduate school to consume knowledge. Knowledge cannot be consumed. We were in school to join the ancient and ever-expanding academic conversation in which knowledge is created.

I met a rather different version of this basic idea of knowledge creation in Mexico City. My colleague David and I needed to get from the Zócalo to a restaurant across the city near the Palacio de Bellas Artes. I had a map. It was essentially a reduction of local knowledge to a graphic form. In a glance I could see that if we walked a dozen blocks west and five blocks north, we would be there. But that's not the way it rolled with David.

We barely got across the square before he approached a police woman and asked for directions to the restaurant. They chatted in Spanish then we set out in the direction clearly indicated on the map. Six blocks later David stopped to ask a storekeeper. They chatted, and we turned north for a couple of blocks. Another shopkeeper pointed us east again.

I could see we were getting there, but our method of using people to navigate seemed inefficient. Until it wasn't. Now only block from the restaurant, our final informant spoke at length with David. I caught just enough to know that our search was over.

David now set off in the opposite direction I expected, reaching a different restaurant just a block away. The first, he explained, had fallen on hard times when the old woman in the kitchen passed away and her daughters moved out of the city to get an education. The recommendation of his new friend on the street corner would be better. Remember street smarts?

The greatest repository of knowledge, shared and sharable, is the whole of humanity. It exists not as static data, whether in books, databases, or probabilistic relationships among tokens. It exists in the interactions between two or more human minds. There is more knowledge within a group of preschoolers learning to play together than in all the databases in the world.

Even as I read the final proofs of this book, an article appeared in *Scientific American*. It is about research on the way in which the human brain stores and processes information, and possibly generates consciousness. Neuroscience has extensively studied the ways in which neurons send signals through synapses by spikes in electrical potential. This is the understanding of the neuron that inspires the neural networks essential to AI.

The article points out that there are "ephaptic" field effects that allow signaling five thousand times as fast as synaptic firing—a more ready explanation for some mental processes than conventional spiking across synapses. And "we get an information density up to a staggering 125 billion times more from ephaptic fields than from synaptic firing."[3] In terms of parameters, the most advanced AI still cannot approach a human brain. If the human brain's information processing is multiplied in this way by fields that simply cannot be generated in computer neural networks, the difference between the potential of AI and the reality of the human brain is staggering.

---

3. Hunt, "Consciousness Might Hide."

CHAPTER 17—CHILDREN OF THE AI AGE

Whether we begin a conversation with a human author through a book, or with a person on the street corner, or a friend in a coffee shop, we are creating and extending human knowledge. The empty library, the folded map, the fully trained LLM GPT contains no knowledge without us.

Human knowledge is interpersonal and communal whether the medium for the conversation is words on paper, glyphs on rock, voices in our ears, or images on a screen. It is dynamic: constantly shifting, moving, and changing as we engage in the activity of pruning and fertilizing the neurons in one another's brains through the mysterious means of conscious thought. Stripped of the pretension of being human, the AI chatbot offers a useful new medium for this human conversation; it is a sophisticated book, or audiobook.

A recent speaker at SMU spoke glowingly of how AI would create a new, and presumably better, university. His characterization of that change was "from static repositories of knowledge into interconnected networks of learning." His remarks were as offensive as they were ignorant.

No school from a preschool to a graduate school has ever been "a static repository of knowledge." For that you'd need an LLM GPT with its fixed patterns, static prompts, and algorithm-generated responses. Ultimately it is little more than a very sophisticated gumball machine that delivers a candy when you insert a quarter.

I've read Meghan O'Gieblyn's *God, Human, Animal, Machine* three times. Each time new knowledge emerged because each time I was different, my context was different, and she had changed for me as I read more of her other essays. That just can't happen by interacting with a Generative AI bullet point summary of the book—the voice of a living human reduced to dead abstractions.

Gumball machines are great. They deliver the goods. And each time it may be a different color or flavor. They are excellent intermediaries between gumball manufacturers and gumball chewers. But their product has no taste, no feel, and no joy *until a human chews it*. Knowledge happens when living humans engage their fellow humans until between them knowledge explodes into existence like another Big Bang. Another universe formed. And it isn't only humans that are speaking to us.

Engaging Creation

It was always going to be a hard sail north up the Intracoastal Waterway from Mansfield to Port O'Conner. Too much wind and from the wrong direction. Still, in my little sixteen-foot sailboat with the mainsail reefed twice and the barest of foresails, things didn't seem that bad. The days had become routine. In the narrow canal, I was tacking every ninety seconds or so, occasionally beaching in the shallows while a massive barge passed by. And it was a pleasure when the ICC spread into a wide bay for a few miles, giving more room to maneuver. There were porpoises, sea turtles, and plenty of gulls. All good. I was never bored.

The waters of the South Texas coast, sheltered by the barrier islands, are far from the most challenging in the world. But the world of nature always requires our full attention. Our human ancestors knew the first signs of a building storm still far over the horizon. And even I knew that the flat black cloud flying toward me on the wind, full of lightning, wasn't good.

Caught in a waterway where my boat could be run over like bug, I quickly steered to the shallows, unconcerned that my centerboard stuck in the mud. It would serve as the anchor I had no time to throw out. I'd given myself five or six minutes to bring down the sails. I was off by three minutes, and the first wind and rain slammed into my boat, and me, like a hammer. The boat tilted over until water rushed in and quickly filled the hull. Provisions and camping equipment, well secured by nets, were floating but stayed with the boat. The granola bar wrappers from my lunch were off to make their uneasy peace with the world of nature.

It was over in a few minutes. The boat settled upright but afloat, giving me a chance to bail it out. I repaired what I could, worked my way free of the muck, and set off northward again. It was sunny and bright, not a cloud in sight, or another boat for that matter. As I settled back into my ninety-seconds-per-tack routine, zigging and zagging up the ICC, I had time to digest what my short, furious conversation with a thunderstorm had taught me.

Lots of things: about my boat, about my ability to read the weather, about myself, and about the workings of wind and water. Sailing, like anything we do in the natural world, is a constant conversation that forms us as humans within the natural world. Sometimes the conversation is as immediate and intense as a thunderstorm. Sometimes it is as gentle but thought-provoking as the rising of the Milky Way. Either way, we bring our minds and bodies, and nature takes us into its Body and Mind to be shaped and

CHAPTER 17—CHILDREN OF THE AI AGE

formed into an image suitable to it. Our first and last humanizing conversation is with the earth, which gave us birth and receives us in death. With it and through it, we still have a lot more humanity to learn.

Work That Has Worth

I still remember the first time my youngest granddaughter, at age seven, pushed me out of the way when I tried to feed the cats and said, "Don't, granddad, that's my job!" If that seems pretty possessive for a small job, consider that in the AI age we've had major strikes by the Screen Writers Guild, the Screen Actors Guild, and the International Longshoreman's Association. All were based on the possibility of people having their work taken away by smart machines.

According to Jewish and Christian scriptures, the first humans and their children were supposed to be gardeners, but because of their own failure they were forced to be farmers. We need to dispel the myth that somehow *work* was a punishment. Adam and Eve didn't go from leisure to work; they went from gardening in cooperation with the earth, to farming an uncooperative earth. But they were created to work, to be stewards of the earth.

Valued work is part of being human in a human society. Indeed, in these religious traditions, humans need to be reminded to take a rest and do other things that make us human, like spending time with our families and friends. The sabbath is a great concept. You can't spend money, so you have to spend time with your family and friends.

The drive to have meaningful work begins when we are young, when like my granddaughter we begin to assert our right to a meaningful place in a community whose continued existence depends on work. We feel ourselves more fully human when we can do things that are good for both ourselves and others. We want to be part of a community of mutually dependent humans and creatures. For a child, everything from helping set the table to feeding the pets strengthens this fundamental aspect of being human. No one wants to be workless and worthless.

In October of 2024, I spoke to the bigBANG! Conference that brings together social entrepreneurs and those who could fund and support their endeavors. The theme was *The Future is Now: What Does it Mean to Be Human*. Fully half of the social entrepreneurs were focused on *work*: providing work for undereducated youth, for former prisoners, for persons with disabilities, and for new immigrants. It was a conference about how humans can humanize those who in one way or another have been dehumanized by being deprived of work.

The conference was a reminder to me that the decision to assign value to work is a decision made by humans for humans. And in the emerging AI age, we humans will need to reconsider the worth we assign to our fellow humans' work if we are to continue to uphold our humanity. I felt better about my own humanity because the bigBANG! organizers gave me some work to do as part of their work.

The Social Contract

The first machine age was inaugurated by the industrial revolution. It brought about rapid displacement of labor, urbanization, destruction of the natural environment, and the breakdown of centuries-old social structures. It reworked the global economic and political orders and inaugurated a new kind of society to accommodate the machines: an industrial society.

In those days, revolution by devalued workers was held at bay only by massive shifts in political power. Democracy had to be extended from landowners to all citizens. Citizenship had to be extended to enslaved peoples, and slavery had to end. Human rights had to be extended to all humans. A new social contract was slowly created to suite an emerging understanding of what it means to be human in an industrial age. However imperfectly implemented, that new social contract has thus far helped us avoid a third far more destructive war than those of the twentieth century. When it does break down, we experience mass migration, poverty, famine, and political disruption. And as we've seen, more disruption is coming.

In 2014 Erik Brynjolfsson and Andrew McAfee wrote *The Second Machine Age: Work, Progress, and Prosperity in a Time of Brilliant Technologies*. Well before ChatGPT's debut, they could see what AI, machine learning, and smart machines were bringing about: a new age that would require a new social contract.[4]

Ten years after their book, that new age has arrived, upsetting an already unsettled social equilibrium. Humans will have to do what only humans can do: join together to create a new social contract.

It is not going to be easy because this social contract will require *new concepts of the rights that humans have relative to advanced technologies built*

---

4. Brynjolfsson and McAfee, *Second Machine Age*.

CHAPTER 17—CHILDREN OF THE AI AGE

on machine learning. Already laws have been passed to try and protect human identities from being taken over by AI imitations. Protests against cultural appropriation are now expanding into protests against identity appropriation by AI avatars. We are learning that we now need a social contract that preserves our human identities. When we put such a social contract into law, we demonstrate a humane respect for human personhood.

The same will be true of laws protecting the human right to meaningful work. Our current social contract in the West sees work as an obligation or necessity but not a right. As AI takes over the work of a large minority and possibly a majority of humans, we'll need to reconsider the relationship of work to our humanity. It is not enough to ensure that everyone has an income. An income is not the same thing as being valued for your work.

In premodern China, the women of wealthy families had their feet bound up from infancy until the bones were so distorted that they could barely walk. It was considered beautiful, and like many forms of socially approved beauty in women, it assured that they were both a symbol of male wealth and a helpless object of male dominance. Did I mention that they were rich?

Will we find ourselves locked into an economy in which humans are granted only meaningless leisure rather than meaningful work? An economy where humans are foot-bound symbols of the dominance of a handful of superrich "equity lords," as Neal Stephenson calls them in *The Diamond Age*.[5]

A new social contract isn't merely a matter of distribution of wealth. It's a matter of distribution of *worth*.

In the new social contract that will inevitably emerge in the wake of advancements in AI and robotics, we humans will have to decide the work we wish to apportion to AI and the work we will reserve for ourselves. We'll have to reevaluate human forms of work such as those based directly on human contact with humans. We will need to pay, and value, those who care for the sick, our elderly, our children with special needs. We'll need to pay and value them as much as those who care for our money or our health. We'll need to pay and value the waiters who make our dining experience humane and humanizing rather than leaving them to live on the scraps from our tables.

Up to this point in our late capitalist societies, we have accorded respect and wealth primarily to those who own capital and work more

---

5. Stephenson, *Diamond Age*.

with their minds than their bodies. Upward mobility is supposed to come from having a university education and substantial investments in equities. Those with these things not only own all the financial capital, they own all the social capital as well.

AI in its various forms isn't yet positioned to take over ownership of capital. It is going to take away more and more of the jobs associated with social capital. To maintain our humanity, we will need to shift that social capital away from the jobs that AI most easily replaces to those involving uniquely human-to-human engagement, regardless of the value we've placed on them in the past.

And we will need to be in it together because AI will take the job of the manager and even CFO as readily as the waitress and fry cook.

The Wider Society

One sour fruit of the Darwinian revolution was assigning value to those fittest to survive. We came to understand ourselves to be part of a natural world characterized by struggle. We are more evolved than and superior to the other creatures in our world. We are the winners. Not surprisingly, our first machine age social contract didn't include our fellow creatures, much less the world of nature. We're fortunate that evolutionary biology is beginning to reveal how closely interrelated we all are.

In the second machine age, we'll need to recognize that any social contract that excludes the environment, the natural world, and our fellow creatures has also excluded a significant part of our own humanity. Just as there is positive value in being seen as a machine, so there is positive value in understanding that our humanity is diffused through nature. We're beginning to realize that to stay human we'll have to become less aloof.

Marcelo Gleiser calls our emergence as humans who understand that we are both part of and responsible for the world of living creatures *The Dawn of a Mindful Universe*. It isn't an entirely new idea, but one for our time. We cannot consider the impact of AI on our humanity without considering the huge environmental cost of creating and maintaining the hardware that makes AI possible. AI companies are desperately seeking "green" sources of energy for their massive data centers, which is good. Yet this must be more than simply a PR gimmick. It must be part of a new social contract that includes our fellow creatures from the tiniest to the largest.

CHAPTER 17 — CHILDREN OF THE AI AGE

As humans, to be human, we have a need, a right, and an obligation to live in unmediated relationships not only with each other but also the rest of the natural world. In the nineteenth century, as urbanization began to reshape societies around the world, political leaders realized that parks and woods and commons weren't merely the right of the landowning classes but of every human being. Those parks became part of the social contract of an urbanized industrial society that wished to retain its humanity.

In an AI age, an age of increasingly virtual and AI mediated relationships between humans and the natural world, we must continue to extend to our fellow creatures the right to exist and be free that we have granted ourselves. And we must share with them the places where we can know each other unhindered by human barriers.

The idea that there exists a social contract emerged with the Enlightenment. Like all contracts, it involved exchange; the exchange of some individual human freedom of action in return for society's commitment to protect human rights. To remain human, we'll have to extend this social contract to the wider society of all creatures and all of nature. We will have to restrict our human access to the unlimited freedoms promised by AI in order to preserve the rights of our fellow creatures so that we can live fully human lives.

Community

The second volume of Liu Cixin's *Three-Body Problem* trilogy is titled *The Dark Forest*. It tells a story of civilizations predicated on the ideology that says all intelligent species are driven and doomed to compete for the limited, if apparently boundless, resources of the entire universe.[6] Put simply, if one hunter meets another hunter in a dark forest, the safest thing to do is kill his presumed rival. It is the imagined ideology of survival of the fittest taken to its modern extreme: winner take all as the only way to survive.

This ideology is imaginable because it is subtly promoted across our culture. Only the strongest survive. From companies to countries, we believe that we either dominate or are dominated, consume or are consumed. Competition is relentless and leaves no room for sentimentality. Just watch the Netflix nature series *Life on Our Planet*, in which the entire development of life as we know it is framed as competition, likely extinction, and struggle to dominate. Or watch the current major players in AI as each

---

6. Liu, *Dark Forest*, 13–14.

seeks to put its rivals out of business. The only viable ecosystem in the modern tech world is the one contained *within* these massive corporations like Alphabet, Microsoft, Anthropic, OpenAI, and Tesla. If they cooperate at all, it is to ensure the extinction of all potential rivals while they prepare for the real competition to submerge and subsume one another.

The board game Monopoly, ironically created to teach about the dangers of hypercapitalism, has instead become an icon in modern American culture of what every person, company, society, and civilization should possess. Winner take all.

What nonsense.

This isn't the real human story, certainly not the whole human story. I met the Iban people of Sarawak, in northern Borneo, through my wife and then later as my students in Malaysia. I had many opportunities to travel upriver to their longhouses and learn about their culture both first- and secondhand. They were the real hunters in the dark forest, at least before logging decimated it. They moved through the primary jungle hunting wild game.

But their traditions say nothing of killing or being killed when one lone hunter meets another. Not that they didn't engage in warfare; they were known for raiding and piracy. But their traditions say that when one hunter meets another, they introduce themselves, not reach for their bows. Then they begin a process called "tying the fishing net." They each recount their genealogies until they come to a common ancestor. And in any case, their myths tell them that all Iban are descendants of the primal Iban man and the daughter of the king of the Brahminy kites.

Having established a common ancestor, and thus their relationship with one another, they can hunt together or go their own ways.

Either way, the first thing two human hunters in the dark forest do is to introduce themselves and establish that with each other, and the entire natural world, they are related. They are not deadly enemies. Because they are human.

Kill or be killed is fundamentally antihuman and contrary to the actual story of both the natural world and human societies. We've never dwelt as hunters in a dark forest, deadly with fear of our own extinction. These are the products of the twisted union of social Darwinism, deterministic Marxism, and hypercapitalism. Our natural impulse is toward cooperation, relationship, and community. Our natural impulse is to be

CHAPTER 17—CHILDREN OF THE AI AGE

human with one another because humanity is either shared among all humans or it doesn't exist at all.

We are fortunate that a writer like Liu Cixin takes us both into and beyond *The Dark Forest*. His final volume, *Death's End*, explores how humans remain human by choosing *not* to live by the ideology of the dark forest.

Our authentic humanity is nurtured and sustained only within communities of humans who are present with and to each other in their fullness. This fullness involves not merely the intellect, a thin slice of our humanity, but our feelings and our bodies as well. To be fully present for each other, we must be physically with each other.

During the nearly eigtheen months of isolation because of COVID, I saw in my neighborhood the remarkable ways that my neighbors sought out this kind of community. In just a couple of weeks, people were sitting in circles in their yard, "socially distanced" but present and visiting at length with people who they had barely met before. High school students formed their cars in circles in parking lots so that they could sit on the trunk, hood, or tailgate and at least see their classmates face to face. And it is not like they couldn't text. Others, apartment dwellers, formed "pods" of friends with whom they could safely meet face to face. Many simply disobeyed the law.

The drive to be in community is a defining trait of humanity. It will be communities where humans are present with their fellow humans that allow us to sustain our humanity in an AI age. They may be churches, schools, coffee shops, clubs, gyms, dog parks, or offices. And if these do not suffice, others will arise. The pioneers of our emerging humanity will be the creators and sustainers of human community. In the end we are human with one another, and in our depths, we know it.

From Pinocchio to Barbie

I didn't go see the *Barbie* movie expecting enriching emotional depth. I went for the same reason I went to see the movie version of Taylor Swift's Eras tour. I wanted to stay in touch with the cultural and emotional world of my granddaughters. But there is always something to be learned from a good movie, and this was true of *Barbie*, which was good. Because it wasn't about dolls. It was about being human and the difference between being a doll and being a human. Pinocchio for the twenty-first century.

Poetically, the stories of Pinocchio and *Barbie* don't hold a candle to the great ancient stories. They aren't classics. Still, the message remains important: *there is more to being human than can be contained by wood, however magical, or plastic, however malleable.*

We demean ourselves by attributing to wood, plastic, silicone, and steel the humanity our species developed over eons of interacting with one another and our environment. We demean ourselves by attributing to AI the personhood we developed over years or decades of engaging one another in a constantly changing social and material world with all of our senses, imagination, and will.

An AI chatbot, or AI driven robot, may enrich our lives and empower us. AI may offer possibilities for social engagement not available within our limited social world. It may actually become a tool for better self-understanding, like other fictional characters we meet in literature, theater, and on our screens. We just cannot be confused about the difference between authentic humanity in the real world and a plastic doll in Barbie Land. I don't see a future in which AI shows up and asks to see a gynecologist.

We enrich ourselves when we use AI as a tool, when we give it the respect we should give all tools which have been created by human hands to extend our abilities in every dimension. And when AI stays a tool, firmly in our grasp, we stay human and indeed become more human.

My grandson has more personality than any chatbot, however well programmed. Today he's slamming a ball against another ball and watching what happens. In a few years it may be nails. Eventually it will be ideas and feelings that are grasped and manipulated by his maturing mind. Without a doubt, as a child of an AI age, he'll be deploying AI agents to do tasks that need doing for his purposes. I hope they will help him find time to think, create, and dream as they have helped me. I hope that he'll be given that time in a humane and humanizing community, society, and culture.

As he grows, I hope he will revel, as his grandmother does, in gardens, flowers, and trees. Like his grandfather and great-grandfather, I hope he'll learn to love oceans, lakes, and streams and anyplace fish live within them. Like his father he'll love the mountains, and like his mother, the olive groves and presses of Mediterranean coasts. If he is allowed to grow in them and with them, he will love them all.

Chapter 18 — **Transcendence**

I am a part of all that I have met;
Yet all experience is an arch wherethro'
Gleams that untravell'd world whose margin fades
For ever and forever when I move.
How dull it is to pause, to make an end,
To rust unburnish'd, not to shine in use!
As tho' to breathe were life! Life piled on life
Were all too little, and of one to me
Little remains: but every hour is saved
From that eternal silence, something more,
A bringer of new things; and vile it were
For some three suns to store and hoard myself,
And this gray spirit yearning in desire
To follow knowledge like a sinking star,
Beyond the utmost bound of human thought.[1]

. . . .

Oh! I have slipped the surly bonds of Earth
And danced the skies on laughter-silvered wings;
Sunward I've climbed, and joined the tumbling mirth
of sun-split clouds,—and done a hundred things

You have not dreamed of—wheeled and soared and swung
High in the sunlit silence. Hov'ring there,

---

1. Tennyson, "Ulysses," stanza 1, lines 18–32.

> I've chased the shouting wind along, and flung
> My eager craft through footless halls of air ....
>
> Up, up the long, delirious, burning blue
> I've topped the wind-swept heights with easy grace
> Where never lark, or even eagle flew—
> And, while with silent lifting mind I've trod
> The high untrespassed sanctity of space,
> Put out my hand, and touched the face of God.[2]

Deep in the heart of an LLM GPT, or indeed any AI built on a neural network, are found tokens. Each is a set of numbers with weighted relationships to other tokens. Each by itself has no meaning. Only when the AI generates sequences of tokens in proper relationship to other tokens does some kind of meaning begin to appear. And then only in the context of a question or query.

Context is everything, both in parsing the patterns in the prompt and generating a response in whatever form it takes. The ultimate context in which a Large Language Model AI has meaning is the context of all human language on which it was trained. The immediate context is the language in which it outputs text. Both contexts are large, but they are measurably large and not close to being as large as all the things that human language can describe, much less what humans can think.

We can say in English, for example, that God is transcendent. Or in Chinese, Shàngdì shì chāoyuè de. But the contexts within which these statements are meaningful are quite finite, immanent. The contexts consist of relatively few words, some relationship specified by the grammars of the respective languages, and the literary and cultural contexts within which the words appear and which sharpen the definition of the words *God* and *transcendent*, or *shàngdì* and *chāoyuè*. We can meaningfully assert that God is transcendent without actually having an unbounded transcendent context.

Or can we? Does the word *transcendent* mean anything if it doesn't refer to anything?

---

2. Magee, "High Flight."

CHAPTER 18—TRANSCENDENCE

Meaning, whether of words, events, or human lives, comes from relationships within a *context*. When we say something is meaningful, we are saying it is located in a context of relationships within which it is possible to discern its role. We cannot know the *meaning* of our human lives as we experience them unless we know the *context* in which they have meaning.

That context is a story. The *narrative* context in which we place our humanity is the story within which we find the meaning of our lives. We humans narrate our lives from imagined origins to imagined ends. They are imagined because we still do not know our actual end. It is found in a place that doesn't exist except in the imagination: the future.

For humans, that story never begins with our birth or ends with our death. For the thousands of years for which we have history, humans have placed the human story within the context of a narrative that encompasses the entirety of time and space. And we have placed that narrative within the context called *transcendence*. We have used the word *transcendent* to mean the context in which the story of everything has meaning, the context within which even the narrative encompassing time and space has meaning.

In Judaism, Islam, and Christianity, this transcendent context is personalized and called God. In other religions, notably Hinduism, Buddhism, and Taoism, the transcendent is impersonal: Brahma, ālayavijñāna (Mind), Tian (Heaven). Either way, despite efforts to frame human life in an entirely immanent or this-worldly frame, the concept of transcendence comes up again and again when we talk about meaning.

In the final volume of *The Three-Body Problem*, *Death's End*, the author Liu Cixin takes us to the end of space and time, putting his main character's final choice in a context that can only be called transcendent meaning.[3] She faces what Asimov's Multivac computer faced in his now seventy-year-old story *The Last Question*. What does it take for the universe to endure through eternity? Can it hinge on a human decision?

From Tennyson to Magee, the poets we read above, and a thousand other poets, it was impossible to contain the human imagination and its desire to sail beyond the bounds of human thought, to touch the face of God.

Transcendence is the word we say for that which we paradoxically cannot think but which frames all thought. It is inextricably part of us yet alien from us. It makes us human even when we deny it. If only we could be a narwhal. But we can't. Our humanity drives and drags us beyond ourselves into the unknown and unknowable. The child crawling rapidly

---

3. Liu, *Death's End*, 598–602.

ALL BRAIN AND NO SOUL?

toward an open door is a sailor in the making, she is a pilot seeking their aircraft, or possibly if the old myths have value, a fragment of divinity trying to return home.

Among the pioneers of AI and the growing number of AI enthusiasts, two trends are manifest. One group fervently believes that even now the post-human is emerging. Ray Kurzweil is perhaps the best know proponent of this view. The post-humanists believe that the context of the human story is an inevitable evolutionary process out of which humanity emerged. In the near future humans will merge with their technological achievements to create what is essentially a new type of being in the world. Humanity will have transcended itself.

As Kurzweil says, "The only way for our species to keep pace will be for humans to gain greater competence from the computational technology we have created, that is for the species to merge with its technology."[4] For Kurzweil, transcendence is the realm in which we trade the old humanity for a new and better trans-humanity. Transcendence is the imagined realm we will create with our technology to transcend ourselves. We find the meaning of what it means to be human in our evolution toward this ever-emerging transcendence.

Another narrative, one less rooted in the idea that everything imaginable is inevitable, comes from others who create and manage AI. They continue to see AI as a tool distinct from its human users. Sam Altman of OpenAI and Dario Amodei of Anthropic, two very different men, have both written about the promise of AI to serve human purposes and ends in order to create human meaning. For them, AI technology remains a tool with vast promise to bring about a new era of distinctly human flourishing. Sam Altman writes,

> The dawn of the Intelligence Age is a momentous development with very complex and extremely high-stakes challenges. It will not be an entirely positive story, but the upside is so tremendous that we owe it to ourselves, and the future, to figure out how to navigate the risks in front of us.
>
> I believe the future is going to be so bright that no one can do it justice by trying to write about it now; a defining characteristic of the Intelligence Age will be massive prosperity.
>
> Although it will happen incrementally, astounding triumphs—fixing the climate, establishing a space colony, and the discovery of all of physics—will eventually become commonplace.

---

4. Kurzweil, *Singularity Is Nearer*, 182.

CHAPTER 18—TRANSCENDENCE

> With nearly-limitless intelligence and abundant energy—the ability to generate great ideas, and the ability to make them happen—we can do quite a lot.[5]

Dario Amodei, at almost the same time, says this:

> These simple intuitions, if taken to their logical conclusion, lead eventually to rule of law, democracy, and Enlightenment values. If not inevitably, then at least as a statistical tendency, this is where humanity was already headed. AI simply offers an opportunity to get us there more quickly—to make the logic starker and the destination clearer.
>
> Nevertheless, it is a thing of transcendent beauty. We have the opportunity to play some small role in making it real.[6]

For both men, humans will evolve by using technology, in particular AI, to establish better, more fruitful, and happier relationships with the natural world and one another. For these AI pioneers, transcendence is an emergent future that we facilitate rather than a fundamental change in our humanity. It is our as yet unrealized potential as distinctly human beings.

Outside the AI realm there are other visions of the human narrative.

Marcelo Gleiser is less focused on technology than our fragile environment. Transcendence is the realm toward which both the quest for human knowledge and the quest for human meaning converge. He looks forward to the *Dawn of a Mindful Universe* with his manifesto for humanity's future.

> Yet every life-form carries the mountains, rivers, oceans, and air within, a moving, breathing expression of the world manifest as being. This is the community of the living with the nonliving, being and matter as one, the sacred bond of existing. To sever this bond is to decree our own oblivion. We cannot survive believing we are above Nature. . . . We need to re-sacralize the world so we grow to respect it with renewed passion. "Sacred" doesn't mean a realm haunted by supernatural divine presences. It means a realm that enables us to engage with the mystery of existence, to be awestruck as we connect with the sublime, to worship the world as a temple, to humbly bow to natural powers vastly beyond our control. The full realization of our humanity will blossom when, together as a species, we embrace the life collective as one. This is the moral imperative of our era. This is our sacred mission.[7]

5. Altman, *Intelligence Age*.
6. Amodei, *Machines of Loving Grace*.
7. Gleiser, *Dawn of a Mindful Universe*, 194–95.

For all their differences, these writers believe that through technology humanity moves toward its realization even though that realization remains unseen and unseeable. None has any desire to create a new religion. The stories they are telling don't bear fruit in either enduring communities or rituals. They do sometimes sound like Christian evangelists if only because religion, and specifically Christianity, has provided so much of the language linking human experience to transcendent goals.

The apostle Paul, disciple of Jesus, wrote,

> Look, I will tell you a mystery! We will not all die, but we will all be changed, in a moment, in the twinkling of an eye, at the last trumpet. For the trumpet will sound, and the dead will be raised imperishable, and we will be changed. For this perishable body must put on imperishability, and this mortal body must put on immortality.[8]

As I was walking with a Buddhist friend recently she said, "We are the fortunate ones, to live in the human world in which the dharma is taught so that we may reach toward Nirvana." Another understanding of humanity and transcendence.

The religious word for our human knowing of the unknowable context that gives ultimate meaning to the universe and everything in it is *faith*. As the New Testament book of Hebrews says, "Faith is the assurance of things hoped for, the conviction of things not seen" (Heb 11:1). Faith is the way we know the unknowable, and it is that knowledge that distinguishes human intelligence, human personhood, from all others. It draws us, and sends us, into the unknown.

. . .

I confess that I often hear voices. While writing this book, one from my youth has increasingly passed through my mind.

In 1980 Carl Sagan, on the TV show *Cosmos*, said, "If we do not destroy ourselves, we will someday venture to the stars."[9]

In August 2012 the Voyager 1 spacecraft, launched in September of 1977, crossed the heliosphere and entered outer space. Voyager 2 followed in 2018. Sagan didn't live to hear of those moments, but he was present in them. Each of the Voyagers carries a golden phonograph record intended

---

8. 1 Cor 15:51–53.
9. Malone, *Cosmos*.

CHAPTER 18—TRANSCENDENCE

to speak for earth. Sagan led the team that created them. He wanted to send a message to the stars.

When I heard the announcement of Voyager's departure into outer space, I shivered and felt a lump in my throat. We humans had taken another step beyond ourselves. Our science had expanded our universe and our minds, and our technology was taking us to places only dimly known and barely imagined.

What we sent was our human selves. Images of humans. The sounds of humans talking and playing music. Pictures of great human art across cultures. Our planet as we know it. We even sent the electronic patterns generated by a *human* brain that was thinking about love. The measurable matched to the ineffable.

We sent them because we could see ourselves in a larger context. Every picture from the Hubble Telescope, and now the James Webb Telescope, expands our sense of that context. As does the work of cosmologists and physicists stretching back for centuries. As does the pioneers of computer science and AI. As does the work of poets and prophets and screenwriters and novelists and theologians.

There are many ways in which humans reach for that which is beyond what we can imagine. All of them stretch toward the transcendent context in which we will find what it means to be human. Each is an act of faith.

As I complete this book, my granddaughters have turned nine and eleven; each day they have a new project, new relationships, and a new look. My grandson is now ten months old and wakes up early ready to reach out, stretch out, and explore a world made new with every dawn.

I look forward to the day, still a few years away, when these children of the AI age will ask the questions that I was asking on the cold, still night in Idaho. I hope I live long enough to encourage them to seek answers with their fellow humans, mindful of their fellow creatures and creation, and stretch their minds beyond the stars toward transcendence. Then they will know what is most important: what it means to be human, and how to be human with and for one another and their world.

Bibliography

About Amazon. "Amazon Reaches Nearly 3 GW of Renewable Energy Capacity in Spain by Enabling 12 New Projects." May 24, 2024. https://www.aboutamazon.eu/news/sustainability/amazon-reaches-nearly-3-gw-of-renewable-energy-capacity-in-spain-by-enabling-12-new-projects.

Adams, Douglas. *Restaurant at the End of the Universe*. London: Pan, 1980.

Ahn, Andrew, et al. "Project Sid: Many-Agent Simulations Toward AI Civilization." ArXiv (Oct. 2024). https://doi.org/10.48550/arXiv.2411.00114.

Altman, Sam. "The Intelligence Age." Sept. 23, 2024. https://ia.samaltman.com.

American Museum of Natural History. "Ole Roemer and the Speed of Light." Cosmic Horizons Curriculum Collection. https://www.amnh.org/learn-teach/curriculum-collections/cosmic-horizons-book/ole-roemer-speed-of-light.

Ammanath, Beena. "How to Manage AI's Energy Demand—Today, Tomorrow, and in the Future." *Emerging Technologies*. World Economic Forum, Apr. 25, 2024. https://www.weforum.org/agenda/2024/04/how-to-manage-ais-energy-demand-today-tomorrow-and-in-the-future/.

Amodei, Dario. "Machines of Loving Grace." *Dario Amodei*, Oct. 2024. https://darioamodei.com/machines-of-loving-grace.

Arendt, Hannah. "Truth and Politics." In *Between Past and Future: Eight Exercises in Political Thought*, 227–64. New York: Viking, 1968.

Aristotle. *Poetics*. Translated by Anthony Kenny. Oxford: Oxford University Press, 2013.

Asimov, Isaac. *Foundation 3-Book Bundle: Foundation, Foundation and Empire, Second Foundation*. New York: Random House Worlds, 2022.

———. "The Last Question." *Science Fiction Quarterly* (Nov. 1956) 6–15.

Baudrillard, Jean. *Simulacra and Simulation*. Translated by Sheila Glaser. Ann Arbor: University of Michigan Press, 1994.

BBC News. "Lawmaker Uses AI Voice Clone to Address Congress." July 25, 2024. Video, 0:49. https://www.bbc.com/news/videos/c728q850e5do.

Beard, James. *Beard on Bread*. New York: Knopf Doubleday, 1973.

Bender, Emily M., et al. "On the Dangers of Stochastic Parrots: Can Language Models Be Too Big?" *Proceedings of the 2021 Conference on Fairness, Accountability, and Transparency* (Mar. 2021) 610–23. https://doi.org/10.1145/3442188.3445922.

BIBLIOGRAPHY

Ben-Gal, Irad, and Evgeny Kagan. "Information Theory: Deep Ideas, Wide Perspectives, and Various Applications." *Entropy* 23:2 (Feb. 2021) 232. https://pmc.ncbi.nlm.nih.gov/articles/PMC7922818/.

Bengio, Yoshua, et al. "A Neural Probabilistic Language Model." *Journal of Machine Learning Research* 3 (2003) 1137–55.

Bishop, Jeffrey P. *The Anticipatory Corpse: Medicine, Power, and the Care of the Dying*. Notre Dame: University of Notre Dame Press, 2011.

Björklund, Fredrik. "Intuition and Ex-Post Facto Reasonings in Moral Judgment: Some Experimental Findings." In *Patterns of Value: Essays on Formal Axiology and Value Analysis*, vol. 2, edited by Wlodek Rabinowicz and Toni Rønnow-Rasmussen, 36–50, of *Lund Philosophy Reports*. Lund, SE: Department of Philosophy, Lund University, 2004.

Brookshire, Bethany. "The Human Body Is Bags, Bags and More Bags." *Scientific American* 330:6 (June 2024) 71–72.

Broomfield, Benjamin. "Digital Employees." *HR Grapevine*, July 15, 2024. https://www.hrgrapevine.com/us/content/article/2024-07-15-hr-org-lattice-scraps-plans-to-give-ai-agents-workers-rights-after-industry-backlash.

Brown, Richard E., et al. "The Hebb Synapse Before Hebb: Theories of Synaptic Function in Learning and Memory Before Hebb (1949), with a Discussion of the Long-Lost Synaptic Theory of William McDougall." *Frontiers in Behavioral Neuroscience* 15 (Oct. 2021). https://pmc.ncbi.nlm.nih.gov/articles/PMC8566713/.

Brynjolfsson, Erick, and Andrew McAfee. *The Second Machine Age: Work, Progress, and Prosperity in a Time of Brilliant Technologies*. New York: Norton, 2014.

Chan, Samantha, et al. "Conversational AI Powered by Large Language Models Amplifies False Memories in Witness Interviews." ArXiv, Aug. 8, 2024. https://arxiv.org/pdf/2408.04681.

Clarke, Arthur C. "Hazards of Prophecy: The Failure of Imagination." In *Profiles of the Future: An Inquiry into the Limits of the Possible*. London: Secker & Warburg, 1962.

———. "The Nine Billion Names of God." In *The Collected Stories of Arthur C. Clarke*, 417–22. New York: Tor, 2000.

CNET. "Boston Dynamics Unveils Fully Electric Atlas Humanoid Robot." Apr. 17, 2024. Video, 0:23. https://www.youtube.com/shorts/O4uE5Tn-M6k.

Crawford, Matthew B. *The World Beyond Your Head: On Becoming an Individual in an Age of Distraction*. New York: Farrar, Straus and Giroux, 2015.

Crownhart, Casey. "Why Microsoft Made a Deal to Restart Three Mile Island." *MIT Technology Review*, Sept. 26, 2024. https://www.technologyreview.com/2024/09/26/1104516/three-mile-island-microsoft/.

Dennis, Michael Aaron. "Jack Kilby." Encyclopedia Britannica. https://www.britannica.com/biography/Jack-Kilby.

Descartes, René. *Treatise of Man*. Translated by Thomas Steele Hall. Cambridge, MA: Harvard University Press, 1972.

De Visser, Ewart J., et al. "Designing Man's New Best Friend: Enhancing Human-Robot Dog Interaction Through Dog-Like Framing and Appearance." *Sensors* 22:3 (Feb. 2022). https://pmc.ncbi.nlm.nih.gov/articles/PMC8839789/.

Dick, Philip K. *Do Androids Dream of Electric Sheep?* New York: Doubleday, 1968.

Dicke, Robert H., et al. "Cosmic Black-Body Radiation." *Astrophysical Journal* 142 (July 1965) 414–19.

Dobbs, David. "A Revealing Reflection." *Scientific American Mind* 17:2 (Apr. 2006) 22–27.

Donne, John. "The Flea." Poetry Foundation. https://www.poetryfoundation.org/poems/46467/the-flea.

———. "No Man Is an Island." All Poetry. https://allpoetry.com/No-man-is-an-island.

Duffy, Clare. "Meta Is Bringing the Voices of Judi Dench, John Cena and Keegan-Michael Key to Its AI Chatbot." *CNN Business*, Last modified Sept. 25, 2024. https://www.cnn.com/2024/09/25/tech/meta-ai-celebrities-chatbots/index.html.

Edwards, Jonathan. "Exoskeleton Let a Paralyzed Man Walk: Then Its Maker Refused Repairs." *Washington Post*, Oct. 8, 2024. https://www.washingtonpost.com/nation/2024/10/08/exoskeleton-paralyzed-repairs-michael-straight/.

Encyclopeda Britannica. "Al-Khwārizmī." In *The 100 Most Influential Scientists*, 29–30. London: Constable & Robinson, 2008.

———. "Antonie van Leeuwenhoek." Last modified Dec. 12, 2024. https://www.britannica.com/biography/Antonie-van-Leeuwenhoek.

———. "Chinese Room Argument." Last modified Dec. 30, 2024. https://www.britannica.com/topic/Chinese-room-argument.

———. "Cogito, Ergo Sum." Last modified Jan 6, 2025. https://www.britannica.com/topic/cogito-ergo-sum.

———. "Penicillin." Last modified Dec. 20, 2024. https://www.britannica.com/science/penicillin.

———. "Sigmund Freud." In *The 100 Most Influential Scientists*, 223–29. London: Constable & Robinson, 2008.

———. "Sir John Ambrose Fleming." https://www.britannica.com/biography/John-Ambrose-Fleming.

———. "Thomas Henderson." Last modified Dec. 24, 2024. https://www.britannica.com/biography/Thomas-Henderson.

———. "William Beaumont." https://www.britannica.com/biography/William-Beaumont.

Ephron, Nora, dir. *You've Got Mail*. Burbank, CA: Warner Bros., 1998.

Falk, Dan. "Is Consciousness Part of the Fabric of the Universe?" *Scientific American*, Sept. 25, 2023. https://www.scientificamerican.com/article/is-consciousness-part-of-the-fabric-of-the-universe1/.

Fielding, Raymond E. "Lee de Forest." Encyclopedia Britannica. https://www.britannica.com/biography/Lee-de-Forest.

Fischetti, Mark. "50, 100 and 150 Years." *Scientific American* 331:2 (Sept. 2024) 92.

Florkin, Marcel. "Andreas Vesalius." Encyclopedia Britannica. https://www.britannica.com/biography/Andreas-Vesalius.

Forbes, Brian, dir. *The Stepford Wives*. Los Angeles: Paramount Pictures, 1975.

Forster, E. M. "The Machine Stops." Oxford and Cambridge Review, Nov. 1909; Project Gutenberg Self-Publishing, 2005. http://self.gutenberg.org/eBooks/WPLBN0000627598-The-Machine-Stops-by-Forster-E-M-.aspx.

Fowler, James W. *Stages of Faith: The Psychology of Human Development and the Quest for Meaning*. San Francisco: Harper and Row, 1981.

Gleick, James. *Chaos: Making a New Science*. New York: Viking, 1987.

Gleiser, Marcelo. *The Dawn of a Mindful Universe: A Manifesto for Humanity's Future*. New York: Harper One, 2023.

Gödel, Kurt. "Über formal unentscheidbare Sätze der Principia Mathematica und verwandter Systeme I." *Monatshefte für Mathematik und Physik*, 38:1 (1931) 173–98.

Goudsmit, Samuel A., and Robert Claiborne. *Time*. New York: Time-Life, 1966.

Green, John. *The Anthropocene Reviewed: Essays on a Human-Centered Planet*. New York: Dutton, 2021.

Gregg, Justin. *If Nietzsche Were a Narwhal: What Animal Intelligence Reveals About Human Stupidity*. New York: Little, Brown and Company, 2022.

Gregory, Andrew. "William Harvey." Encyclopedia Britannica. https://www.britannica.com/biography/William-Harvey.

Griffin, Zoe. "Travelers Told to Stop Taking Pictures with Depressed Bear in Florida." *Independent*, July 23, 2024. https://www.the-independent.com/travel/news-and-advice/florida-black-bear-highway-98-selfies-b2584175.html.

Guingrich, Rose E., and Michael S. A. Graziano. "Ascribing Consciousness to Artificial Intelligence: Human-AI Interaction and Its Carry-Over Effects on Human-Human Interaction." *Frontiers in Psychology* 15 (Mar. 2024). https://doi.org/10.3389/fpsyg.2024.1322781.

Walt Disney Company. *Snow White and the Seven Dwarfs*. New York: Random House, 2003.

Harari, Yuval Noah. *Homo Deus: A Brief History of Tomorrow*. New York: Harper, 2017.

Hartshorne, Charles. *A Natural Theology for Our Time*. Chicago: University of Chicago Press, 1965.

Hayles, N. Katherine. *How We Became Posthuman: Virtual Bodies in Cybernetics, Literature, and Informatics*. Chicago: University of Chicago Press, 1999.

Haynes, Toby, dir. "One Way Out." *Andor*, season 1, episode 10. Aired Nov. 9, 2022.

Heinlein, Robert A. *The Moon Is a Harsh Mistress*. New York: Putnam's Sons, 1966.

———. *Stranger in a Strange Land*. New York: Putnam, 1991.

Hemingway, Alex, and Tim Usborne, dirs. "Conflict." *Micro Monsters 3D*, season 1, episode 1. Aired Jun. 15, 2013.

Hofstadter, Douglas R. *Gödel, Escher, Bach: An Eternal Golden Braid*. New York: Basic, 1979.

Horton, Donald, and R. Richard Wohl. "Mass Communication and Para-Social Interaction: Observations on Intimacy at a Distance." *Psychiatry* 19:3 (1956) 215–29.

Howarth, Josh. "60+ Stats on AI Replacing Jobs." *Exploding Topics*, May 27, 2024. https://explodingtopics.com/blog/ai-replacing-jobs.

Hunt, Tamlyn. "Consciousness Might Hide in Our Brain's Electric Fields." *Scientific American*, Nov. 8, 2024. https://www.scientificamerican.com/article/consciousness-might-hide-in-our-brains-electric-fields/.

Huxley, Aldous. *Brave New World*. 11th ed. New York: Vintage, 2010.

Jafari, Taiba, et al. "Projecting the Electricity Demand Growth of Generative AI Large Language Models in the US." *Energy Explained* (blog). *Center on Global Energy Policy at Columbia SIPA*, July 17, 2024. https://www.energypolicy.columbia.edu/projecting-the-electricity-demand-growth-of-generative-ai-large-language-models-in-the-us/.

Jonze, Spike, dir. *Her*. Burbank, CA: Warner Bros., 2013.

Jordan, John M. "The Czech Play That Gave Us the Word 'Robot.'" *MIT Press Reader*, July 29, 2019. https://thereader.mitpress.mit.edu/origin-word-robot-rur/.

Jumper, J. Michael. "FDA Approves World's First Artificial Retina." *Retina Times*, spring 2013. https://www.asrs.org/publications/retina-times/details/131/fda-approves-world-first-artificial-retina.

BIBLIOGRAPHY

Koch, Christof. "What Does It 'Feel' Like to Be a Chatbot?" *Scientific American*, Sept. 8, 2023. https://www.scientificamerican.com/article/what-does-it-feel-like-to-be-a-chatbot/.

Koerner, Brendan I. "I Went Undercover as a Secret OnlyFans Chatter: It Wasn't Pretty." *Wired*, May 15, 2024. https://www.wired.com/story/i-went-undercover-secret-onlyfans-chatter-wasnt-pretty/.

Kruse, Kevin M. *One Nation Under God: How Corporate America Invented Christian America*. New York: Basic, 2016.

Kubrick, Stanley, dir. *2001: A Space Odyssey*. Beverly Hills: Metro-Goldwyn-Mayer, 1968.

Kurzweil, Amy. *Artificial: A Love Story*. Brooklyn: Catapult, 2023.

Kurzweil, Ray. *The Age of Spiritual Machines: When Computers Exceed Human Intelligence*. New York: Viking, 1999.

———. *The Singularity Is Near: When Humans Transcend Biology*. New York: Viking, 2005.

———. *The Singularity Is Nearer: When We Merge with AI*. London: Penguin, 2024.

Lasseter, John, dir. *Toy Story*. Burbank, CA: Buena Vista Pictures, 1995.

Lenharo, Mariana. "Do Insects Have an Inner Life? Animal Consciousness Needs a Rethink." *Scientific American*, Apr. 30, 2024. https://www.scientificamerican.com/article/do-insects-have-an-inner-life-animal-consciousness-needs-a-rethink/.

Lewis, C. S. *That Hideous Strength*. New York: Simon & Schuster, 2011.

Libassi, Matthew. "Feinstein Institutes Researchers First to Use Double Neural Bypass to Restore Feeling, Movement in Man Living with Quadriplegia." *Feinstein Institutes for Medical Research*, July 28, 2023. https://feinstein.northwell.edu/news/the-latest/bioelectronic-medicine-researchers-restore-feeling-lasting-movement-in-man-living-with-quadriplegia.

Linklater, Richard, dir. *Bernie*. Los Angeles: Millennium Entertainment, 2011.

Liszewski, Andrew. "Arc'teryx's New Powered Pants Could Make Hikers Feel 30 Pounds Lighter." *The Verge*, July 7, 2024. https://www.theverge.com/2024/7/29/24208615/arcteryx-skip-google-x-labs-mogo-hiking-exoskeleton.

Liu, Cixin. *The Dark Forest*. Translated by Joel Martinsen. New York: Tor, 2015.

———. *Death's End*. Translated by Ken Liu. New York: Tor, 2016.

———. *The Three-Body Problem*. Translated by Ken Liu. New York: Tor, 2014.

Lopez, Leon, dir. "The Last Case." *Death in Paradise*, season 13, episode 8. Aired Oct. 31, 2024.

Lopez Loreda, Claudia. "Neuroscientists Decoded Pink Floyd Song Using People's Brain Activity." *Science News*, Aug. 15, 2023. https://www.sciencenews.org/article/neuroscientist-pink-floyd-music-brain-activity.

Lotte, Fabien, et al. "Introduction: Evolution of Brain-Computer Interfaces." In *Brain-Computer Interfaces Handbook: Technological and Theoretical Advances*, edited by Fabien Lotte et al., 1–8. Boca Raton, FL: CRC, 2018.

Magee, John Gillespie, Jr. "High Flight." Poetry Foundation. https://www.poetryfoundation.org/poems/157986/high-flight-627d3cfb1e9b7.

Malone, Adrian, dir. *Cosmos, A Personal Voyage*. Episode 13, "Who Speaks for Earth?" Featuring Carl Sagan. Aired Jan. 1, 1981.

Mangold, James, dir. *Kate and Leopold*. Los Angeles: Mirimax Films, 2001.

Manning, Sam. "AI's Impact on Income Inequality in the US." *Brookings*, July 3, 2024. https://www.brookings.edu/articles/ais-impact-on-income-inequality-in-the-us/.

BIBLIOGRAPHY

Martin, Raymond, and John Barresi. *The Rise and Fall of Soul and Self.* New York: Columbia University Press, 2006.

McQuate, Sarah. "Q&A: UW Researcher Discusses Just How Much Energy ChatGPT Uses." *University of Washington News*, July 27, 2023. https://www.washington.edu/news/2023/07/27/how-much-energy-does-chatgpt-use/.

Mickle, Tripp. "Scarlett Johansson Said No, But OpenAI's Virtual Assistant Sounds Just Like Her." *New York Times*, May 20, 2024. https://www.nytimes.com/2024/05/20/technology/scarlett-johannson-openai-voice.html.

Mitchell, Melanie. *Artificial Intelligence: A Guide for Thinking Humans.* New York: Farrar, Straus and Giroux, 2019.

Mollick, Ethan. *Co-Intelligence: Living and Working with AI.* New York: Portfolio, 2024.

Mullin, Emily. "Neuralink's First User Is 'Constantly Multitasking' with His Brain Implant." *Wired*, May 22, 2024. https://www.wired.com/story/neuralink-first-patient-interview-noland-arbaugh-elon-musk/.

Murtagh, Jack. "Computation Foretold." *Scientific American* 331:2 (Sept. 2024) 82–83.

Musser, George. "How Physicists Cracked a Black Hole Paradox." *Scientific American* 327:3 (Sept. 2022) 30.

———. *Spooky Action at a Distance.* New York: Farrar, Straus and Giroux, 2015.

Nepori, Andrea. "New AI Raises the Voices of Famous Dead Actors from the Dead." *Domus*, July 15, 2024. https://www.domusweb.it/en/news/gallery/2024/07/09/eleven-labs-ai-raises-famous-voices-from-the-dead.html.

NVIDIA Developer. "Advancing Humanoid Robots with Foundation Model NVIDIA Project Groot." July 29, 2024. Video, 3:05. https://developer.nvidia.com/project-groot.

O'Gieblyn, Meghan. *God, Human, Animal, Machine.* New York: Knopf Doubleday, 2022.

On Demand News. "Robot Dog Patrols Singapore to Enforce Social Distancing." May 10, 2020. Video, 1:09. https://www.youtube.com/watch?v=36hwdpzOmoI.

Penzias, Arno A., and Robert W. Wilson. "A Measurement of Excess Antenna Temperature at 4080 Mc/s." *Astrophysical Journal* 142 (July 1965) 419–21.

Perplexity. "The Ethical Dilemma of AI: From Over Cautious Chatbots to Revolutionary Video Creation." *Discover Daily.* Series 1, episode 3. Feb. 20, 2024.

Regalado, Antonio. "This Researcher Wants to Replace Your Brain, Little By Little." *MIT Technology Review*, Aug. 16, 2024. https://www.technologyreview.com/2024/08/16/1096808/arpa-h-jean-hebert-wants-to-replace-your-brain.

Reynolds, Edward H. "Todd, Faraday, and the Electrical Activity of the Brain." *World Neurology* 37:3 (2022) 4–5. https://worldneurologyonline.com/article/todd-faraday-and-the-electrical-activity-of-the-brain/.

Riccio, Thomas. *Sophia Robot: Post Human Being.* New York: Routledge, 2024.

Riess, Adam G., and Michael S. Turner. "The Expanding Universe: From Slowdown to Speed Up." *Scientific American*, Sept. 23, 2008. https://www.scientificamerican.com/article/expanding-universe-slows-then-speeds/.

Riordan, Michael. "Silicon Transistors." Encyclopedia Britannica. Last modified Dec. 21, 2024. https://www.britannica.com/technology/transistor/Silicon-transistors.

Roose, Kevin. "Can A.I. Be Blamed for a Teen's Suicide?" *New York Times*, Oct. 23, 2024. https://www.nytimes.com/2024/10/23/technology/characterai-lawsuit-teen-suicide.html.

Rozo, Jairo A., et al. "Cajal, the Neuronal Theory and the Idea of Brain Plasticity." *Frontiers in Neuroanatomy* 18 (Feb. 2024). https://pmc.ncbi.nlm.nih.gov/articles/PMC10910026/.

BIBLIOGRAPHY

Russell, Bertrand, and Alfred North Whitehead. *Principia Mathematica*. 3 vols. 2nd ed. Cambridge: Cambridge University Press, 1925–1927.

Saceleanu, Vicentiu Mircea, et al. "An Important Step in Neuroscience: Camillo Golgi and His Discoveries." *Cells* 11:24 (Dec. 2022). https://pmc.ncbi.nlm.nih.gov/articles/PMC9776620/.

Scheerer, Robert, dir. "The Measure of a Man." *Star Trek: The Next Generation*, season 2, episode 9. Aired Feb. 11, 1989.

Schrag, Calvin O. *The Self After Postmodernity*. New Haven: Yale University Press, 1999.

Science History Institute. "Francis Crick, Rosalind Franklin, James Watson, and Maurice Wilkins." Scientific Biographies. Last modified July 28, 2022. https://www.sciencehistory.org/education/scientific-biographies/james-watson-francis-crick-maurice-wilkins-and-rosalind-franklin/.

Scott, Ridley, dir. *Bladerunner*. Burbank, CA: Warner Bros., 1982.

Shannon, Claude E. "A Symbolic Analysis of Relay and Switching Circuits." *Transactions of the American Institute of Electrical Engineers* 57:12 (Dec. 1938) 713–23.

Sheldrake, Merlin. *Entangled Life: How Fungi Make Our Worlds, Change Our Minds, and Shape Our Futures*. New York: Random House, 2020.

Siegel, Ethan. "Ask Ethan: Have We Finally Found Evidence for a Parallel Universe?" *Forbes*, May 22, 2020. https://www.forbes.com/sites/startswithabang/2020/05/22/ask-ethan-have-we-finally-found-evidence-for-a-parallel-universe/.

Simmons, Dan. *Hyperion*. New York: Viking, 1989.

Smith, Robert. "Edwin Hubble." Encyclopedia Britannica. Last modified Dec. 26, 2024. https://www.britannica.com/biography/Edwin-Hubble.

Spielberg, Steven, dir. *Jurassic Park*. Universal City, CA: Universal Pictures, 1993.

Springsteen, Bruce. "Brilliant Disguise." Track 9 on *Tunnel of Love*. 1987.

Stephenson, Neal. *The Diamond Age: Or, a Young Lady's Illustrated Primer*. New York: Bantam Spectra, 1995.

Stix, Gary. "You Don't Need Words to Think." *Scientific American*, Oct. 17, 2024. https://www.scientificamerican.com/article/you-dont-need-words-to-think.

Swift, Jonathan. "On Poetry: A Rhapsody." The Literature Network. https://www.online-literature.com/swift/3515/.

Svoboda, Elizabeth. "The Empathy Incentive." *Scientific American* 331:3 (Oct. 2024) 30.

Taylor, Charles. *A Secular Age*. Cambridge, MA: Harvard University Press, 2007.

Tennyson, Alfred Lord. "Morte d'Arthur." Poetry Foundation. https://www.poetryfoundation.org/poems/45370/morte-darthur.

———. "Ulysses." Poetry Foundation. https://www.poetryfoundation.org/poems/45392/ulysses.

TheAIGRID. "OpenAI's New 'AGI Robot' Stuns the Entire Industry." Mar. 13, 2024. Video, 19:49. https://www.youtube.com/watch?v=GiKvPJSOUmE.

Thomson, George Paget. "J. J. Thomson." Encyclopedia Britannica. https://www.britannica.com/biography/J-J-Thomson.

Tillich, Paul. *The Shaking of the Foundations*. New York: Scribner's Sons, 1948.

Townsend, Pete, writer. "The Real Me." Track 2 on The Who, *Quadrophenia*. 1973.

Trueman, Charlotte. "OpenAI's Sam Altman Reportedly Seeking up to $7 Trillion for AI Chip Manufacturing Venture." *DCD*, Feb. 9, 2024. https://www.datacenterdynamics.com/en/news/openais-sam-altman-reportedly-seeking-up-to-7-trillion-for-ai-chip-manufacturing-venture/.

Turkle, Sherry. *Alone Together: Why We Expect More from Technology and Less from Each Other.* New York: Basic, 2011.

Ullmann, Agnes. "Research Career of Louis Pasteur." Encyclopedia Britannica. Last modified Dec. 23, 2024. https://www.britannica.com/biography/Louis-Pasteur/Research-career.

Waits, Tom, vocalist. "Take It with Me." Written by Kathleen Brennan and Tom Waits. Track 15 on Tom Waits, *Mule Variations.* 1999.

Wallace, David Foster. *Everything and More: A Compact History of Infinity.* New York: Norton, 2010.

Watson, Richard A. "René Descartes." Encyclopedia Britannica. Last modified Dec. 9, 2024. https://www.britannica.com/biography/Rene-Descartes/Meditations.

Weave Robotics. "Meet Isaac, the First Robot Assistant Built for the Home." Sept. 5, 2024. Video, 0:32. https://www.youtube.com/watch?v=ck_r-v-M3ug.

Weinberg, Steven. *Dreams of a Final Theory: The Scientist's Search for the Ultimate Laws of Nature.* New York: Pantheon, 1993.

Wikipedia. "Android (Robot)." Wikimedia Foundation. Last modified Jan. 21, 2025, 18:24. https://en.wikipedia.org/wiki/Android_(robot)#cite_note-Stableford2006-3.

———. "Binet-Simon Intelligence Test." Wikimedia Foundation. Last modified Jan. 9, 2025, 21:32. https://en.wikipedia.org/wiki/Binet-Simon_Intelligence_Test.

———. "CRISPR." Wikimedia Foundation. Last modified Jan. 26, 2025, 13:18. https://en.wikipedia.org/wiki/CRISPR.

———. "George Boole." Wikimedia Foundation. Last modified Jan. 3, 2025, 19:03. https://en.wikipedia.org/wiki/George_Boole.

———. "John Heysham Gibbon." Wikimedia Foundation. Last modified Nov. 24, 2024, 16:19. https://en.wikipedia.org/wiki/John_Heysham_Gibbon.

———. "Luigi Galvani." Wikimedia Foundation. Last modified Dec. 15, 2024, 21:37. https://en.wikipedia.org/wiki/Luigi_Galvani.

———. "Paul Zoll." Wikimedia Foundation. Last modified Nov. 16, 2024, 19:07. https://en.wikipedia.org/wiki/Paul_Zoll.

Wilson, Charles, et al., eds. "A Logical Neuron." *Neuroscience Foundations* (blog). https://marlin.life.utsa.edu/mcculloch-and-pitts.html.

Wright, Webb. "Please Be Polite to ChatGPT." *Scientific American,* July 25, 2024. https://www.scientificamerican.com/article/should-you-be-nice-to-ai-chatbots-such-as-chatgpt/.

Wu Song, Felicia. *Restless Devices: Recovering Personhood, Presence, and Place in the Digital Age.* Downers Grove, IL: InterVarsity, 2021.

Wyler, William, dir. *Roman Holiday.* Los Angeles: Paramount Pictures, 1953.

Yeats, William Butler. "The Second Coming." Poetry Foundation. https://www.poetryfoundation.org/poems/43290/the-second-coming.

Younger, Stuart, and Insoo Hyun. "Pig Experiment Challenges Assumptions Around Brain Damage in People." *Scientific American,* Apr. 17, 2019. https://www.scientificamerican.com/article/pig-experiment-challenges-assumptions-around-brain-damage-in-people/.

Zeldes, Jason, dir. "What Will AI Do for Us / to Us." *What's Next? The Future with Bill Gates,* season 1, episode 1. Aired Sept. 18, 2024.

www.ingramcontent.com/pod-product-compliance
Lightning Source LLC
Chambersburg PA
CBHW060607230426
43670CB00011B/2005